Mathematics
— LEVELS 3 & 4 —

DAVID ALCORN

CAUSEWAY PRESS

Published by Causeway Press Ltd
PO Box 13, Ormskirk, Lancs L39 5HP

First published 1991

British Library Cataloguing in Publication Data
Alcorn, David
  Mathematics: Levels 3 and 4.
  I. Title
  510

  ISBN 0946183864

Typesetting by Alden Multimedia Ltd., Northampton
Printed by Alden Press, Oxford

Preface

Mathematics: Levels 3 & 4 has been written mainly for pupils who are of secondary school age. It is based on covering the requirements of levels 3 and 4 of the National Curriculum, but also provides consolidation of earlier levels as appropriate, and allows a pupil to demonstrate abilities commensurate with a higher level.

For some pupils, the book will be used as a basis for a year's work, whilst for others it provides a firm foundation from which they might aspire to higher levels more quickly. The teacher can decide how best to use the book with a particular group of pupils or with a particular class. (There are some notes for teachers on page *x*.)

I should like to thank Jean Holderness for her invaluable help, the tireless support and the encouragement that she has given whilst I was writing this book.

The people who have helped with the production of this book have my thanks, Sue, Andrew, the staff at Alden Multimedia (Northampton) and the staff at Alden Press (Oxford). Thanks are also due to all at Causeway Press, especially Mike, who have encouraged me throughout this project.

Finally, I wish to thank Barbara and Timothy for their support and encouragement, especially Timothy who has tested much of the material contained in this book.

David Alcorn

To Barbara and Timothy

Acknowledgements

Artwork and page design Susan and Andrew Allen

Cover Andrew Allen/IPC

Photography Andrew Allen

Copyright photographs

Ed Buziak pp. 12 (top), 13 (top right), 30 (bottom left), 60 (bottom left), 60 (bottom right), 77 (bottom left), 90 (top right), 91 (left), 145 (left), 145 (right), 157 (top right), 193 (bottom left), 193 (bottom right), 210, 248 (top), 264 (bottom right), 265 (bottom left)

Sally and Richard Greenhill pp. 13 (bottom left), 50 (top right), 119 (middle), 169 (top left), 193 (middle left), 230, 263

Popperfoto pp. 12 (bottom), 30 (middle right), 60 (top left), 119 (left), 119 (right), 193 (top left), 248 (bottom)

Science Museum pp. 10, 31 (top right), 31 (bottom right), 61 (top)

Topham Picture Source pp. 1 (bottom), 1 (bottom right), 13 (bottom right), 30 (top left), 30 (bottom right), 77 (bottom right), 153, 169 (bottom left), 169 (top right), 193 (top right), 249 (top), 249 (bottom), 264 (top), 264 (bottom left), 265 (top left), 265 (top right), 265 (middle left), 265 (middle right), 265 (bottom right)

Contents

Miscellaneous Section C

Topics for Activities (included in the miscellaneous sections)

To the teacher

Mathematics: Levels 3 & 4 can be used in different ways. It is intended for pupils of secondary school age who require thorough coverage of the work contained in levels 3 and 4 of the National Curriculum. It may also be used to consolidate work that pupils have previously encountered and to bolster confidence whilst allowing the teacher to establish a common platform from which pupils may aspire to higher levels at a faster pace. The book also allows teachers to liaise with feeder primary schools who may find this book beneficial for some of their mathematicians.

Although the main focus of the book is levels 3 and 4, work from earlier levels is covered where appropriate. This allows pupils to consolidate work which they have found difficult when the topic was first encountered.

There are plenty of opportunities for the pupils to display their specific abilities and strengths in areas beyond level 4.

The book is organised as follows:- For each chapter there is an introductory section called 'Thinking About . . .' You could use these sections, or part of them, for class discussion, for group work or for individual work. The section could take a brief few minutes or several lessons. You might find that by extending the ideas there you are covering the work of the chapter quite adequately and very little follow-up work will be needed.

The main part of the chapter consists of bookwork, worked examples and straightforward exercises. Each part of a chapter is designed so that pupils may practise a skill or concept in small manageable amounts. The bookwork and worked examples enable a pupil to cover work on their own, or with the help of an adult, and provide useful reference for later revision. The teacher may use a more practical introduction to some topics and may only use the bookwork and worked examples for reference.

The last exercise of a chapter is more varied, giving ideas for applications and activities of various lengths. They may be used for individual work, group work or as a whole class activity. The teacher can best decide how to use this exercise effectively.

The book contains 17 chapters. There are miscellaneous sections after Chapters 7, 14 and 17, which provide aural questions, revision questions and more suggestions for longer activities. There are puzzle questions fitted in at the ends of chapters where there is space. They are in no particular order and are there to give further interest.

In many instances greater reinforcement of a concept can be achieved by using a practical approach. In order to provide a practical aspect to the vast amount of number work that is contained in levels 3 and 4 I have used abacus charts, number lines, number ladders, one-hundred squares, etc. as well as more abstract approaches. The best way to learn how to use various measuring instruments is to actually use them, and ample opportunity is provided in the activities sections.

Calculators. A basic calculator is recommended though pupils should be encouraged to work, at times, without a calculator.

Graph paper. Centimetre squared paper and 2 mm graph paper are the only types of graph paper used. Only use 2 mm graph paper if the smaller divisions are required, otherwise centimetre squared paper is easier for pupils to use.

Computers. Suggestions for computer work are given and I hope you have the facilities to make use of computers and the vast amount of software that is now available. Specific reference to any particular computer is difficult due to the many and varied machines that are currently used in schools.

Answers. The answers begin on a right-hand page, so that if you do not want a class to have them, they may be cut out of the book. Answers are provided to the straightforward questions, but not always for the activities questions, where it is important that the pupils make their own discoveries. The puzzle answers are not given either.

I hope that you and your pupils find this book useful and that it provides, or is the focal point, for many enjoyable lessons.

David Alcorn

Numbers everywhere

Make a list of all the places in your home, or in your local area, where numbers are used.
Include numbers on doors, on dials, serial numbers, etc.

Why do you think numbers are used in everyday life ?

Sometimes numbers are combined with letters, e.g. the postcode. Can you think of other examples where this is done.

Serial numbers are used on electrical appliances. What information is given here ?

How are numbers used on this remote control machine ?

House numbers

The numbering of houses began in Paris, in 1463.
The first numbering of houses in Great Britain was in Prescot Street, London. The people in Prescot Street at the time were mostly from Europe and it is believed that they brought the idea of numbering houses with them.
By 1763 about a dozen roads and streets in London had numbered houses.
By 1765 all houses in London were numbered, except for those houses which had names.
Why do you think some houses have numbers as well as names ?
At which end of a road does the numbering of houses start ?

Who lives here ?

Different number systems

People have always counted. However, the way in which they wrote their numbers was different. Here are some numbers from the ancient world together with the Modern Arabic system that we use today.

Which numbers look nearly the same in these different number systems?

Modern Arabic	O	I	2	3	4	5	6	7	8	9	10
Early Arabic	o	I	2	3	2	4	6	∧	8	9	1o
Hindu	O	8	2	3	8	2	3	∪	I	6	8o
Babylonian		▼	▼▼	▼▼▼	▼▼▼▼	▼▼▼▼▼	▼▼▼▼▼▼	▼▼▼▼▼▼▼	▼▼▼▼▼▼▼▼	▼▼▼▼▼▼▼▼▼	◀
Mayan	◯	•	••	•••	••••	—	•̱	••̱	•••̱	••••̱	=
Egyptian		I	II	III	IIII	III I	III III	IIII III	IIII IIII	III III III	∩
Roman		I	II	III	IV	V	VI	VII	VIII	IX	X

Roman numbers or Roman numerals are still used.
Where might you see them in use today?

Games that use numbers

Many games use numbers. Sometimes dice are used to play a game. Some games are played on boards which have numbers written on them.
Make a list of games in which numbers are used.

Place your list of games in order, starting with your favourite game.

How could you find out which was the most popular game that uses numbers in your class?

Hampton Court accounts from the time when Henry VIII ruled

1 Numbers

Reading and writing numbers

Numbers play a great part in our lives. It is very difficult to exist without coming into contact with numbers. They will be seen written in figures, written in words, or they will be heard.

Here are some of the numbers we use and how they are spelt.

1 one	11 eleven	10 ten
2 two	12 twelve	20 twenty
3 three	13 thirteen	30 thirty
4 four	14 fourteen	40 forty
5 five	15 fifteen	50 fifty
6 six	16 sixteen	60 sixty
7 seven	17 seventeen	70 seventy
8 eight	18 eighteen	80 eighty
9 nine	19 nineteen	90 ninety
10 ten	20 twenty	100 one hundred

The abacus chart

The **abacus chart** can be used to show numbers.
The headings at the top of the chart are:

H	T	U

U = units
T = tens   10 units = 1 ten
H = hundreds   10 tens = 1 hundred

Examples

1 Write the number 64 in words.

64 is written as sixty-four.

2 What number does this abacus chart show ?

There are 5 tens = 50
            6 units =   6
The abacus chart shows the number 56 or fifty-six.

H	T	U
	oo o oo	ooo ooo

Exercise 1.1

1. Write the following numbers in figures.

   1 twenty-four   **6** ninety-eight
   2 seventeen   **7** thirty-one
   3 eighty-six   **8** forty-five
   4 seventy-four   **9** twenty-two
   5 fifty   **10** sixty-three

2. Write the following numbers in words.

   1 13   **5** 79   **8** 33
   2 27   **6** 81   **9** 95
   3 38   **7** 40   **10** 67
   4 52

3. What number is shown on each of these abacus charts ?
   Write your answers in figures.

4. What number is shown on each of these abacus charts ?
   Write your answers in words.

5.   Draw an abacus chart to show each of these numbers.
      Write the number in words below each chart.
      1   23   **2**   44   **3**   15   **4**   30

Larger numbers

In the first exercise you looked at numbers which were less than 100. There are many more numbers which are greater than 100.
Some are shown below with their spellings.

100 one hundred
1000 one thousand
10 000 ten thousand
100 000 one hundred thousand
1 000 000 one million

We can use these numbers together with the ones you met earlier as the basis for writing many other numbers.
The abacus chart can be used to show any number, but we rarely use one to show large numbers. You may add extra columns to an abacus chart. For example, thousands, tens of thousands, etc.

Place value

The position that a figure has in a number is called its **place value**.
Our number system is made up of the 10 digits
0, 1, 2, 3, 4, 5, 6, 7, 8 and 9
Using these digits we can write all the numbers we need.

Examples

Give the value of the underlined figure in the following.

1   3<u>5</u>8

The 5 is in the tens column and is worth 50.

2   1<u>7</u> 452

The 7 is in the thousands column and is worth 7 000.

3   2<u>8</u>34

The 8 is in the hundreds column and is worth 800.

4   Write 276 in words.

Two hundred and seventy-six.

5   Write 27 423 in words.

Twenty-seven thousand, four hundred and twenty-three.

6   Write one hundred and thirty-six thousand, four hundred and seven in figures.

This can be split into two parts.
The number of thousands is 136.
The last three figures of the number are 407.
This gives the number 136 407.

Exercise 1.2

1.   Give the value of the underlined figure in the following.

1	31<u>5</u>	**6**	174<u>3</u>	**11**	<u>6</u>8 674
2	2<u>6</u>4	**7**	2<u>6</u>01	**12**	740 <u>3</u>72
3	<u>3</u>70	**8**	100<u>7</u>	**13**	<u>1</u> 500 762
4	57<u>2</u>	**9**	34 <u>0</u>02	**14**	4 762 <u>1</u>80
5	<u>8</u>06	**10**	17<u>2</u>5	**15**	5 243 1<u>9</u>4

2.   Write the following numbers in figures.
   1   one hundred and twenty-six
   2   three hundred and seventeen
   3   five hundred and nine
   4   seven hundred and forty
   5   one thousand, six hundred and thirty-nine
   6   four thousand, eight hundred
   7   fifteen thousand
   8   forty-nine thousand, five hundred
   9   one hundred and sixty-seven thousand, two hundred and twelve
   10   one million and forty-two

3.   Write the following numbers in words.

1	245	**5**	1420	**8**	12 500
2	150	**6**	2500	**9**	12 349
3	278	**7**	3768	**10**	156 437
4	902				

4.   John wanted to write the number five hundred and four.
      In a hurry he wrote 54.
      1   What is wrong ?
      2   Write the number correctly.

5.   2478 = 2 thousands + 4 hundreds + 7 tens + 8 units
      Write these numbers out in the same way.
      1   374   **4**   720
      2   526   **5**   1437
      3   304   **6**   5070

Ascending and descending order

You can place a group of numbers in order of size.
If you put the numbers in **ascending order** you start with the smallest number and
finish with the largest number.
If you put numbers in **descending order** you start with the largest number and finish
with the smallest number.

Examples

1   Put the numbers 37, 124, 56, 39 and 86 in descending order.

124 is the largest number because it is the only number with a figure in the
hundreds column.
You next look for the number with the highest figure in the tens column. This is 86
This gives 124, 86 and then 56.
You now have to look more closely at 37 and 39.
They both have the same figure in the tens column.
To put these numbers in order you must look at the units column.
This gives 39 and then 37.
You now get 124, 86, 56, 39, 37 in descending order.

2   Use all the figures 3, 8, 1 and 2 to write the smallest possible number.

The smallest possible number is 1238.

3   Use all the figures 3, 8, 1 and 2 to write the largest possible number.

The largest possible number is 8321.

Exercise 1.3

1. Write the following numbers in ascending order (lowest to highest).
    1   15, 34, 26.
    2   78, 24, 59, 38.
    3   127, 131, 130, 141.
    4   2745, 2764, 2746, 2753.
    5   14 726, 15 135, 14 762, 15 014.

2. Write the following numbers in figures and then put them in ascending order.
    1   thirty-seven, seven, twenty-nine, fifteen.
    2   ninety-four, eighty-six, ninety-nine, seventy.
    3   one hundred and eight, five, one hundred and ten, one hundred and twenty.
    4   three thousand four hundred and six, three thousand four hundred, three thousand three hundred and ninety-nine.
    5   one million and one, nine hundred and ninety-nine thousand and sixty-four, one million one thousand and seventy-eight.

3. Write the following numbers in descending order.
    1   57, 63, 75, 19, 39.
    2   87, 45, 53, 48, 67.
    3   102, 129, 145, 137, 178.
    4   1324, 1426, 2638, 2739, 989, 1726.
    5   1, 34, 3, 123, 134, 143, 4.

4. Use all the figures to make the smallest possible number.
    1   4, 1, 2   **6**   5, 6, 8, 3
    2   3, 5, 1   **7**   1, 3, 2, 4
    3   7, 4, 2   **8**   4, 2, 3, 9
    4   3, 8, 6   **9**   7, 4, 1, 4
    5   7, 1, 4   **10** 4, 3, 5, 8, 9

5. Use all the figures to make the largest possible number.
    1   2, 7, 4   **6**   7, 1, 5, 8
    2   3, 9, 2   **7**   6, 3, 1, 4
    3   5, 7, 3   **8**   2, 1, 0, 5
    4   9, 3, 8   **9**   4, 1, 3, 6, 4
    5   8, 4, 9   **10** 3, 9, 8, 4, 7

Even and odd numbers

An **even number** can be divided exactly by 2.
The figure in the units column of an even number is 0, 2, 4, 6 or 8.

When you divide an **odd number** by 2 you always get a remainder of 1.
The figure in the units column of an odd number is 1, 3, 5, 7 or 9.

Consecutive numbers

Examples

1 Write five consecutive numbers starting at 8 and going upwards.

   8, 9, 10, 11, 12

2 Write four consecutive odd numbers starting at 7 and going upwards.

   7, 9, 11, 13

Exercise 1.4

1.   Make a copy of the one-hundred square.

1	2	3	4	5	6	7	8	9	10
11	12	13	14	15	16	17	18	19	20
21	22	23	24	25	26	27	28	29	30
31	32	33	34	35	36	37	38	39	40
41	42	43	44	45	46	47	48	49	50
51	52	53	54	55	56	57	58	59	60
61	62	63	64	65	66	67	68	69	70
71	72	73	74	75	76	77	78	79	80
81	82	83	84	85	86	87	88	89	90
91	92	93	94	95	96	97	98	99	100

1 Shade all the even numbers in one colour.
2 Shade all the odd numbers in another colour.

2. Using your one-hundred square write down
   1 the first five odd numbers,
   2 the eighth odd number,
   3 the even numbers between 59 and 71,
   4 four consecutive even numbers starting at 40 and going upwards,
   5 five consecutive odd numbers starting at 91 and going downwards,
   6 the twenty-third even number.

3. **1** What is the next even number after 160 ?
   2 What is the biggest odd number before 173 ?
   3 What is the biggest odd number before 301 ?
   4 What is the biggest even number before 1000 ?
   5 How many even numbers are there between 121 and 131 ?
   6 How many odd numbers are there between 320 and 342 ?

Exercise 1.5 Applications and Activities

1. **Guessing and counting**

Group A   *Group B*

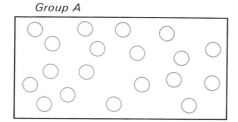 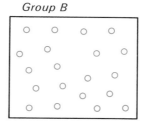

1 Guess the number of circles that are in Group A.
2 Guess the number of circles in Group B.
3 Count the number of circles in Group A.
4 Count the number of circles in Group B.

It is very difficult to guess the number of objects in a group.
We can group objects together in patterns.
This makes counting easier.

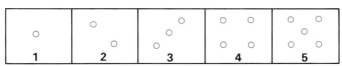

Draw patterns for 6, 7, 8, 9 and 10.
Can you think of anywhere where objects are put into a pattern to make
counting easy? A domino is an example.

2. The bus queue

Sam   Helen   Roy   Larry   Hanif   Georgina   Rachel   Robert   George

These children are waiting to catch the bus home after school.

1   How many children are in the queue ?
2   Who is third in the queue ?
3   Name the last four people in the queue.
4   Who is sixth from the back of the queue ?
5   Who is in the middle of the queue ?
6   Who is second in line behind Georgina ?
7   Who is five places in front of Rachel ?

3. Inventions

Here is a list of inventions in alphabetical order.
The year of invention is also given.

Aeroplane 1903
Air Balloon 1782
Braille System 1834
Bunsen Burner 1852
Dynamo 1831
Kaleidoscope 1816
Laughing Gas 1772

What is the earliest invention in the list ?
Put the inventions in chronological order (earliest invention, second earliest invention, and so on).

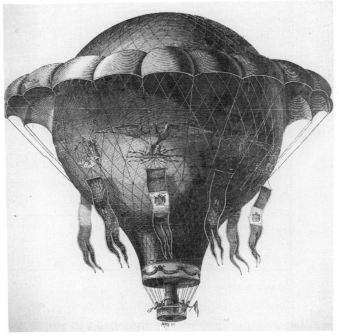

Try to find out more about the inventions and the people who invented them.

4. **The Great Lakes**

The Great Lakes are in North America.
The length of each lake in miles is:

Lake Erie 241 miles,
Lake Huron 206 miles,
Lake Michigan 307 miles,
Lake Ontario 193 miles,
Lake Superior 360 miles.

Put the lakes in order of length starting with the longest.

5. **Make an abacus chart**

Make an abacus chart.
Use the headings H, T and U.
Put counters on your abacus chart to show a number.
Ask a friend to read your abacus chart.
Take it in turns making and reading numbers.

6. **Numbers everywhere**

Make a list of the places in school where numbers are used.
Include room numbers, etc.
See how many different uses you can find.
Why is it important to use numbers ?
Do all lessons use numbers ?

7. **Numbers in newspapers**

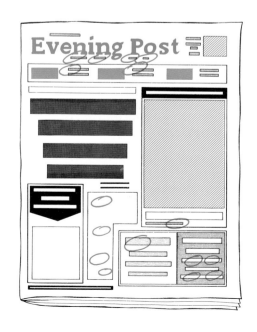

How many times are numbers used on
one page of a newspaper ?
To find out, choose a page from a
newspaper and use a bright colour to
circle where numbers appear on the
page.
Do not use the financial pages (money
pages) or the sports pages.
Numbers may be written in words, or in
figures. They may appear in diagrams.
Do some pages use numbers more than
other pages ?

You could also look at different
newspapers, magazines, comics, etc.

2 Thinking about angles and directions

Viewpoint

In school, stand facing in the direction of North. Turn to face in the direction of different places, such as the hall, the playground, the school gate, and so on.

An angle measures the amount of turning between two directions. You can draw your own viewpoint and describe the angles through which you turn to face in the direction of various places.

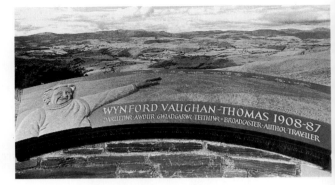

A viewing point at Foel Fadian, Wales

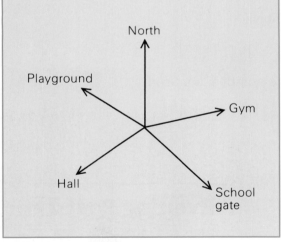

Vertical

Some buildings are not upright, or vertical, and lean at an angle.
Are there any buildings near where you live that are not vertical ?
Why does the Leaning Tower of Pisa not fall over?
Try to find out why it leans.

The Leaning Tower of Pisa

A weather vane

How does a weather vane work ?

What information does a weather vane give ?

Why might this information be useful ?

Design your own weather vane to represent a sport, e.g. cricket, a job, e.g. a blacksmith, or something of your own choice. You might like to actually make a weather vane.

Look for weather vanes in your local area. Where are they usually found ?

A weather vane

Finding your way

How might directions be useful in these situations ?

Hampton Court Maze

Spaghetti Junction, Birmingham

2 Angles and Directions

Giving directions

If you are visiting a town you may have to ask for directions in order to find somewhere. It is important that the instructions are clear and simple.

You may have to give directions to someone. For example, someone who is visiting your school.

Left and right

The instructions 'left' and 'right' are used a lot when giving directions. Do you know your left from your right ?

Left   Right

Back

Always think of directions from your point of view. That is looking forwards. What is on your left could well be on someone else's right.

Exercise 2.1

1. Jane lives at 37 Wye Close.
    To get to school she
    turns right out of her house,
    turns right into Thames Road,
    turns left into Severn Road,
    turns left into Waterfield Road and
    the school is on the right.

    1   John lives at 15 Fine Lane.
        Give directions for John to get
        to school.

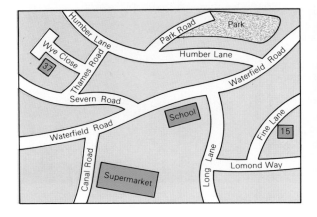

2   What route should John's father take to get home from the supermarket ?

3   Umar turned right out of school, left into Humber Lane and then first right. Which road did Umar end up in ?

On Saturday morning John and Jane play in the park.

4   Give directions for Jane to get home from the park.

5   Give directions for John to get home from the park.

2.   This plan shows a new building development.
       It is just being built. The roads have not been named yet.
       Each house is given a number from 1 to 150.
       All delivery lorries must stop at the gate to get directions.

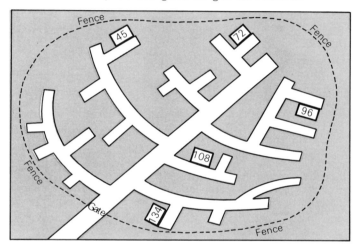

1   Which house do you get to if from the gate you take this route ? Third right, first left and second right.

2   Give directions to get from the gate to house number 108.

3   Give directions to get from the gate to house number 134.

4   Give directions to get from the gate to house number 45.

5   Give directions to get from house number 72 back to the gate.

6   Give directions to get from house number 108 to house number 45.

7   Give directions to get from house number 96 to house number 72.

3.   This diagram shows where four friends sat at the dinner table.

1   Who is sat opposite to Sally ?

2   Who is sat on Alf's left ?

3   Who is sat on Sid's right ?

4   Who is sat opposite to Sid ?

5   Who is sat on Sally's right ?

6   Who is sat on Laura's left ?

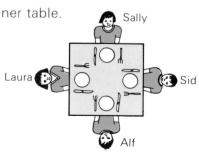

Angles

An angle measures the amount of turning or
the change in direction between two lines.

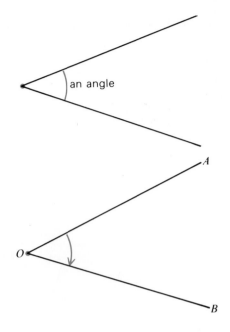

The size of an angle

Imagine that you are standing at the point O
and you are facing A.
You now turn and face B.
To do this you turn through the angle shown.

The size of an angle is measured in **degrees**.

A full-turn is 360°
A half-turn is 180°
A quarter-turn is 90°

The little circle by the last figure means degrees.

Compass directions

This diagram shows the four main directions North, East, South and West.
The angle between any two compass directions that are next to each other is 90°.

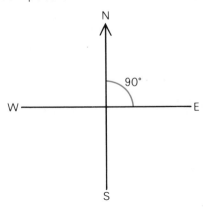

These are eight-point compass directions.
They include North-East, South-East,
South-West and North-West.

This type of compass is often called a
mariner's compass because sailors used them.
The angle between any two eight-point
compass directions that are next to each other is
45°.

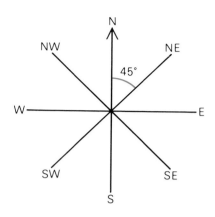

Examples

1   Face North. Turn 90° anti-clockwise. In which direction would you be facing ?

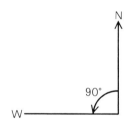

You would now be facing West.

Remember: **Anticlockwise** is the opposite
direction to which the hands
of a clock turn.
The hands of a clock turn in a
clockwise direction.

2   Face East. What is the smaller angle you have to turn through to face South-West ?

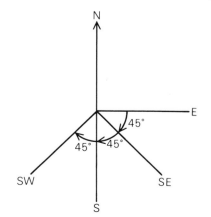

You could turn clockwise or anticlockwise
to face SW.
The smaller angle is found by turning
clockwise.
The angle is 3 × 45° = 135°.

Remember: The angle between eight-point
compass directions that are
next to each other is 45°.

3   Face North-West. Turn a quarter turn clockwise. In which direction would you be facing ?

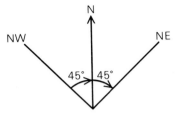

You would now be facing North-East.

The North line has been put in the diagram to help you. The North line is always drawn on diagrams and maps. It is the direction in which the compass needle points.

Exercise 2.2

1.   Face North. Turn to face South. Through how many degrees have you turned ?

2.   Face West. Turn clockwise to face North. Through how many degrees have you turned ?

3.   Face South. Turn 90° anticlockwise. In which direction are you now facing ?

4.   Face NW. Turn through 90° anticlockwise. In which direction are you now facing ?

5.   **1**   Face SW. Turn 90° clockwise. In which direction are you now facing ?
      2   Face SW. Turn 90° anticlockwise. In which direction are you now facing ?

6.   **1**   Face North. Turn clockwise to face East. How many degrees did you turn through ?
      2   Face North. Turn anticlockwise to face East. How many degrees did you turn through ?

7.   Copy and complete this table.

	Turn from	Number of degrees if turning clockwise	Number of degrees if turning anticlockwise
1	S to W		
2	SW to N		
3	W to SE		
4	NE to E		
5	NW to SW		
6	NE to SW		

7   What do you get if you add the number of degrees clockwise to the number of degrees anticlockwise ?

8.   Look at this map.

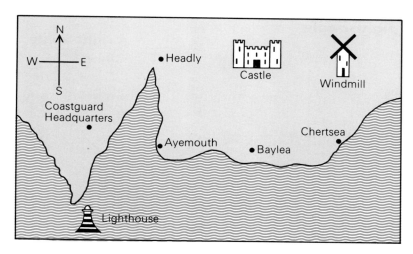

The Coastguard Headquarters is North of the lighthouse.
1   Which village is North of Ayemouth ?
2   Which village is South of the castle ?
3   What can be found South-West of Ayemouth ?

Copy and complete these sentences by filling in the missing words. Use the map to help you.
4   The _____ is North of Chertsea.
5   Headly is _____ of Baylea.
6   Chertsea is _____ of the castle.
7   The windmill is _____ of Baylea.
8   The Coastguard Headquarters is South-West of _____
9   The windmill is _____ of the castle.

Types of angle

Acute angle

An **acute angle** is an angle between 0° and 90°.

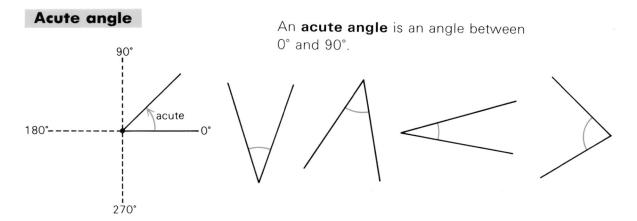

Right-angle

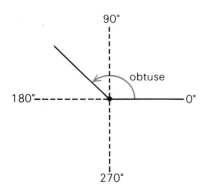

A **right-angle** is exactly 90°.
We label the angle as shown in the diagram.
90° is a quarter-turn.

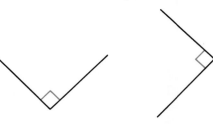

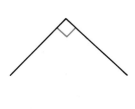

Obtuse angle

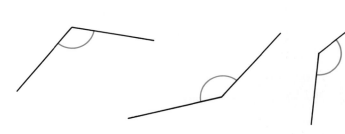

An **obtuse angle** is an angle between 90° and 180°.

Straight-angle

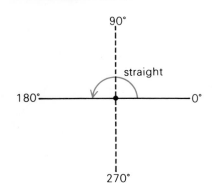

A **straight-angle** is exactly 180°.
180° is a **half-turn**.

Reflex angle

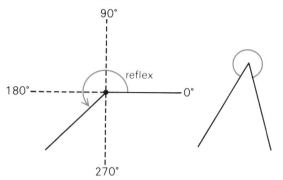

A **reflex angle** is an angle between 180° and 360°.

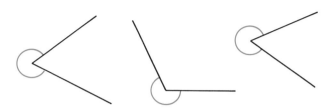

Full-turn

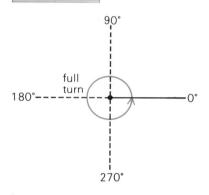

A **full-turn** is exactly 360°.

Exercise 2.3

1. Look at these angles. Say whether each angle is an acute angle or an obtuse angle.

1

2
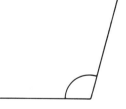

3
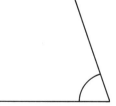

4
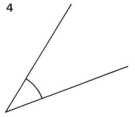

5
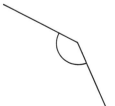

6
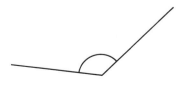

2. Look at each angle. Say whether each angle is an acute angle, a right-angle, an obtuse angle or a reflex angle.

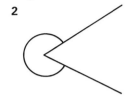

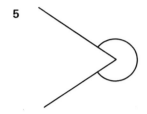

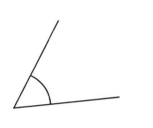

3. Look at this list of angles.
    54°, 138°, 180°, 7°, 290°, 90°, 360°, 300°, 272°, 45°, 178°, 315°, 1°, 182°, 100°.
    1   List the acute angles.
    2   List the obtuse angles.
    3   List the reflex angles.
    4   List the angles that you have not already listed in parts **1**, **2** or **3**.

Types of lines

Naming lines

The diagram shows how to label a line.
We call the line *AB* because it runs from *A* to *B*.
We could also call the line *BA* because it runs from *B* to *A*.

Vertical lines

Vertical lines are important in building and decorating.

To get a **vertical line** decorators use a plumb-line. This is a length of string with a weight tied to the end.
They hold the string against the wall at the top and let the plumb-bob (weight) hang. When it is perfectly still the string hangs in a vertical line.

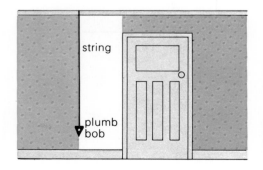

Horizontal lines

A **horizontal line** is a level line.
It is at right-angles to a vertical line.

Builders use a spirit level to check that their
work is horizontal or level.

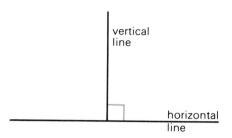

Oblique lines

An **oblique line** is a line which is slanted to
the vertical.

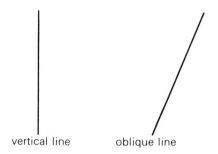

Perpendicular lines

If two lines are at right-angles to each other
they are **perpendicular**.

You can check if two lines are perpendicular by
using a **set-square**.

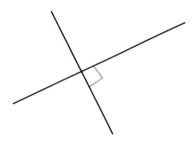

These lines are perpendicular.

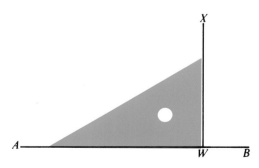

Line *WX* is perpendicular to
line *AB*.

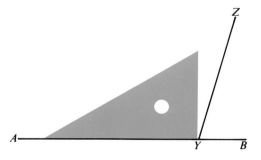

Line *YZ* is not perpendicular to
line *AB*.

A **vertical line** is perpendicular to a **horizontal line**.

Parallel lines

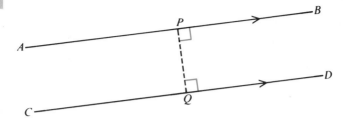

Lines which are always the same distance apart are called **parallel lines**.
Parallel lines never meet or cross.
In the diagram above *AB* is parallel to *CD*. To show that the lines are parallel we put
an arrowhead on each line.

The line *PQ* shows the shortest distance between *AB* and *CD*.
The angles at *P* and *Q* are right-angles.
You can use a set-square to draw the line *PQ*.
The distance from *P* to *Q* is called the **perpendicular distance** between *AB* and *CD*.

Points of intersection

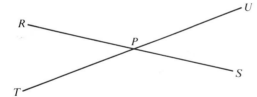

The lines *RS* and *TU* cross at the point *P*.
P is called the **point of intersection**.

Exercise 2.4

1.

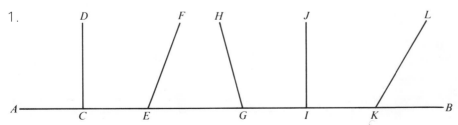

AB is a horizontal line drawn on a vertical wall.
Using a set-square, find
1   which lines are vertical lines,
2   which lines are oblique lines.

2.   In each diagram say whether the pairs of lines are perpendicular or not.

1

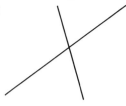

2

3

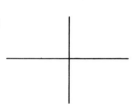

4

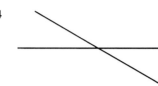

3.   Are the two lines parallel ?

1

2

3

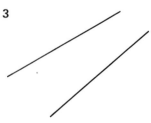

4

4.   Look at the diagram on the right.
   1   Which line is parallel to *CD* ?

Name the points of intersection where
these pairs of lines cross.
   2   *AB* and *GH*
   3   *EF* and *CD*
   4   *AB* and *EF*
   5   *CD* and *GH*
   6   *EF* and *GH*

5. Write down the missing word or words from these sentences.
   1   If two lines meet at _____ angles they are perpendicular to each other.
   2   The size of the angle between perpendicular lines is _____ degrees.
   3   _____ never meet.
   4   The point where two lines meet is called the point of _____ .
   5   A vertical line is perpendicular to a _____ line.
   6   To check if lines are perpendicular you can use a _____ .

Exercise 2.5   Applications and Activities

1. What type of angle is the smaller angle between the hands of these clocks ?
   You can choose from acute angle, right-angle, obtuse angle or straight angle.

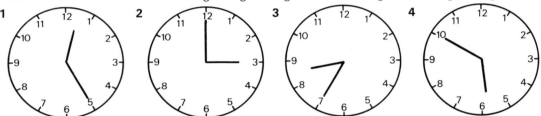

   What type of angle is the smaller angle between the hands of a clock at the
   following times ? You may draw the clock if you wish.
   5   six o'clock   7   half-past three
   6   ten o'clock   8   quarter-past seven

2. This is a map of two islands. Boats deliver goods from port to port. The ports are
   marked by letters.

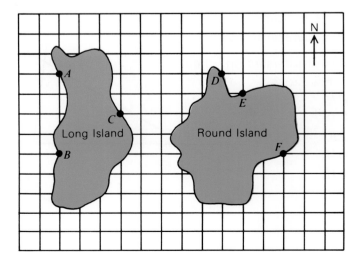

Boats can sail from one port to another by sailing along the sides of the squares.
The length of the side of a square is 1 mile.
Example: A possible route from *A* to *F* is:
        1 mile west, 7 miles south, 12 miles east and 3 miles north.
        Total distance: 23 miles
Remember: You can only sail along the black lines which are the sides of squares.

1   Write a route to get from port *A* to port *B*.
2   How long is your route from *A* to *B* ?
3   Write a route to get from port *C* to port *D*.
4   How long is your route from *C* to *D* ?
5   Write the shortest route from port *E* to port *F*.
6   What is the length of the shortest route from *E* to *F* ?
7   A boat sails from port *C*. It sails 1 mile east, 5 miles south, 5 miles west, 3 miles north and 1 mile east. At which port does the boat dock ?
8   A boat sailed 2 miles in going from one port to another. Which were the two ports the boat sailed between ?
9   A boat sailed from port *C* round Long Island and back to port *C*. The boat took the shortest route. How far did the boat sail ?
10 Another boat left port *F* and sailed round Round Island. It took the shortest route. How far did the boat sail ?

3. Look around your classroom. Try to find examples of
    1   vertical lines,
    2   horizontal lines,
    3   perpendicular lines,
    4   parallel lines,
    5   oblique lines.

4. **Tour guide**

    Write directions that someone could follow.
    Direct them on an interesting walk in your area.
    Draw a simple map or plan that they could use.
    This would help them to follow your directions.
    If there are places of interest on your tour, write
    some information about them, and mark these places
    on your map.

5. **Giving directions**

Write instructions to direct someone from the school gate
1   to the headteacher's room,
2   to the dining room,
3   to the gym.

6. **Investigating angles**

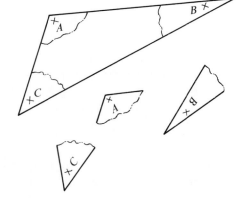

Draw a triangle of any shape on paper
and cut it out.
Label the angles *A*, *B* and *C*.
Mark a little cross at each angle, as shown
in the diagram.
Tear each angle from the triangle.

Fit the three angles together in any order,
with their points meeting and their sides
touching.

What do you notice ?

Repeat the experiment with another triangle and see what happens.

Then try this experiment with the angles
of a four-sided figure.
Investigate using different four-sided
figures.

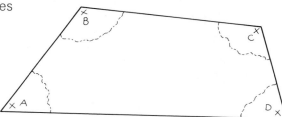

PUZZLES

1. How many triangles can you count in this diagram ?

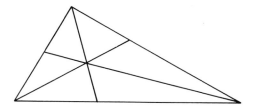

2. A boy has 7 brown socks and 8 black socks in his sock drawer. If he gets dressed in the dark, what is the smallest number of socks he must take from the drawer in order to get a pair ?

3. Where will you go if you keep travelling in the direction North-East for as long as possible ?

4. A person claimed to have dug up an ancient pot, dated 354 BC, when digging the foundations for a house. Is the pot genuine ?

5. How many times do you write down the digit 8 when writing all the numbers from 1 to 100 ?

6. 12.34 pm on 5th June is unusual because it could be written using the first 6 numbers in order (June is the 6th month). Can you make up any other dates, times, etc. which consist of consecutive numbers ?

7. In a stable there are 5 black horses, 3 brown horses and 2 white horses. How many of the 10 horses can say that they are the same colour as another of the horses in the stable ?

8. Can you draw this shape without taking your pencil off the paper, or going over the same line twice ?

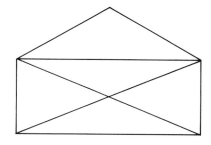

9. If you take 3 oranges from a basket of 5 oranges, how many oranges do you have ?

10. Frank is 12 years old. His father is 56 years old.
    Each year Frank's father promises to buy his son a car.
    His father will only buy the car if Frank is exactly one-third of his age that year.
    How long does Frank have to wait for his car ?

3 Thinking about addition and

Addition and subtraction in sports and games

Many sports and games involve the addition and subtraction of numbers. The following pictures show just a few. Can you think of some more?

Basketball

Darts

Ten-pin bowling

3-day eventing

Snooker

subtraction

The Japanese Abacus

The Japanese abacus is used by some people instead of a calculator. Indeed, some operators of the abacus can do calculations quicker than some people using calculators.

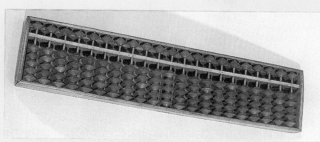

A Japanese abacus

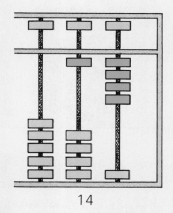

14

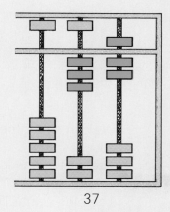

37

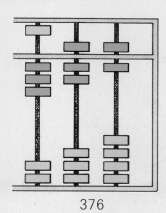

376

Babbage's Difference Engine

People have always tried to design and make devices to perform calculations.

Charles Babbage was such a person. He started work in 1823 using £17 000 from the government and £6000 of his own money. However, the precision engineering that Babbage needed for his project was too difficult for the engineers of the day.

Finally, having lost interest, Babbage gave up working full-time on the project in 1842. He continued to experiment with calculating devices until he died in 1871.

Babbage's Difference Engine

3 Addition and Subtraction

Addition using an abacus chart

In Chapter 1 you used an abacus chart to display numbers.
You can use the same abacus chart to do addition and subtraction questions.

Example

Use an abacus chart to add 15 and 18 together.

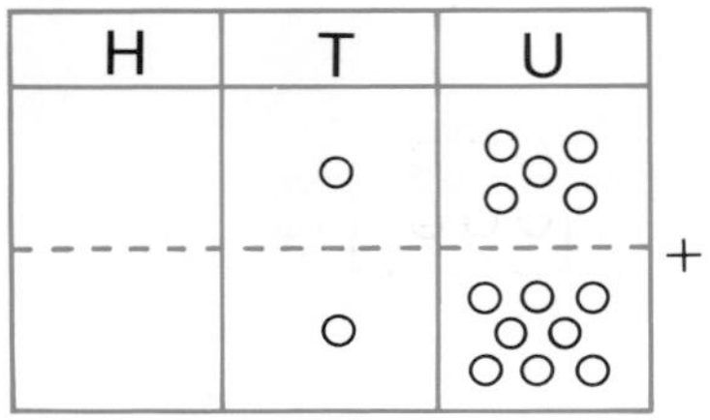

We can show the numbers 15 and 18 on an abacus chart.
The dotted line keeps the two numbers apart.
The plus sign is there to remind us that we have to add the numbers together.

To add 15 and 18 you work out the total number of counters on the chart.
Remember: You can exchange 10 counters in the units column for 1 counter in the tens column.
The abacus chart now looks like this.

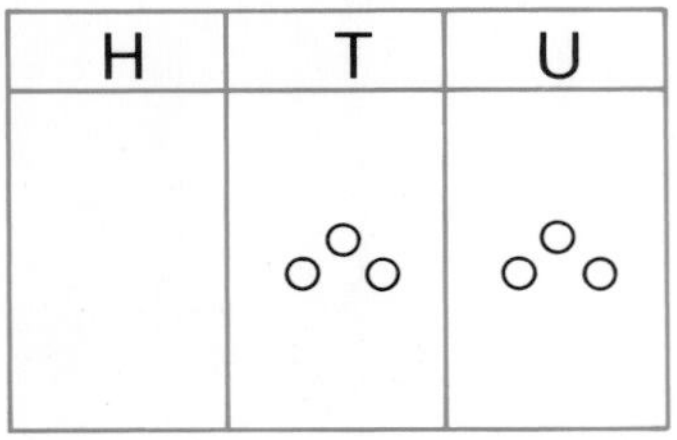

The abacus chart shows 33.
So 15 + 18 = 33

Exercise 3.1

1. This abacus chart shows 32 + 45.
   What is 32 + 45 ?

H	T	U
	o o o	o o
	o o o o	o o o o o

2. This abacus chart shows 16 + 17.
   What is 16 + 17 ?

H	T	U
	o	o o o o o o
	o	o o o o o o o

3. This abacus chart shows 47 + 26.
   What is 47 + 26 ?

H	T	U
	o o o o	o o o o o o o
	o o	o o o o o o

4. Draw abacus charts to show the following additions.
   Write the answer to each sum below your abacus chart.

1	31 + 15	**4**	36 + 17
2	23 + 18	**5**	45 + 28
3	27 + 34	**6**	56 + 36

5. This abacus chart shows 152 + 173.
   1 How many counters in the tens
   column can be exchanged for one
   counter in the hundreds column ?
   2 Work out 152 + 173.

H	T	U
o	o o o o o o	o o
o	o o o o o o o	o o o

6. This abacus chart shows 258 + 374.
   Work out 258 + 374.

H	T	U
o o	o o o o o o	o o o o o o o o o
o o o	o o o o o o o	o o o o

Subtraction using an abacus chart

Examples

1   Use an abacus chart to work out 38 − 26.

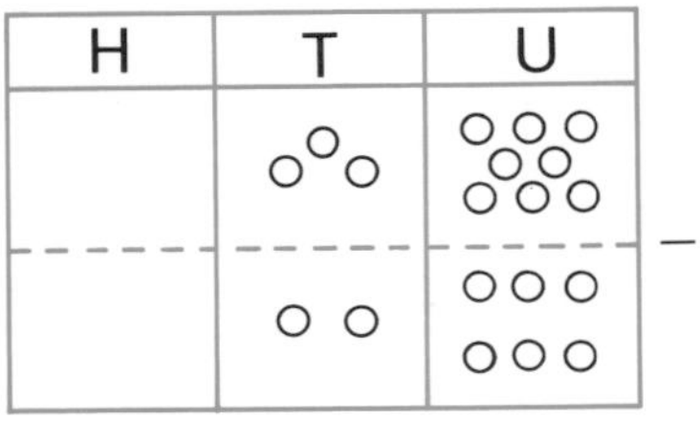

H	T	U
	o°o	ooo ooo
	o o	ooo ooo

We can show the numbers 38 and 26 on an abacus chart.
The dotted line keeps the two numbers apart.
The minus sign is there to remind us that we have to subtract the numbers.

When you subtract you must take the number of counters below the line away from the number of counters above the line.

In the units column 8 − 6 = 2.
In the tens column 3 − 2 = 1.

The abacus chart now looks like this.

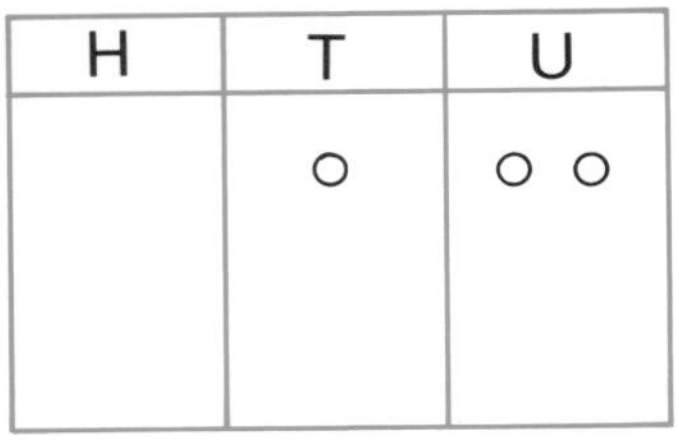

H	T	U
	o	o o

The abacus chart shows 12.
So 38 − 26 = 12.

2   Use an abacus chart to work out 41 − 16.

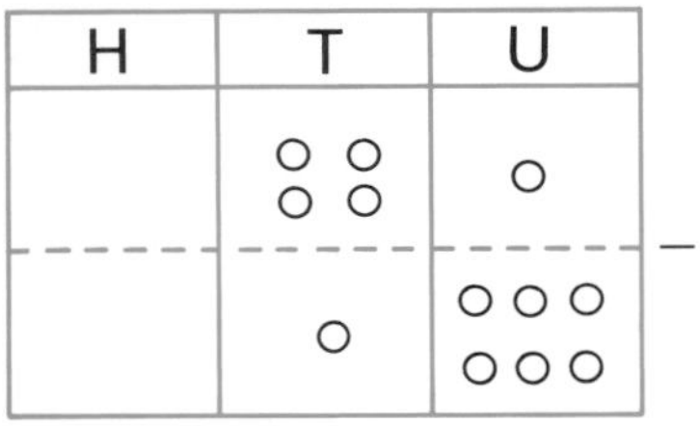

H	T	U
	o o o o	o
	o	ooo ooo

Remember: You must take the number of counters below the line away from the number of counters above the line.

In the units column we have to take 6 counters away from 1 counter.
This cannot be done.
Change 1 counter in the tens column for 10 counters in the units column. This exchange must take place **above** the dotted line.
The abacus chart now looks like this.

H	T	U
	o o o (5 above)	o o o o / o o o o / o o o o (11 above)
	o	o o o / o o o

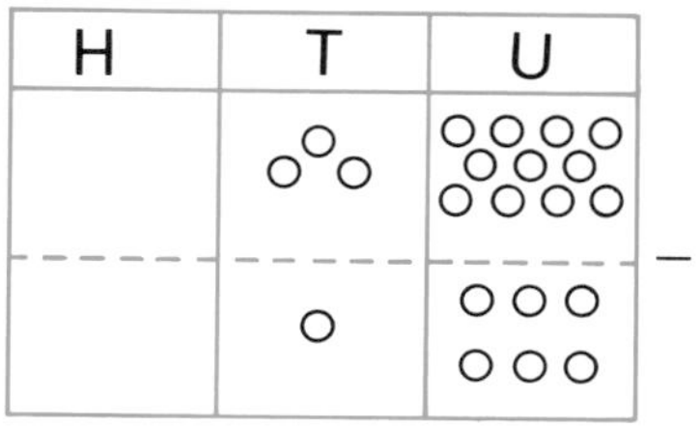

In the units column $11 - 6 = 5$.
In the tens column $3 - 1 = 2$.
The abacus chart now looks like this.

H	T	U
	o o	o o o / o o o

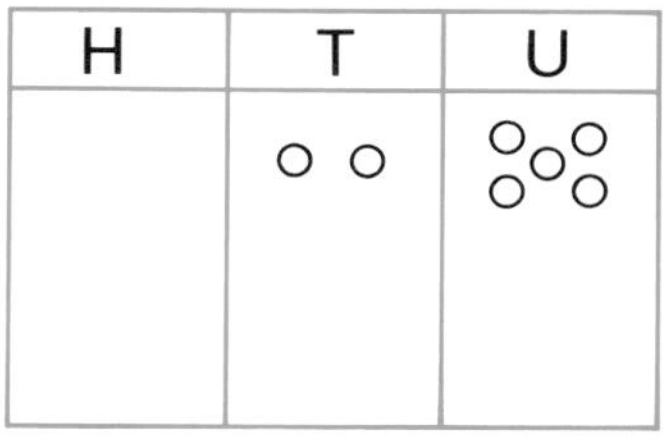

The abacus chart shows 25.
So $41 - 16 = 25$.

Exercise 3.2

1. This abacus chart shows $35 - 12$.
    1 What is $5 - 2$?
    2 What is $3 - 1$?
    3 What is $35 - 12$?

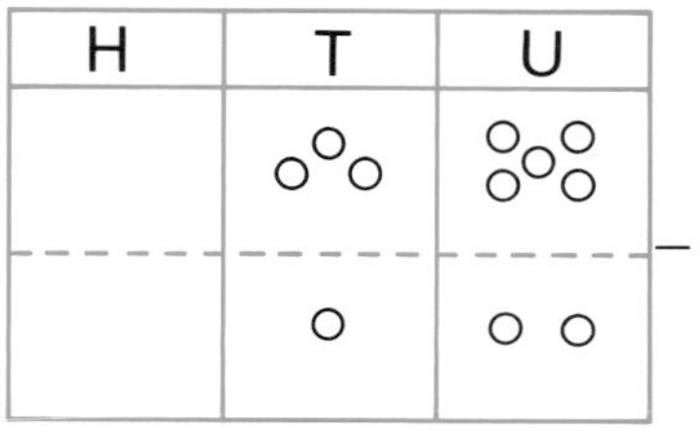

H	T	U
	o o o	o o o / o o o
	o	o o

2. This abacus chart shows $47 - 24$.
    Work out $47 - 24$.

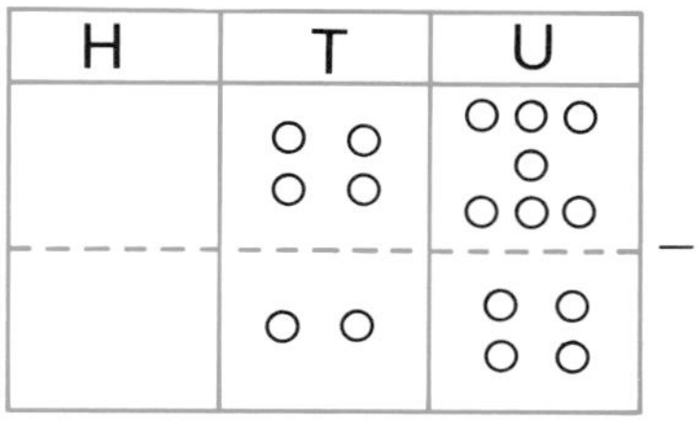

H	T	U
	o o / o o	o o o / o / o o o
	o o	o o / o o

3. This abacus chart shows 346 − 103.
    What is 346 − 103 ?

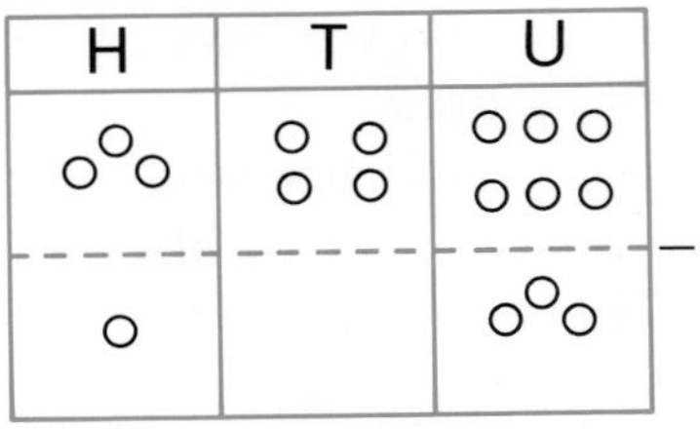

H	T	U
o o o	o o / o o	o o o / o o o
o		o o o

4. Draw abacus charts to show each of these subtraction sums, and write down the answers.

    1 27 − 14   **3** 36 − 24
    2 45 − 21   **4** 57 − 35

5. This abacus chart shows 31 − 14.
    You cannot work out 1 − 4 in the units column.
    Change 1 ten for 10 units in the number above the dotted line.

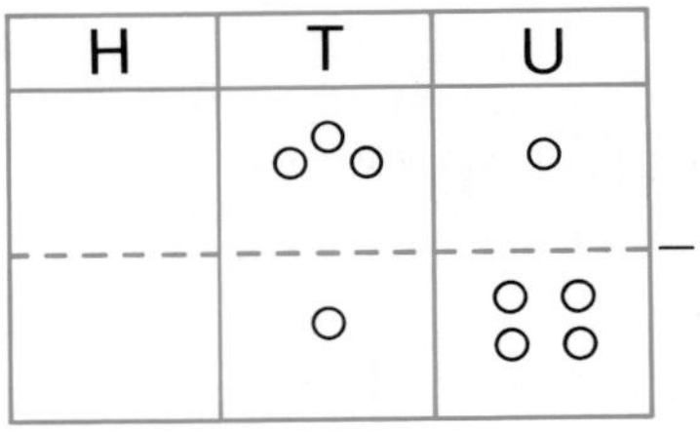

H	T	U
	o o o	o
	o	o o o o

    The abacus chart now looks like this.
    What is 31 − 14 ?

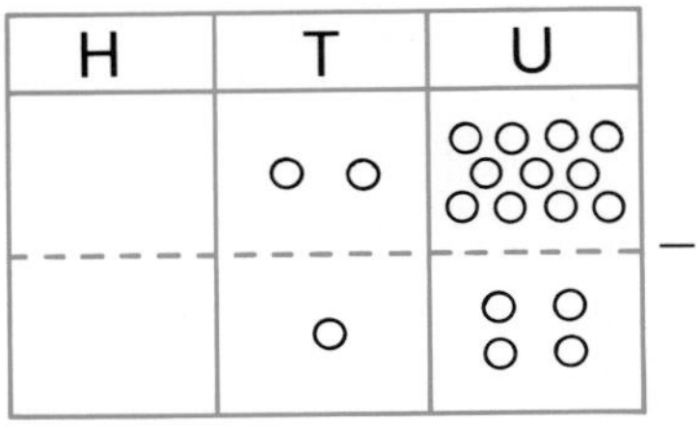

H	T	U
	o o	o o o o o o o o
	o	o o o o

6. This abacus chart shows 43 − 25.
    Work out 43 − 25.

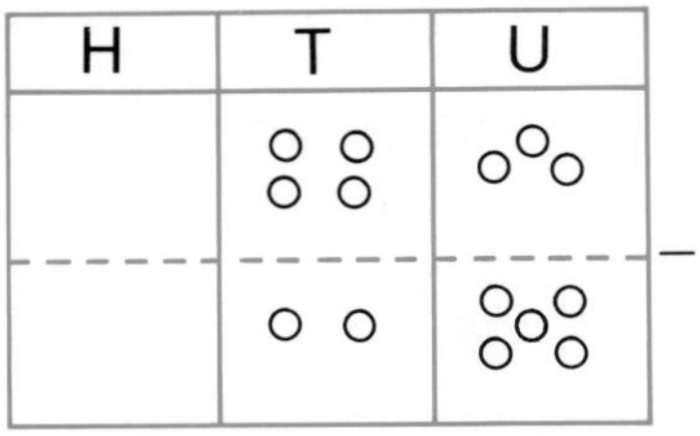

H	T	U
	o o o o	o o o
	o o	o o o o o

7. This abacus chart shows 54 − 28.
    Work out 54 − 28.

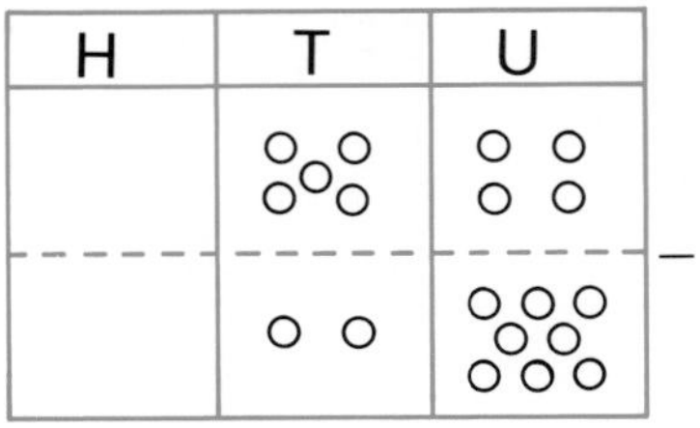

H	T	U
	o o o o o	o o o o
	o o	o o o o o o o o

8.   Draw an abacus chart to show the following subtraction sums.
     Write the answer to each question below the second abacus chart.
     1   32 − 17   **4**   71 − 25
     2   53 − 25   **5**   93 − 37
     3   40 − 24   **6**   54 − 38

9.   This abacus chart shows 324 − 176.
     Work out 324 − 176.
     Remember: 1 counter in the hundreds
     column is equal to 10 counters in the tens
     column.

H	T	U
o oo o	o o	o o / o o
o	ooo o ooo	ooo / ooo

Addition and subtraction without an abacus chart

The abacus chart is very useful if we want to show what is happening when two
numbers are added or subtracted.
We often do addition and subtraction sums by writing the numbers in tidy columns.

Addition

Example

   Work out 174 + 258.

```
  1 7 4
  2 5 8
  ─────
      2
    1
```
Add the figures in the units column together
first.
4 + 8 = 12
12 = 1 ten and 2 units.
Carry the 1 ten to the tens column and write
the 2 in the units column.

```
  1 7 4
+ 2 5 8
  ─────
    3 2
  1 1
```
Next, add together the figures in the tens
column.
7 + 5 + 1 = 13
Remember to add the carried figure.
13 tens = 1 hundred and 3 tens.
Carry the 1 hundred to the hundreds column
and write the 3 tens in the tens column.

```
  1 7 4
+ 2 5 8
  ─────
  4 3 2
  1 1
```
Finally, add together the figures in the
hundreds column.
1 + 2 + 1 = 4
Write 4 in the hundreds column.

1 It does not matter in which order you add the numbers together.
174 + 258 is the same as 258 + 174.

2 You always work from the **right**. That is, you add together the figures in the units
column, then you add together the figures in the tens column (including any
carried from the units column), and so on, until you have completed the addition.

3 If the figures in a column add up to 10 or more you will have to do some
carrying.
If the figures in a column add up to less than 10 there is no carrying to be done,
and the answer is written between the lines.

Subtraction

There are several methods that you can use for subtraction.
Here are examples of one method.

Example

Work out 372 − 134.

```
  3 7 2
− 1 3 4
───────
```

You must do 372 − 134.
The bottom number is taken away from the
top number.
Start in the units column.
2 − 4 cannot be done.
Change 1 ten in the tens column for 10
units in the units column.
This must be done on the top line.

```
      6
  3 ⁷¹2
− 1 3 4
───────
  2 3 8
```

Now in the units column we have
12 − 4 = 8
In the tens column 6 − 3 = 3
In the hundreds column 3 − 1 = 2

So 372 − 134 = 238

1 The order in which the numbers is written down is important.
134 − 372 is not the same as 372 − 134.

2 Any exchanges (e.g. 1 ten for 10 units) that take place must be carried out on the
top number.

3 If there are no tens (i.e. the figure in the tens column is 0) you cannot exchange 1 ten for 10 units.

When this happens you must first exchange 1 hundred for 10 tens, and then exchange 1 ten for 10 units.

Example

Work out 400 − 132

$$\begin{array}{r}{}^{3}\\ \cancel{4}\ {}^{1}0\ \ 0\\ -\ 1\ \ 3\ \ 2\\ \hline\end{array}$$
Exchange 1 hundred for 10 tens

$$\begin{array}{r}{}^{3}\ \ {}^{9}\\ \cancel{4}\ {}^{1}\cancel{0}\ {}^{1}0\\ -\ 1\ \ 3\ \ 2\\ \hline\end{array}$$
Exchange 1 ten for 10 units

$$\begin{array}{r}{}^{3}\ \ {}^{9}\\ \cancel{4}\ {}^{1}\cancel{0}\ {}^{1}0\\ -\ 1\ \ 3\ \ 2\\ \hline 2\ \ 6\ \ 8\\ \hline\end{array}$$
Do the subtractions 10 − 2 = 8, 9 − 3 = 6 and 3 − 1 = 2

You may already use a method of subtraction that is different to the one used above. It is important that you use the method which you find the easiest to use.

Exercise 3.3

Work these questions out by writing the numbers in columns.
Do not use a calculator.

1.	43 + 34	6.	58 − 27	11.	420 − 214
2.	58 + 23	7.	63 − 18	12.	500 − 324
3.	336 + 114	8.	743 − 235	13.	700 − 418
4.	278 + 147	9.	632 − 245	14.	603 − 256
5.	366 + 278	10.	301 − 126	15.	807 − 439

Using a number line

A number line shows a different method for adding and subtracting numbers.

Examples

1   Work out 27 + 34.

27 + 34 is the same as 34 + 27.
When you use a number line to add numbers together it is easier to start with the larger number.

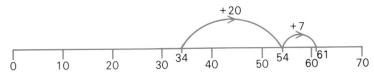

Start at 34 and add on 27.
This means go 27 places to the right on the number line.

Remember: 27 = 2 tens and 7 units.
You can add 27 in two steps.
34 + 20 = 54   (adding the 2 tens)
54 + 7 = 61   (adding the 7 units)
So 27 + 34 = 61.

2   Work out 53 − 37.

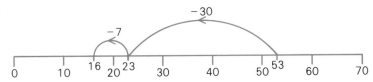

Start at 53 and take away 37.
This means go 37 places to the left on the number line.

Remember: 37 = 3 tens and 7 units.
You can take away 37 in two steps.
53 − 30 = 23   (taking away 3 tens)
23 − 7 = 16   (taking away 7 units)
So 53 − 37 = 16.

When you use a number line you start from a number and add (or subtract) the number of tens first. Then you add (or subtract) the number of units.

Exercise 3.4

1.   Here is a number line for 25 + 13.

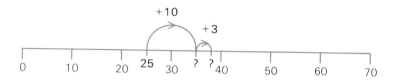

   Start at 25.
   1   What is 25 + 10 ?
   2   What is 25 + 13 ?

2.   Here is a number line for 34 + 18.

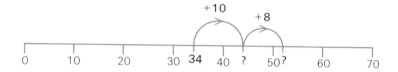

   Start at 34.
   1   What is 34 + 10 ?
   2   What is 34 + 18 ?

3.   Draw a number line for each of the following sums and work out the answers.
   1   24 + 15   **4**   42 + 24
   2   18 + 16   **5**   49 + 24
   3   34 + 19   **6**   15 + 47

4.   Here is a number line for 52 − 27.

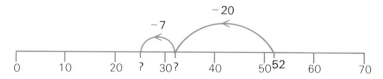

   Start at 52.
   1   What is 52 − 20 ?
   2   What is 52 − 27 ?

5.   Here is a number line for 38 − 16.

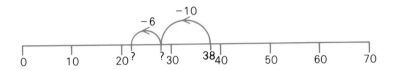

      Start at 38.
      1   What is 38 − 10 ?
      2   What is 38 − 16 ?

6.   Draw a number line for each of the following sums and work out the answers.
      1   27 − 15   **4**   51 − 19
      2   47 − 23   **5**   55 − 37
      3   32 − 17   **6**   63 − 35

Mental calculations

We often need to do calculations without a calculator.
Sometimes we do calculations without pencil or paper.
When you do calculations in your head they are called **mental calculations**.

Have you ever been in a supermarket and stood in the queue at the checkout hoping
that you had enough money ?
A mental calculation is needed to put your mind at rest.

Work these questions out in your head.
1.   7 + 2   5.   30 − 1   8.   60 + 20
2.   5 + 3   6.   40 − 2   9.   80 − 10
3.   4 + 8   7.   30 + 20   10.   70 + 30
4.   8 + 5

These questions should have been fairly easy for you to do.

Imagine that you had to buy items costing 33p and 18p.
You only have 50p in your pocket.
Will you have enough money to buy the two items ?

18 = 10 + 8
So 33 + 18 = 33 + 10 + 8
          = 43 + 8   (adding the 10 first)
          = 51   (adding the 8)

The items cost a total of 51p, so you would not have enough money to buy both
items.

Examples

Work out the following in your head.

1 24 + 43

It is easier to start with the larger number.
43 + 24 is the same as 24 + 43.

24 = 20 + 4
So 43 + 24 = 43 + 20 + 4
         = 63 + 4   (adding 43 and 20)
         = 67

You could do the same question another way.
43 + 24 = 43 + 20 + 4
         = 47 + 20   (adding 43 and 4)
         = 67

2 47 + 29

29 = 30 − 1
So 47 + 29 = 47 + 30 − 1
         = 77 − 1   (adding 47 and 30)
         = 76

If the figure in the units column is a 9 it is often easier to work from the ten above.
For example, 29 = 30 − 1.

3 56 − 34

34 = 30 + 4
So 56 − 34 = 56 − 30 − 4 (You must take away 30 then
         = 26 − 4   **take away** 4)
         = 22

Exercise 3.5

Do this exercise without using a calculator. It is an exercise in mental calculation.

1.   Work out the following questions in your head.

    1   14 + 13   **4**   18 + 14
    2   23 + 15   **5**   35 + 26
    3   34 + 22   **6**   48 + 27

2. Use a method like the one used in example **2** to work these questions out.
    1   24 + 19   **3**   53 + 29
    2   35 + 29   **4**   42 + 39

3. Work out these questions in your head.
    1   28 − 10   **4**   31 − 12
    2   36 − 20   **5**   84 − 31
    3   76 − 32   **6**   73 − 35

The calendar

There are 7 days in a week.
Sunday, Monday, Tuesday, Wednesday, Thursday, Friday, Saturday.

There are 12 months in a year.
January, February, March, April, May, June, July, August, September, October,
November, December.

Do you know this rhyme ?

Thirty days hath September,
April, June and dull November,
All the rest have 31,
Excepting February alone,
Which has 28 days clear,
And 29 in each leap year.

JULY 1992						
Sun	Mon	Tu	Wed	Th	Fri	Sat
			1	2	3	4
5	6	7	8	9	10	11
12	13	14	15	16	17	18
19	20	21	22	23	24	25
26	27	28	29	30	31	

You can use your fingers to work out the number of days in a month.

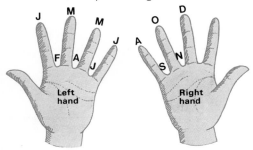

All the months at the tops of your fingers have
31 days.
All the months at the bottoms of your fingers
have 30 days.
Except February which has 28 days usually,
and 29 days if it is a leap year.

7 days   = 1 week
12 months = 1 year
365 days   = 1 year
366 days   = 1 leap year

A leap year occurs every 4 years.

If the number of the year can be divided exactly by 4 then it is a leap year. (A number divides exactly by 4 if its last two figures divide by 4.)

For example. The number 2008 can be divided by 4,

 so the year 2008 will be a leap year.

 (The last two figures are 08 and 8 divides by 4.)

When will the next leap year be ?

Exercise 3.6

Use a calendar to help you to answer these questions.

1.   How many days are there in January ?

2.   How many days are there in August ?

3.   How many days are there in June ?

4.   Which month has the least number of days ?

5.   How many days are there from September 8th to September 29th ?
 Do not count the day you start from.

6.   How many days are there from January 27th to February 3rd ?

7.   Bill is going on holiday in 12 days time. If today is January 25th on what date does Bill go on holiday ?

8.   If today is February 20th and it is a Leap Year what will the date be in 15 days time ?

9.   If today is 15th March what was the date 7 days ago ?

10.   If today is 5th May what was the date 17 days ago ?

11.   Mary and Jill were born in the same year.
 Mary was born on April 5th.
 Mary is 24 days older than Jill.
 On what date was Jill born ?

12. Steve likes Formula One motor racing.
    The first Grand Prix of the season was held on March 13th.
    The next race took place three weeks later.
    On what date did the second race take place ?

13. Alison is looking forward to the summer holidays.
    School finishes on July 22nd.
    If today is 21st June how many days will Alison have to wait until the end of term ?

14. Stuart's birthday is three weeks after William's birthday.
    If William's birthday is on the 12th November on what date is Stuart's birthday ?

15. Alex has a dental appointment on March 18th and he has an important exam on April 21st. How many days after his dental appointment does Alex have his exam ?

Exercise 3.7   Applications and Activities

1. Lopa bought a pencil costing 25 pence and a ruler costing 47 pence. How much did she spend altogether ?

2. Tracey and Adam are playing darts. Each player starts at 301 and takes away the total they score with 3 darts.
   1   Tracey throws first. She scores 8, 15 and 20. What did Tracey score altogether ?
   2   What number is left when Tracey takes away her score from 301 ?
   3   Adam throws next. He scores 13, 14 and 2. What did Adam score altogether ?
   4   What number is left when Adam takes his score away from 301 ?

3. How much change would you get from 50p if you spent 37p ?

4. Find numbers which could replace the asterisks to make these sums correct.

1
```
    2 4
  + 2 *
  -----
    4 7
```

5
```
    2 * 7
  + 1 4 8
  -------
    4 1 5
```

8
```
    6 2
  - * 4
  -----
    1 8
```

2
```
    3 *
  + 2 5
  -----
    5 7
```

6
```
    * 3 6
  + 2 7 5
  -------
    8 1 1
```

9
```
    4 1
  - 1 *
  -----
    2 9
```

3
```
    * 2
  + 4 3
  -----
    8 5
```

7
```
    4 7
  - 2 *
  -----
    2 2
```

10
```
    2 4 *
  - 1 1 6
  -------
    1 2 5
```

4
```
    3 6
  + 2 *
  -----
    6 3
```

5. Gordon was looking at his English Essay book. He had written 5 pages for his first essay, 3 pages for his second essay, 4 pages for the third, 6 for the fourth and 7 for the fifth.
   1   How many pages of essays had Gordon written altogether ?
   2   His Essay book contained 64 pages. How many pages were still blank ?

6. **Magic square**

   Copy the diagram on the right.
   Write the numbers 1 to 9 in the squares so
   that each row and each column adds up
   to 15.
   You can only use each number once.

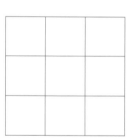

7. **Opposites**

   Write an opposite of each of these.
   1   Open the door.
   2   Spend £5.
   3   Fill the kettle.
   4   Get dressed.
   5   Tie your shoelace.
   6   Take away 5.

The opposite of subtracting is adding.
We can check subtraction sums by doing an addition sum.
15 − 6 = 9   so   9 + 6 = 15   or   6 + 9 = 15
12 − 5 = 7   so   7 + 5 = 12   or   5 + 7 = 12

Write addition sums to check each of these.
7   11 − 4 = 7
8   23 − 8 = 15
9   17 − 6 = 11

The opposite of adding is subtracting.
We can check addition sums by doing a subtraction sum.
5 + 6 = 11   so   11 − 6 = 5   or   11 − 5 = 6
12 + 8 = 20   so   20 − 8 = 12   or   20 − 12 = 8

Write subtraction sums to check each of these.
10   8 + 7 = 15
11   21 + 8 = 29
12   14 + 12 = 26

8.   **The Dice Game**

This game can be played by two or more
people. You need 4 dice and a sheet of
paper on which to record the scores.
Players take turns to roll the 4 dice.
On your first turn you roll the 4 dice and
add together in your head the 4 numbers
shown. This is your score for that turn.
Record it on the paper.

On your next turn add your new score to your score for the first throw.

Play continues and you keep on adding to your previous scores.
The first player to score 100 or more is the winner.

You can play this game on your own. Record your scores in the usual way.
Play several games and find the lowest number of throws you took to score
100 or more.

9. **The Take Away Game**

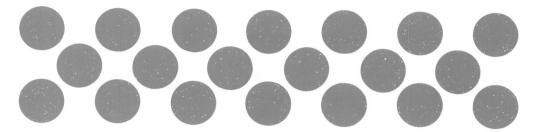

You need 20 counters and a partner.
Take it in turns to remove counters from the pile.
You must take either 1, 2 or 3 counters when it is your turn.
The person who takes the last counter is the winner.

Play several games. Take it in turns to be the first to start.

Try recording your games on paper. Can you find a method of playing so that you always win ?

Does it matter whether you start first, or not, in each game ?

Try starting with a different number of counters.
For example, start with 100 counters.
Change the rules so that you may take away more counters.
For example, you may take any number of counters from 1 to 10 when it is your turn.

PUZZLES

11. Copy this diagram.
     Write the numbers 1 to 6 in the circles so that
     each side of the triangle adds up to 10.
     Each number can only be used once.

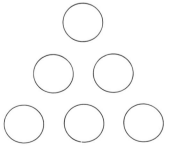

12. The village clock only gives the correct time
     twice a day. Can you explain this ?

4 Thinking about collecting information

Different ways of collecting information

Describe how information is being collected in each of these pictures. Why do you think the information is being collected ?

In what other ways can information be collected ?

A scientist at work

A street survey

A postal survey

A telephone survey

An observatory

Information from tables

A lot of information can be presented neatly in the form of a table. The table below shows the final placings after a 5-a-side football tournament between the depots of a timber company.

	Played	Won	Lost	Drawn	Goals For	Goals Against	Points
Birch	4	3	1	0	10	4	6
Deal	4	2	1	1	7	8	5
Ash	4	2	2	0	7	7	4
Cedar	4	1	2	1	7	10	3
Elm	4	1	3	0	5	7	2

1 Which team came second ?
2 How many goals did Cedar score ?
3 Which two teams were involved in the drawn game ?
4 Which team had a total of 4 goals scored against them during the whole competition ?

Make up questions of your own using the table and ask a friend to answer them. Make sure you know the answers.

Pop music charts

The first chart appeared in *Billboard* in New York on 4 January 1936.
The Top-Ten record sales chart appeared in the *New Musical Express* on 14 November 1952.
How could you find the most popular record in your class ?
Look at a recent pop music chart.
How many of the records in the chart are new records and not old records that have been re-released, or old records that have been re-recorded ?

What type of records are played on juke-boxes ?

4 Collecting Information

Information can be collected from many different places.
At one time information came mainly from books, newspapers and magazines.
Before that, the method of passing information was to tell someone.

Nowadays information can be obtained from television (Teletext and Oracle), radio, computers, videos, audio cassettes etc.

You may collect information for yourself. This may involve looking, listening, asking questions, etc. You will have to record your observations in a suitable way.

Information from tables

A clear method of giving information is to use a **table**.
One table can show many pieces of information.
You may only be interested in part of the table.

Example

This is a table which shows the costs of a holiday at Hotel Sunnyland.

First day of holiday	Cost per person.	Children half-price.
	7 nights	10 nights
June	£112	£128
July	£129	£147
August	£142	£162
September	£117	£134

Mr and Mrs Trindle have one child.
They decided to go to Hotel Sunnyland for 10 nights.
Their holiday started on 12th August.
What was the total cost of their holiday ?

The cost is £162 per person

Cost for Mr Trindle   £162
Cost for Mrs Trindle £162
Cost for the child   £ 81   (Half-price for children)
Total cost of hotel = £405

Exercise 4.1

1. This table shows the number of meals served in the school canteen each day to pupils in each year group.

	Mon	Tues	Wed	Thurs	Fri	Total
Year 7	53	51	47	56	42	
Year 8	48	42	46	52	45	
Year 9	47	54	53	51	49	
Year 10	43	41	37	47	43	
Year 11	38	41	47	39	42	
Total						

1 How many meals were served to pupils in Year 10 on Thursday ?

2 How many meals were served to pupils in Year 7 on Tuesday ?

Make a copy of the table.

3 Complete the right-hand column. This shows the number of meals served to each year.

4 Complete the bottom row. This shows the total number of meals served each day.

5 How many meals did the canteen serve during the week ?

2. A sports shop sells a range of sweatshirts.
This table shows the various colours, sizes and costs of the sweatshirts.

	Small	Medium	Large	Extra Large
Green	£10.50	£11.25	£12.00	£12.75
Red	£10.25	£10.80	£11.20	£11.55
Blue	£10.60	£10.90	£11.20	£11.50

Find the cost of the following from the table.

1 A small red sweatshirt.

2 A large blue sweatshirt.

3 An extra large green sweatshirt.

4 A medium blue sweatshirt.

5 A small blue sweatshirt.

6 Which sweatshirt costs £10.80 ?

7   Which is the most expensive sweatshirt ?

8   How much more does a large green sweatshirt cost than a large blue sweatshirt ?

9   How much more does an extra large green sweatshirt cost than a medium blue sweatshirt ?

10   What is the total cost of buying a small red and a small blue sweatshirt ?

3.

First day of holiday	Cost per person. Children half-price.		
	7 nights	10 nights	14 nights
March	£ 84	£108	£144
April	£ 98	£126	£168
May	£ 98	£126	£168
June	£112	£144	£192
July	£132	£170	£226
August	£142	£183	£243
September	£120	£154	£206

The table shows the cost of staying at Hotel Greenfields.
For example, if you start your holiday on the 29th June, for 10 nights it will cost you £144.

1   What is the cost for one person, starting a holiday on 12th August, for 7 nights ?

2   What is the cost for one person, starting a holiday on 26th May, for 14 nights ?

3   What is the cost for a child, starting a holiday on 1st July, for 10 nights ?

4   Mr and Mrs Wright have one child. They start their holiday on 22nd June, for 7 nights. What will their hotel bill be ?

5   Mr and Mrs Arkwright have booked a 10 night holiday starting on 25th March. What will the holiday cost ?

6   How much more will a 10 night holiday cost if it starts in July instead of in March ?

7   How much extra does it cost to stay for 14 nights than to stay for 10 nights in September ?

8   Mr Malhotra paid £183 for his holiday.
How long did he stay at the hotel ?

9   Mr and Mrs Banks paid a total of £224 for their holiday.
In what month did they start their holiday ?
How long did they stay at the hotel ?

Tally marks

If you had to count the number of people in your class it would be very easy. You only have to count one group of people.

Suppose you had to count the different colours of cars passing the school. It is difficult to keep count of more than one group of things at a time.

A method of keeping count is to use **tally marks**.
Each time a red car passes the school you put a tally mark against red.
For a blue car you would put a tally mark against blue.
You could do this for many different colours.
It could look like this.

RED | | | | | | | | | | | | | | | | | | | |
BLUE | | | | | | | | | | | | |

How many red cars passed the school ?
I counted 20 tally marks. So 20 red cars passed the school.

It is difficult to count tally marks when they are written like this.
Tally marks are easier to count if they are grouped together.
We group tally marks into groups of 5.   卅
The fifth tally mark goes across the first four.

The survey now looks like this.

RED   卅   卅   卅   卅
BLUE   卅   卅 | |

20 red cars passed the school. $4 \times 5 = 20$
12 blue cars passed the school. $(2 \times 5) + 2 = 10 + 2 = 12$

Exercise 4.2

1.   Write the numbers represented by these tally marks.

1 卅 | 6 卅 卅 卅 | |
2 卅 卅 | | 7 卅 卅 |
3 | | | | 8 卅 卅 卅 卅 卅 | | |
4 卅 | | | | 9 卅 卅 卅 卅 | | |
5 卅 卅 卅   10 卅 卅 卅 卅

2.   Represent the following numbers using tally marks.
      1   3
      2   8
      3   14
      4   22
      5   10

Collecting data

Data is the name given to information that is collected.
You must have an easy method of recording your data.
To record data you use a **data collection sheet**.

IMPORTANT: If you do a survey out of school make sure that you are looked after by
a teacher or a responsible adult. Do not go near dangerous roads or talk to strangers.
The most important part of a survey is your safety.

Example

Each time a boy passed the classroom door Pam wrote a letter B on her paper.
When a girl went by she wrote a letter G on her paper.
Here is her record.

B   G   B   B   G   G   B   G   G   B
G   B   B   G   G   B   G   B   B   B

Design a data collection sheet that uses tally marks.

	Tally	Total
Girl	ⅢⅠ ⅠⅠⅠⅠ	9
Boy	ⅢⅠ ⅢⅠ Ⅰ	11

This data collection sheet is easy to use.
It is quicker to write down tally marks than to write B or G, and the totals are easier
to see.
You can see that 9 girls and 11 boys passed the classroom.

Exercise 4.3

1. Robin likes cats and dogs.
   He asked all the people in his form if they had a cat or a dog. He wrote down
   their replies.

cat	cat	neither	cat	dog	cat	neither
neither	dog	cat	dog	neither	neither	dog
dog	dog	neither	neither	dog	neither	

   1 Copy this data collection sheet.
        Complete it for the data Robin collected.

Reply	Tally	Total
Cat		
Dog		
Neither		

   2 How many people did Robin ask ?
   3 Which was the more common pet ?

2. Hilary and Suzanne want to study the choices of food, for the pupils in their year.
   In the canteen pupils can have chips, baked potato or mashed potato.
   The girls started collecting data one lunch-time.
   They noted the following choices:

   chips, mash, neither, baked potato,
   baked potato, mash, chips, chips,
   mash, neither, chips, baked potato,
   chips, neither, chips, chips.

   Hilary and Suzanne collected 16 observations.
   Not every person was observed. This was because they could not write quickly
   enough.

   1 Design a data collection sheet that Hilary and Suzanne could use.
   2 Enter the 16 observations they made on your data collection sheet.

Exercise 4.4   Applications and Activities

1. **The Planets of the Solar System**

Planet	Distance from the Sun (km)	Number of moons	Diameter (km)	Time to rotate once on axis	Time for 1 orbit round the Sun
Mercury	58 000 000	0	4 900	59 days	88 days
Venus	108 000 000	0	12 100	244 days	225 days
Earth	150 000 000	1	12 800	24 hours	365 days
Mars	228 000 000	2	6 800	25 hours	687 days
Jupiter	778 000 000	16	143 000	10 hours	11.9 years
Saturn	1 427 000 000	17	120 000	10 hours	29.5 years
Uranus	2 870 000 000	5	52 000	17 hours	84 years
Neptune	4 500 000 000	3	48 000	18 hours	165 years
Pluto	*5 970 000 000	1	3 000	6.4 days	248 years

* Pluto has an unusual orbit. At times it is closer to the Sun than Neptune. Try to find out more about Pluto.

1   Which is the nearest planet to the Sun ?

2   How long does it take Mars to orbit the Sun ?

3   How far is Saturn from the Sun ?

4   What is the diameter of Neptune ?

5   How long does it take Neptune to rotate on its own axis ?
       The Earth takes 1 day, which is equal to 24 hours.

6   Which planet is 2 870 000 000 km from the Sun ?

7   How many moons does Mars have ?

8   Which planet takes the longest time to rotate on its own axis ?

9   Which planet has the smallest diameter ?

10 Which planet has the largest diameter ?

11 How much further is the Earth away from the Sun than Venus is ?

12 Which planets have only one moon ?

13 How much bigger is the diameter of Earth than the diameter of Venus ?

14 How much longer does it take Pluto to orbit the Sun than Neptune takes ?

15 Which planets have no moons ?

2.   **Favourite book**

You read books in school and you may enjoy reading books at home.
Some newspapers list the best selling
books.

These lists rarely include your opinions. So
you are going to design a data collection
sheet which you could use to get the
opinions of pupils in your class.

You might want to find the most popular
book. This could be difficult. Your data
collection sheet might not be big enough.
Why ?

You could find the most popular 'type' of book.
The data collection sheet could include science fiction, adventure, horror, etc.

Collect data from people in your form.
The survey could be extended to include people in your year.
Comment on the results of your survey.

3.   **Television programmes**

Design a data collection sheet to discover which is the most popular television
programme.
Make sure that your data collection sheet is easy and quick to use.

Survey people in your form.
If possible survey people in another form.
How can you make sure that someone has not been surveyed more than once ?
Comment on the results of your survey.

PUZZLE

13.   The diagram represents a cherry in a glass.
By moving two straws change the diagram so
that the cherry is no longer in the glass.

5 Thinking about multiplication and

At work

How might these people use multiplication and division in their jobs ?
Can you think of any other job in which a person might use multiplication and division ?

A clerk working in the foreign exchange at a bank

A farmer sowing seeds

A painter and decorator

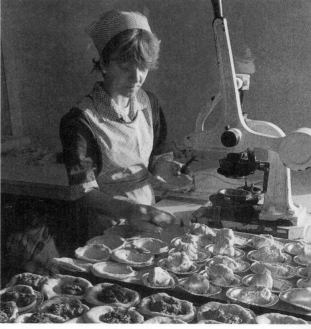

A caterer

division

The first mechanical calculator

As early as 1642, Blaise Pascal, a young French mathematician, designed and made the first mechanical calculator. Pascal was only 19 years old at the time.

The machine did multiplication by repeated addition. So 23 × 4 was calculated by doing 23 + 23 + 23 + 23. How many different ways can you think of for calculating 23 × 4 ?

Try to find out how a modern calculator performs calculations.

Blaise Pascal's calculator

A basic calculator

The modern calculator

There are two types of calculator, the basic calculator and the scientific calculator. Both are very light and can be carried easily.

When Charles Babbage designed his Difference Engine he was unable to complete the project, which he worked on from 1823 to 1842, because engineers found it was impossible to build. Had the project been completed its weight would have been about 2 tonnes. Hardly a pocket calculator !

How many modern calculators would you need to make a 2 tonne load of calculators ?

What other devices can you use to do calculations ?

Try to find out when the first electronic calculator was invented.

A scientific calculator

5 Multiplication and Division

Multiplication

Tables Square

×	0	1	2	3	4	5	6	7	8	9	10
0	0	0	0	0	0	0	0	0	0	0	0
1	0	1	2	3	4	5	6	7	8	9	10
2	0	2	4	6	8	10	12	14	16	18	20
3	0	3	6	9	12	15	18	21	24	27	30
4	0	4	8	12	16	20	24	28	32	36	40
5	0	5	10	15	20	25	30	35	40	45	50
6	0	6	12	18	24	30	36	42	48	54	60
7	0	7	14	21	28	35	42	49	56	63	70
8	0	8	16	24	32	40	48	56	64	72	80
9	0	9	18	27	36	45	54	63	72	81	90
10	0	10	20	30	40	50	60	70	80	90	100

It is important that you know your tables.

For example, suppose you wanted to buy some spare fuses from the DIY shop. You want 5 fuses, and they cost 9p each. $5 \times 9p = 45p$.

Multiplying a number by 10

Work out 18 × 10.

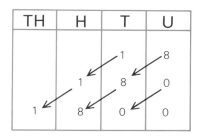

When you multiply a number by 10 each figure becomes 10 times bigger, so each figure on the abacus chart moves **one** place to the **left**.

18 × 10 = 180.

Multiplying a number by 100

Work out 18 × 100.

TH	H	T	U
		1	8
	1	8	0
1	8	0	0

100 = 10 × 10, so you are multiplying by 10, and then by 10 again.
When you multiply a number by 10 each figure on the abacus chart moves one place to the left.

Multiply by 10 again. Each figure moves one more place to the left.

So to multiply by 100 move each figure on the abacus chart **two** places to the **left**.

18 × 100 = 1800

Exercise 5.1

1. Work out the following.

    1 6 × 10   **5** 30 × 10   **8** 100 × 65

    2 6 × 100   **6** 124 × 100   **9** 10 × 73

    3 174 × 10   **7** 306 × 100   **10** 100 × 7486

    4 27 × 100

2. What is the cost of 10 footballs if one football costs £8 ?

3. The price of a ticket to watch a rugby match was £4.
    What would 100 tickets cost ?

4. How many pence are there in £12 ?

5.   Susan travels to work by car. She lives 8 miles from work.
       What is the total distance Susan drives to and from work each week ? She works
       a 5-day week.

6.   What number can the box be replaced by in each of these questions ?
       1 $13 \times 10 = \square$ **4** $\square \times 42 = 4200$
       2 $\square \times 51 = 510$ **5** $123 \times \square = 1230$
       3 $37 \times \square = 370$ **6** $\square \times 574 = 57400$

7.   A school organised a trip to London.
       The return train fare for a pupil was £15.
       The return train fare for a teacher was £23.
       100 pupils and 10 teachers went on the trip.
       1   What was the total cost of the train tickets for the pupils ?
       2   What was the total cost of the train tickets for the teachers ?
       3   How much was spent on train tickets altogether ?

Multiplication without a calculator

Work out 53×6.

If you know your tables up to 10×10 you can do this question.
Here are three ways of looking at this question.
See which method you prefer. You may even have a method of your own. If your
method works keep using it.

Method 1

Draw a diagram to show 53×6.

$53 = 50 + 3$ or 5 tens + 3 units.

$50 \times 6 = 300$
$3 \times 6 = 18$

So $53 \times 6 = 300 + 18$
$= 318$

	50	3	
	50×6	3×6	6
	$= 300$	$= 18$	

Method 2

You can use an abacus chart to work out 53 × 6.

H	T	U
	○○○ ○○○ (5)	○○○ (3)

This abacus chart shows the number 53.
Multiply the number of counters in the tens and units column by 6.

H	T	U
	30 counters	18 counters

Your abacus chart would look like this. The number of counters in each column has been written in.
Exchange 10 units counters for
      1 tens counter.
Exchange 10 tens counters for
      1 hundreds counter.
Do this as many times as you can.

H	T	U
○○○	○	○○○ ○○○

Your abacus chart will end up looking like this. It shows 318.

So 53 × 6 = 318.

Method 3

This method is very similar to the abacus chart method. It is much easier because you do not have lots of counters to sort out.

Step 1

```
   5 3
 ×   6
 ─────
     8
   1
```

6 × 3 = 18
18 = 1 ten and 8 units.
The 8 units are placed in the units column.
The 1 ten is carried to the tens column. We have written it below the answer line.

Step 2

```
   5 3
 ×   6
 ─────
 3 1 8
   1
```

6 × 5 = 30
This is 6 × 5 tens = 30 tens.
Add on the 1 ten carried from the units column.
31 tens = 3 hundreds and 1 ten.

So 53 × 6 = 318.

Method 3 becomes quite easy after you have practised using it.

Exercise 5.2

Do this exercise without using a calculator. You can check you answers afterwards using a calculator.

1. Work these out. Use whichever method you find the easiest.

    1 23 × 3   **5** 36 × 2   **8** 43 × 8

    2 12 × 4   **6** 28 × 5   **9** 54 × 9

    3 24 × 4   **7** 39 × 6   **10** 65 × 7

    4 15 × 5

2. Mrs Clarke bought a chocolate bar for each of her three children. Each chocolate bar cost 24p. How much did Mrs Clarke pay for the three chocolate bars ?

3. A gardener planted 5 rows of cabbage plants.
    He planted 14 plants in each row.
    How many plants did the gardener plant altogether ?

4. Six classes lined up for a fire drill, on the playground.
    There were 28 pupils in each class.
    What was the total number of pupils lined up for the fire drill ?

5. Claire has a paper round.
    She delivers 53 papers each day.
    Claire delivers papers every day except Sunday.
    How many papers does she deliver in a week ?

6. The caretaker sets out the chairs for assembly.
    He set out 16 rows of chairs. There were 8 chairs in each row.
    How many chairs did the caretaker set out altogether ?

7. This is a type of hoop-la game.
    A player throws 6 hoops at the pegs. The score for each peg is written at the bottom of the peg.
    What is the total score for the 6 hoops in the diagram ?

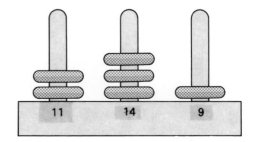

8.   Sarah is playing darts. She scores double 13, treble 20 and a single 8. What is Sarah's total score for the three darts ?

9.   Rajendra has made a grid of squares.
     He spilt some paint on his paper.
     1   How many squares did the grid have ?
     2   What two numbers did you multiply together to get your answer ?

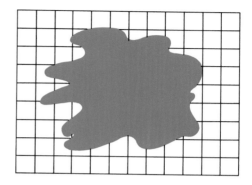

10. A classroom block of a school has 3 floors. On each floor there are 5 classrooms. Each classroom contains 5 windows, 4 cupboards, 30 desks and 30 chairs.
     1   How many classrooms are there in the block ?
     2   What numbers did you multiply together to get your answer ?
     3   How many cupboards are there in the block ?
     4   What numbers did you multiply together to get your answer ?
     5   How many desks are there on each floor of the block ?
     6   What numbers did you multiply together to get your answer ?
     7   How many desks are there in the block ?
     8   What numbers did you multiply together to get your answer ?

Making calculations easier

Try to work out 17×8 in your head.
It is not very easy!
Can we make the question easier ?

$8 = 2 \times 4$ So to multiply by 8 multiply by 2 then by 4.

$$17 \times 8 = 17 \times 2 \times 4 \qquad \text{Multiply 17 by 2}$$
$$= 34 \times 4$$
$$= 34 \times 2 \times 2 \qquad \text{Because } 4 = 2 \times 2$$
$$= 68 \times 2 \qquad \text{Multiplying by the first 2}$$
$$= 136 \qquad \text{Multiplying by the second 2}$$

So $17 \times 8 = 136$

Multiplying by numbers such as 2, 3, 5 and 10 is much easier than multiplying by numbers such as 4, 6, 8, 9, 12.

Examples

1   Work out 21×12 without using a calculator. Show each step of your working.

$$
\begin{aligned}
21 \times 12 &= 21 \times 2 \times 6 \\
&= 42 \times 6 \\
&= 42 \times 2 \times 3 \\
&= 84 \times 3 \\
&= 252
\end{aligned}
$$

Because $12 = 2 \times 6$
Multiplying 21 by 2
Because $6 = 2 \times 3$
Multiplying 42 by 2
Multiplying 84 by 3

So $21 \times 12 = 42 \times 6 = 84 \times 3 = 252$

2   Work out 29×30 without a calculator. Show each step of your working.

$$
\begin{aligned}
29 \times 30 &= 29 \times 3 \times 10 \\
&= 87 \times 10 \\
&= 870
\end{aligned}
$$

Because $30 = 3 \times 10$
Multiplying 29 by 3
Multiplying 87 by 10

So $29 \times 30 = 87 \times 10 = 870$

Exercise 5.3

1.   Copy and complete the following.

1   $29 \times 8 = 29 \times 2 \times \ldots$
$= 58 \times 4$
$= 58 \times 2 \times \ldots$
$= 116 \times 2$
$= \ldots$

2   $37 \times 6 = 37 \times \ldots \times 3$
$= \ldots \times 3$
$= \ldots$

3   $17 \times 24 = 17 \times \ldots \times 12$
$= 34 \times \ldots$
$= 34 \times \ldots \times 6$
$= 68 \times \ldots$
$= 68 \times 2 \times \ldots$
$= 136 \times \ldots$
$= \ldots$

4   $31 \times 40 = 31 \times \ldots \times 10$
$= 124 \times \ldots$
$= \ldots$

2.   Work out the following without using a calculator.

1	43 × 4	**4**	52 × 6	**7**	19 × 16
2	27 × 8	**5**	23 × 30	**8**	41 × 40
3	14 × 9	**6**	41 × 12		

Division

Divide 48 by 3.

Method 1

You can use an abacus chart to work this out.

H	T	U
	○ ○ ○ ○	○○○ ○○○ ○○

This abacus chart shows the number 48.
When you divide by 3 you have to split the abacus chart into three equal sections.

H	T	U
	○	○○○ ○○○
	○	○○○ ○○○ ○○○
	○	○○○

Always start at the **left**.
When you split the 4 tens into three equal sections there is 1 ten left over.
Exchange this 1 ten for 10 units and add them to the 8 units already in the units column.

Now split the 18 units into three equal sections.

H	T	U
	○	○○○ ○○○
	○	○○○ ○○○
	○	○○○ ○○○

Your abacus chart should now look like this.
Each of the three sections shows the number 16.

So 48 ÷ 3 = 16

This method is not very good for dividing by large numbers.
It is very good for explaining what is happening when you divide one number by another number.

Method 2

This method is very similar to the first method.

$$\begin{array}{r} 1\ 6 \\ \hline 3\overline{)4\ ^18} \end{array}$$

Step 1 $4 \div 3 = 1$ and 1 left over.
Step 2 The 1 left over is 1 ten.
1 ten = 10 units.
Step 3 Add the 10 units to the 8 units making 18 units.
Step 4 $18 \div 3 = 6$

So $48 \div 3 = 16$

Exercise 5.4

1. Work out these questions without using a calculator.

1	$26 \div 2$	**5**	$91 \div 7$	**8**	$90 \div 6$
2	$36 \div 3$	**6**	$54 \div 3$	**9**	$96 \div 8$
3	$60 \div 5$	**7**	$72 \div 4$	**10**	$189 \div 9$
4	$52 \div 4$				

2. There are 98 days to go until it is Greta's birthday.
    How many weeks is this ?

3. Sarah is paid £84 for working 7 hours of overtime on Sunday.
    How much is Sarah paid for one hour's work on Sunday ?

4. James shares 96 conkers equally among his 5 friends and himself. How many conkers does each person get ?

5. A school paid £64 for 4 calculators. What is the cost of one calculator ?

6. Five railway tickets cost £80. What is the cost of one ticket ?

7. A man drives a distance of 86 miles. He stops exactly half-way for lunch. How far did he drive before lunch ?

8. Mr Taylor planted a total of 72 lettuce plants in 6 rows.
    How many lettuce plants did he plant in each row ?

9.   Amanda saves £3 a week from her Saturday job. So far Amanda has saved £75.
      For how long has Amanda been saving ?

10.   There are 196 books on 7 shelves in the library. All the books are the same size
      and there are the same number on each shelf.
      How many books are on each shelf ?

Remainders

Sometimes when one number is divided by another we get a remainder.
In practical situations we often have to **round up** or **round down**.

Rounding up

Example

23 people are waiting to use the lift to get to the top of a building. The lift can only
carry 4 people at a time.
How many trips must the lift make to take everyone to the top of the building ?

$23 \div 4 = 5$ exactly and 3 left over.
We sometimes say "5 remainder 3".
On a calculator $23 \div 4 = 5.75$

If the lift makes only 5 trips, 3 people will be left at the bottom of the building.
So the lift has to make 6 trips. On one of the trips there will only be 3 people in the
lift.

We had to **round up** to 6, because 5 trips were not enough.

Rounding down

Example

A bookshelf is 67 cm long. How many books can be put on the shelf if each book
is 5 cm thick ?

$67 \div 5 = 13$ remainder 2
On a calculator $67 \div 5 = 13.4$

There are 13 books on the shelf.

We have had to **round down** here. You cannot fit the 14th book on the shelf. The
remainder 2 tells us that there is a 2 cm gap.

Exercise 5.5

1. Samantha works at a florist's. She has to put different types of flowers into
    bunches. There must be 8 flowers in a bunch.
    How many bunches can be made with these flowers ?
    1   25 roses   **4**   53 freesias
    2   46 lilies   **5**   84 gladioli
    3   36 tulips   **6**   97 daffodils

2. Cars, each 4 m long, are parked in a straight line on a small ferry. The parking
    space on the ferry is 22 m long.
    1   Write down a division sum that you can use to find the greatest number of
            cars that the ferry can carry.
    2   What is the greatest number of cars that the ferry can carry ?
    3   Did you have to round up or round down ?

3. A boat can carry 6 people. How many boats are needed to take 45 people across
    to an island ?

4. Alf has to drive people to a basketball match.
    His van can carry nine people at a time.
    How many trips must he make to transport 47 people ?

5. Barry is packing eggs into boxes of six ready for market.
    How many boxes containing 6 eggs can he send if he starts with 83 eggs ?

6. After he finished packing the eggs Barry weighed potatoes into 5 kg bags. How
    many full bags of potatoes did he pack if he started with 63 kg of potatoes ?

7. Bob makes wooden toys. He sells each toy for £3. How many wooden toys must
    Bob sell in order to make at least £40 ?

8. How many wooden blocks each 9 cm long could be placed end to end in a box
    which is 30 cm long ?

Exercise 5.6   Applications and Activities

1.   Jack is 10 times older than Sally. If Sally is 3 years old how old is Jack ?

2.   Charlene saves £2 a week for her summer holidays. How much will Charlene save in 48 weeks ?

3.   Charles is playing darts. He scores double 14, single 7 and treble 8.
   1   What did Charles score altogether with three darts ?
   2   If he needed to score 501 altogether what has Charles still to score ?

4.   One side of an office block has 8 windows on each floor.
   There are 72 windows on this side of the office block.
   How many floors does the office block have ?

5.   There are seven rows of coat pegs in the cloakroom.
   Each row of pegs can hold 45 coats.
   How many coats can be hung in the cloakroom ?

6.   Four people win £92 on the football pools. They share the money equally. How much does each person get ?

7.   Marie is packing toys into boxes. She packs eight toys into each box. How many boxes can she fill with 57 toys ?

8.   **Opposites**

   1   Write down the number 5.
   Multiply 5 by 8. Write your answer down.
   Divide your answer by 8. Write down this answer.
   What do you notice about this answer ?

   The opposite of multiplication is division.
   $3 \times 8 = 24$ so $24 \div 8 = 3$ or $24 \div 3 = 8$
   $7 \times 5 = 35$ so $35 \div 5 = 7$ or $35 \div 7 = 5$

   Division can be used to check multiplication sums.

   Write a division sum to check each of these multiplication sums.
   2 $3 \times 6 = 18$
   3 $5 \times 4 = 20$
   4 $9 \times 8 = 72$
   5 $6 \times 8 = 48$

The opposite of division is multiplication.

$24 \div 4 = 6$ so $6 \times 4 = 24$ or $4 \times 6 = 24$

$27 \div 9 = 3$ so $3 \times 9 = 27$ or $9 \times 3 = 27$

Multiplication can be used to check division sums.

Write multiplication sums to check each of these division sums.

6 $12 \div 2 = 6$

7 $30 \div 6 = 5$

8 $42 \div 7 = 6$

9 $48 \div 4 = 12$

9. **Tables race**

You first need to make a large tables square like the one on page 62. Do it as follows.

1   Cut out 144 squares of paper. Each square should measure 4 cm by 4 cm.

2   Place the squares into the shape of the tables square.

3   Using a red pen write each of the numbers of the top row on separate squares of paper.

4   Using a red pen write each of the numbers of the first column on squares of paper.

5   Use a red pen to write a multiplication sign on one square.

6   Using a blue pen write all the other numbers of the tables square. Write each number on a separate square of paper.

7   Check very carefully that your tables square is complete and correct.

Now mix all the pieces of paper up.

Either on your own or with a partner see how quickly you can re-make the tables square.

You could time how long it takes to re-make the square. Keep a record of your best time and see if you can improve on it.

Store your pieces of paper in an envelope. You can use them to practise your tables if you have a few minutes to spare.

10. **Dice Multiplication Game**

This game can be played by two or more players. You need 3 dice and a sheet of paper on which to record the scores.

Players take it in turns to roll the 3 dice.

On your turn you roll the 3 dice and multiply together the 3 numbers shown by the dice. If any of the dice shows a 6 it counts as a 0 so you score 0 for that turn.

Play continues with players adding to their previous scores.
The first player to score 200 or more is the winner.

You can play this game on your own. Play the game several times and find the lowest number of throws you took to score 200 or more.

11. **The Division Maze**

Copy this number square on squared paper.

Find the path through the maze taken by three contestants.
They enter from the bottom edge into a square on the bottom row and travel from square to square going horizontally (side-to-side) or vertically (up or down), but not diagonally. They get out across the top edge from a square on the top row.

End this side

28	8	17	26	10	32	44	72
7	3	66	15	60	12	81	18
56	42	98	700	112	217	49	98
52	24	9	75	30	25	4	287
61	19	11	31	33	55	100	91
50	85	70	140	21	77	35	14
95	36	63	90	45	5	20	13
40	6	28	88	16	23	22	64

Start this side

Alex can only enter squares with numbers which divide exactly by 5. Which square on the bottom row does he enter first ? Find his complete route and mark it on your copy by drawing a coloured line.

Basil can only enter squares with numbers which divide exactly by 3.
Which square on the bottom row does he enter first ? Find his complete route and mark it on your copy, using a different colour.

Chris can only enter squares with numbers which divide exactly by 7.
Which square on the bottom row does he enter first ? Find his complete route and mark it on your copy, using a third colour.

You can make a maze for yourself, for your friend to try, with the rule that he/she can only draw through squares with numbers which divide exactly by 4. Plan the route first, and then put numbers on so that all squares on your route have numbers which divide by 4, and all the other squares do not. Then make a copy of the number square without the route shown and let your friend try to find the way.

6 Thinking about coordinates

Coordinates

Coordinates are used to describe the position of something.
The window, marked x in this office block
could be described as the window which
is 2nd from the left on the 3rd floor.
A popular game which uses coordinates is
Battleships.
Can you think of any other situations in
which you might use coordinates to
describe the position of something ?

Noughts and crosses

You probably know the game of noughts and crosses, but have you ever tried to play
against someone at the other end of a telephone line ?

How would you play ?

Try this method.
The rows are labelled top, middle
and bottom.
The columns are labelled left,
centre and right.
The cross shown is in the
bottom-right position.

Draw a noughts and crosses grid.
The following game took place between two people over the telephone. The first
person to play used crosses and the second person used noughts.
To win a player must have 3 crosses (or noughts) in a line, horizontally, vertically or
diagonally.
Each turn was recorded as follows.
>   bottom-right
>   top-left
>   bottom-left
>   bottom-centre
>   top-right
>   middle-right
>   middle-centre
Did the player using noughts or the player using crosses win ?
Where was the winning line ?
Try playing noughts and crosses using coordinates.

Chess

One method of labelling a chess board is shown in the diagram.

The board is always used this way round with white playing up the board.

Each row, called a *rank*, is labelled from 1 to 8.

Each column, called a *file*, is labelled from A to H.

A typical opening move by white is E2 to E4.

Games of chess are sometimes played by telephone or post, using this system of instructions.

Try giving someone instructions to move a chess piece on the board using coordinates.

Maps

The art of drawing a map is called cartography.

A person who draws maps is called a cartographer.

How do maps use coordinates ?

How might a rescue helicopter pilot use coordinates ?

Someone plotting information on a map

 Coordinates

Describing the position of a point

Coordinates are used to describe the position of a point.
Two lines are drawn at right-angles to each other.
Squared paper or graph paper is used.
Each line is called an **axis**.

The horizontal line is called the **x-axis**.
The vertical line is called the **y-axis**.

The plural of axis is **axes**.
The axes can be numbered as shown.
The point where the x-axis meets the y-axis is
called the **origin**.

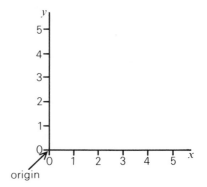

To locate a point

Suppose you want to tell someone where the
point A is located.
Follow these directions:
Start at the origin,
go across 4 squares,
now go up 3 squares.

So A is at the position 4 across and 3 up.

We can write this as:

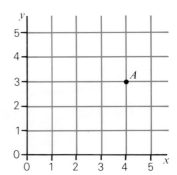

$$A\ (4,\ 3)$$

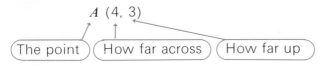

The **coordinates** of A are (4, 3).

The first number is called the **x-coordinate**.
The second number is called the **y-coordinate**.

You can use this method to describe the position of any point on the grid.

Example

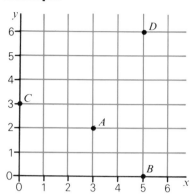

What are the coordinates of the points *A*, *B*, *C* and *D* ?

A has coordinates (3, 2).
B has coordinates (5, 0).
This means 5 across and 0 up.
0 up means the point is on the *x*-axis.
C has coordinates (0, 3).
This means 0 across and 3 up.
0 across means that the point is on the *y*-axis.
D has coordinates (5, 6).

Exercise 6.1

1. What are the coordinates of these points ?
    1   *A*
    2   *B*
    3   *C*
    4   *D*
    5   *E*

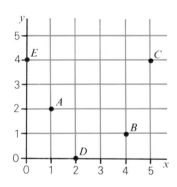

2. What are the coordinates of these points ?
    1   *P*
    2   *Q*
    3   *R*
    4   *S*
    5   *T*
    6   *U*
    7   What do you notice about the *x* and *y* coordinates of each point ?

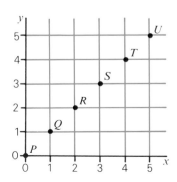

3. Debbie has described the coordinates of
    some points.
    Can you work out which point Debbie has
    described ?
    Give the letter for each.
    1   The first number is 3.
    2   The x-coordinate is 2.
    3   The point is on the x-axis.
    4   The first number is 0.
    5   The x and y coordinates are the same.
    6   The y-coordinate is twice as
           big as the x-coordinate.

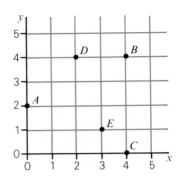

4. The grid below contains the 26 letters of the alphabet.

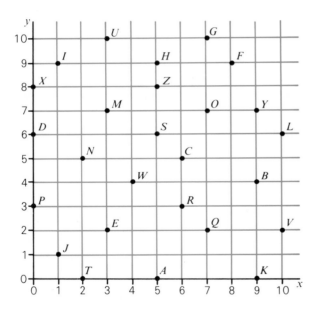

You can use the grid to write messages in code.
For example: (10, 6) (7, 7) (2, 5) (0, 6) (7, 7) (2, 5) is the code for London.

Name the places given by these codes.
1   (10, 6) (3, 2) (3, 2) (0, 6) (5, 6)
2   (7, 7) (9, 4) (5, 0) (2, 5)
3   (9, 7) (7, 7) (6, 3) (9, 0)
4   (7, 10) (10, 6) (7, 7) (3, 10) (6, 5) (3, 2) (5, 6) (2, 0) (3, 2) (6, 3)
5   (3, 7) (5, 0) (6, 3) (7, 10) (5, 0) (2, 0) (3, 2)

6   (5, 9) (1, 9) (7, 10) (5, 9)/(4, 4) (9, 7) (6, 5) (7, 7) (3, 7) (9, 4) (3, 2)
        This is two words.
7   Write the code for Bristol using the grid.
8   Write the code for Cardiff.
9   Write your name in this code.

Plotting points

In the first exercise you had to write down the information given by a point. You are now going to **plot** points.

Points are plotted using a small pencil cross or a dot.
We use a pencil to plot points so that mistakes can be rubbed out.
Small pencil crosses are better than dots because they are easier to see.

Example

Draw x and y axes on graph paper or squared paper.
Number each axis from 0 to 5.
Plot the points A (1, 1), B (5, 1), C (5, 5) and D (1, 5).
Join the points in order. Join the last point to the first point to make a shape.

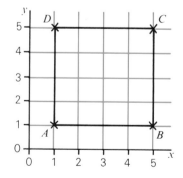

Remember: When you plot a point:
          Start at the origin.
          Go across first,
          then go up.

The shape made is a square.

When you draw a grid make sure that
1   you number the x and y axes correctly,
2   you label the axes x and y.

Exercise 6.2

1. **1** Copy the grid.
    2 Plot the point A (2, 1).
    3 Plot the point B (4, 5).
    4 Plot the point C (1, 0).
    5 Plot the point D (0, 4).

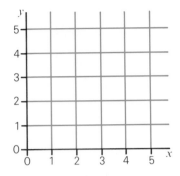

2. **1** Draw x and y axes on graph paper or squared paper.
        Number each axis from 0 to 6.
    2 Use small pencil crosses to plot the points
        (6, 3) (4, 5) (4, 4) (0, 4) (0, 2) (4, 2) (4, 1)
    3 Join the points in order, using a ruler.
        (i.e. Draw a straight line from (6, 3) to (4, 5), (4, 5) to (4, 4) and so on.
        Finally join (4, 1) to (6, 3) to complete the shape.)
    4 What shape have you drawn ?

3. **1** Draw x and y axes on graph paper or squared paper.
        Number each axis from 0 to 7.
    2 Plot the following points using small pencil **dots**.
        (5, 4) (4, 5) (3, 4)
        Join the points in order.
        Join the last point to the first point.
    3 On the same graph plot these points.
        (6, 5) (6, 6) (5, 6) (5, 5)
        Join the points in order and join the last point to the first point.

    Do the same for parts **4**, **5** and **6**, using the same graph.
    4 (2, 6) (2, 5) (3, 5) (3, 6)
    5 (6, 3) (6, 2) (2, 2) (2, 3)
    6 (1, 1) (1, 7) (7, 7) (7, 1)
    7 What does your drawing show ?

4. Draw x and y axes on graph paper or squared paper.
    Number each axis from 0 to 8.
    Join the following points in order.
    (3, 1) (5, 1) (6, 3) (8, 4) (6, 4) (3, 5) (3, 6) (2, 7) (0, 5) (1, 4) (2, 5) (2, 3)
    (1, 1) (2, 1) (3, 3) (5, 2) (3, 2) (3, 1)

    Draw a large dot at the point (2, 6).
    What have you drawn ?

Maps

Grid references

Grid references are used to give the positions of places on a map.
Grid references are like coordinates.

The numbers along the horizontal axis are called **eastings**.
The numbers along the vertical axis are called **northings**.

Eastings and northings always have two figures.
03 is used instead of 3.

A place can be located using a **four-figure grid reference**.
The first 2 figures tell us the eastings, the next 2 figures tell us the northings.
For example, point A in the diagram below has grid reference 0301.

Not all the places marked on a map are where
eastings and northings cross. Some places are found
inside squares.
When this happens we give the grid reference
of the bottom left-hand corner of the square.
For example. The grid reference 0102 refers to
any place which is on the thick line or in the
shaded square.

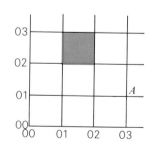

Remember: When giving a grid reference:
  The first two figures give the **eastings** (across),
  the second two figures give the **northings** (up).

Exercise 6.3

1. The grid reference of Harburg is 0607.
    Name the place with grid reference
    1 0206
    2 0404
    3 0102

    Tebay has grid reference 0104.
    Give the grid references for
    4 Vale,
    5 Flint,
    6 Maple.

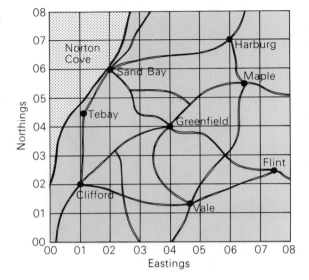

2. This map shows more detail.
    It is part of a bigger map.
    Notice that the eastings and
    northings do not start at 00.
    1 Give the grid references of
         Bywell, Ford and Waine.
    2 Give the grid references of the
         four farms on the map.
    3 Give the grid references of
         Waine Station and Ford
         Station.
    4 There are three bridges where
         the road goes **under** the
         railway.
         Give the grid reference of
         each bridge.
    5 What can be found at the place with grid reference 4437 ?
    6 What can be found at the place with grid reference 4540 ?
    7 What can be found at the place with grid reference 4539 ?

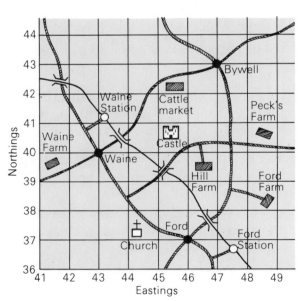

Exercise 6.4   Applications and Activities

1. **Coordinates in the classroom**

    Mr Cart's classroom looks like this.

Row 5	Chris			
Row 4		Hilda	Cath	Sam
Row 3	Richard		Paula	Hilary
Row 2	Graham			Philip
Row 1		Kylie		

    Line 1   Line 2   Line 3   Line 4   Line 5

    Mr Cart

    Pupils always sit in the same places.
    Mr Cart has written coordinates on the front of each exercise book.
    Paula's book has (4, 3) written on it. Paula sits in the fourth line and in the third row.
    Graham's book has (1, 2) written on it.

    1   How many pupils' desks are in the classroom ?

    2   Copy the plan of the classroom on squared paper.
           Write the name of each pupil on your plan.

    What coordinates are written on the top of the book belonging to these pupils ?

    3   Chris   **6**   Sam   **9**   Kylie

    4   Philip   **7**   Cath   **10**   Hilda

    5   Richard   **8**   Hilary

    Write the names of these pupils in their correct places.

    11   Gordon (5, 1)   **14**   Henry (3, 2)

    12   Elton (1, 1)   **15**   Nerys (1, 4)

    13   Leena (2, 2)   **16**   Kapil (4, 1)

    17   Rachel spilt ink on her exercise book.
            Mr Cart could only read the first coordinate.
            It was 5. Where did Rachel sit ?

    18   How many pupils were in the class ?

2. **Secret codes**

The 26 letters of the alphabet are contained in this grid.

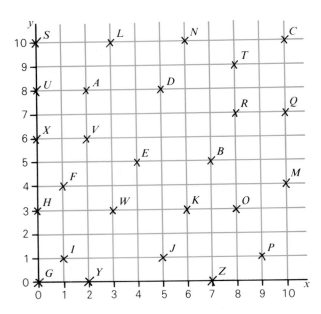

You can use the grid to send secret codes.
Use the grid to decode these messages.

1 (8, 9) (0, 3) (1, 1) (0, 10)/(10, 7) (0, 8) (4, 5) (0, 10) (8, 9) (1, 1) (8, 3)
(6, 10)/(1, 1) (0, 10)/(2, 8) (7, 5) (8, 3) (0, 8) (8, 9)/(10, 10) (8, 3)
(8, 3) (8, 7) (5, 8) (1, 1) (6, 10) (2, 8) (8, 9) (4, 5) (0, 10).

2 (3, 3) (0, 3) (4, 5) (8, 7) (4, 5)/(3, 3) (1, 1) (3, 10) (3, 10)/(2, 0) (8, 3)
(0, 8)/(1, 4) (1, 1) (6, 10) (5, 8)/(7, 0) (4, 5) (7, 5) (8, 7) (2, 8)
(0, 10)/(2, 8) (6, 10) (5, 8)/(9, 1) (4, 5) (3, 10) (1, 1) (10, 10) (2, 8)
(6, 10) (0, 10) ?

3 (10, 10) (8, 7) (8, 3) (0, 10) (0, 10) (1, 1) (6, 10) (0, 0)/(8, 9) (0, 3)
(4, 5)/(8, 7) (8, 3) (2, 8) (5, 8).

Make up your own coded messages.
Ask a friend to decode your messages.
Make sure you both use the same grid!

3. **Six-figure grid references**

When a large scale is used much more detail can be seen on the map.
One square can contain many features.
It is often necessary to locate something within a square.

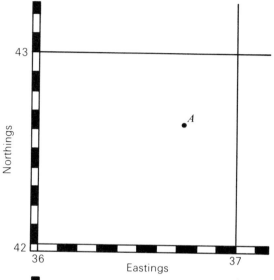

Giving the grid reference of A as 3642
is not very accurate.

Each square can be divided up into 100
smaller squares.

The grid reference of A is

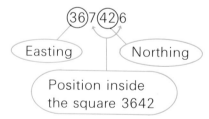

This is called a **six-figure bearing**.

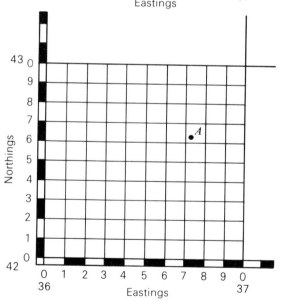

The 10 by 10 grid can be drawn on tracing paper.
Neither this grid nor the small numbers appear on the map.
They would clutter up the map and make it difficult to read.
Notice the black and white 'beading' is drawn to help you to divide the big
squares into smaller squares.

Country park

This map shows a country park.

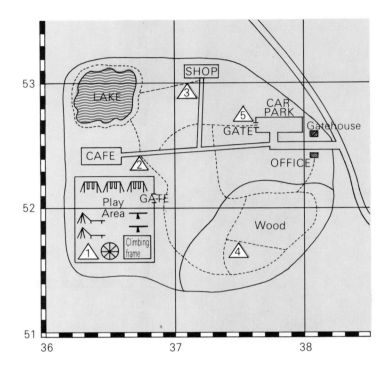

People using the country park must park their cars in the car park and use the footpaths.

Pathways are shown by dotted lines.

Litter bins are shown by triangles with numbers in, just like the one on the right.

1   What can be found at 381526 ?
2   What can be found at 368521 ?
3   What can be found at 371525 ?
4   Give the six-figure grid reference for each of the five litter bins.
5   Unfortunately there has been a problem with litter in certain parts of the park.
    4 extra litter bins have been bought to overcome the problem. Give the six-figure grid references of where you would put the bins. Explain how you decided where to put the litter bins.

Try to borrow an Ordnance Survey map of your own area. Find some local landmarks on it, e.g. railway station, church, school, park, hospital, golf course, well-known building. Make a list of these and work out their 6-figure grid references.

Give the list of grid references to a friend and ask him/her to discover what is at each place.

Your friend can then make a list of places for you to find.

4. **What is this ?**

On 2 mm graph paper draw and label the axes as shown, using 1 small square for each unit, so that the thicker lines 2 cm apart are used for 10, 20, etc.

Plot the points whose coordinates are given below.

Join each point to the next one with a straight line (working downwards in columns).

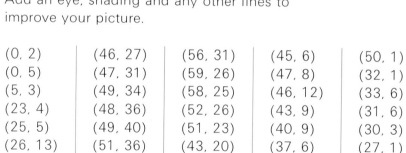

Add an eye, shading and any other lines to improve your picture.

(0, 2)	(46, 27)	(56, 31)	(45, 6)	(50, 1)
(0, 5)	(47, 31)	(59, 26)	(47, 8)	(32, 1)
(5, 3)	(49, 34)	(58, 25)	(46, 12)	(33, 6)
(23, 4)	(48, 36)	(52, 26)	(43, 9)	(31, 6)
(25, 5)	(49, 40)	(51, 23)	(40, 9)	(30, 3)
(26, 13)	(51, 36)	(43, 20)	(37, 6)	(27, 1)
(29, 21)	(52, 40)	(49, 15)	(37, 3)	(5, 0)
(35, 35)	(54, 35)	(50, 9)	(47, 3)	(0, 2)
(43, 25)	(54, 33)	(49, 6)		

PUZZLE

14. **The snail**

A snail climbs slowly up a wall which is 10 metres high.
It climbs 3 m every day, but it slips 2 m down every night.
How long will it take the snail to get to the top of the wall ?

7 Thinking about measures and the

The metric system

The metric system was devised by a group of French scientists around the time of the French Revolution.
It was made legal in England in 1864.

Today we still use the old system of British units (inches, pints, etc.) as well as metric units of measurement (centimetres, litres, etc.)
However, we are moving more and more towards the metric system. The first metric road signs giving distances in metres appeared in 1991.

A signpost showing distances in miles

A combination of old and new units

A metric road sign

Do you know your weight in kilograms or stones ?

The price of petrol given in pence per litre.

metric system

Measuring time

The Dutch scientist Christian Huygens made the first pendulum clock at The Hague, in December 1656.
The clock was powered by a pendulum which swung from side to side.
Galileo, the Italian astronomer and physicist, had studied the motion of the swinging pendulum 70 years earlier.

How does a pendulum power a clock ?
Why do clocks using a pendulum need to be wound up ?

How many different ways can you think of measuring time ?

A sundial, Kew Gardens

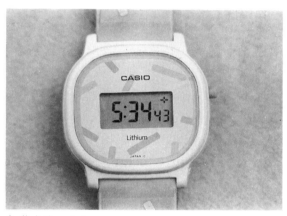

A digital watch

Record of silence

John Cage, an American composer, recorded an unusual record which lasted 4 minutes and 33 seconds, in 1952. It was very popular on juke boxes at the time. The record was unusual because there was 4 minutes and 33 seconds of complete silence. People actually paid money for the record to be played. Why do you think they did this ?

7 Measures and Metric Units

The metric system

There are two main systems of measurement, the British system and the metric system. The advantage of the metric system is that it is based on the number 10, or multiples of 10.

The metric system is being used more nowadays.
Petrol is now measured in litres instead of gallons.
Gallons is a British unit.
We still use some British units such as ounces, pounds, pints, miles.

Metric units

Length

Units of length are used when you are measuring distances.
The distances can be long or short.
You use the unit of length that is suitable for what you are measuring.

Length is based on the **metre** (m).
This is divided into 100 parts which each equal 1 centimetre, or
1000 parts which each equal 1 millimetre.
1000 metres make 1 kilometre.

1 metre (m)	= 1000 millimetres (mm)	
1 metre	= 100 centimetres (cm)	(so 1 cm = 10 mm)
1 kilometre (km)	= 1000 metres	

Weight

Weights can either be light or heavy.
That is why there are different units.
Weight is based on the **gram** (g).

1 gram (g)	= 1000 milligrams (mg)
1 kilogram (kg)	= 1000 grams
1 tonne	= 1000 kilograms

Capacity

The amount a container can hold is called its **capacity**.
Capacity is based on the **litre** (ℓ).

1 litre (ℓ) = 1000 millilitres (ml)	
1 litre = 100 centilitres (cl)	(so 1 cl = 10 ml)
1 kilolitre (kl) = 1000 litres	

Measuring

Whenever we measure something we only get an approximate answer.
For example, if you measure the length of your school field you would probably give
the answer to the nearest metre.
If you wanted a more accurate answer you would measure to the nearest centimetre.

No matter what distance you measure you will have to round off, depending on the
accuracy you require.

You have to do these things when measuring:
1   Choose the most appropriate unit to measure in.
2   Choose a suitable piece of equipment to measure with.
3   Read the measurement and record it.

Estimates

It is very useful if you can guess:
    − how long or high things are
    − the weight of an object
    − how much liquid a container holds
    − a length of time
These guesses are called **estimates**.

Reading scales

When you take a measurement you read a **scale** or **dial**.
The main numbers are shown on the scale.
The distance between these numbers is divided up using marks called **graduations**.
It is useful to be able to work out what one graduation is equal to.

Examples

1   How much liquid is in this beaker ?

There are 5 graduation marks from
100 to 200.
That is 5 marks for 100 ml.
$100 \div 5 = 20$
So 1 mark = 20 ml.
The level of the liquid is 1 mark above 100 ml.
The beaker contains 120 ml of liquid.

2   What weight do the scales show ?

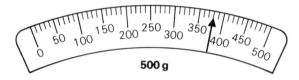

There are 5 graduation marks from 350 to 400.
That is 5 marks for 50 g.
$50 \div 5 = 10$
So 1 mark = 10 g
The arrow is 3 marks more than 350 g
$350 g + 30 g = 380 g$
The scales show 380 g

3

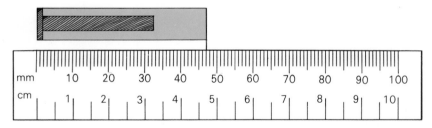

What is the length of the pen top ?

The ruler is marked in centimetres and millimetres. We could give the measurement
in different ways.

To the nearest centimetre

If you want a rough answer measuring to the nearest centimetre will do.
The length of the pen top is nearer to 5 cm than to 4 cm.
So the length of the pen top is 5 cm, to the nearest centimetre.

To the nearest millimetre

This gives a more accurate answer than the first method.
The length is nearer to 47 mm than to 48 mm.
So the length of the pen top is 47 mm, to the nearest millimetre.

Using centimetres and millimetres

1 cm = 10 mm
So 47 mm = 4 cm and 7 mm
The length of the pen top is 4 cm and 7 mm.

Length

Exercise 7.1

1.   Measure the length of each line.
     Give your answers to the nearest centimetre.

     1   _____

     2   _____

     3   _____

     4   _____

2.

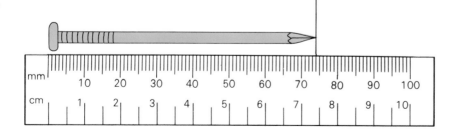

     1   What is the length of the nail to the nearest centimetre ?
     2   What is the length of the nail to the nearest millimetre ?
     3   Which is the more accurate answer ?

3.   This ruler is marked in centimetres.

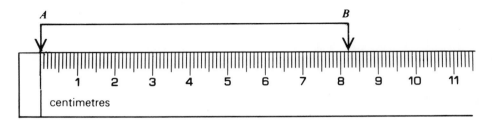

    1   How many graduation marks are there from 1 cm to 2 cm ?
    2   What length does each graduation mark represent ?
    3   What is the length of *AB* in centimetres and millimetres ?

4.

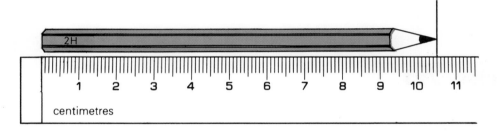

What is the length of the pencil ?
Give your answer in centimetres and millimetres.

5.

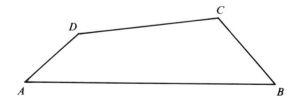

    1   What is the length of *AB* in millimetres ?
    2   What is the length of *BC* in millimetres ?
    3   What is the length of *CD* in millimetres ?
    4   What is the length of *DA* in millimetres ?
    5   The distance all the way round a shape is called the **perimeter**. Find the
        perimeter of the shape.

6.   *A* ●   ● *B*
   1   Estimate the distance between the dots, in millimetres.
   2   Measure the distance between the dots, in millimetres.

Weight

Examples

1   What is 1300 g in kilograms and grams ?

   1 kg = 1000 g
   So 1300 g = 1 kg 300 g

2   What is 3 kg 200 g in grams ?

   3 kg = 3 × 1000 g = 3000 g
   So 3 kg 200 g = 3200 g

3   Mr Smith bought two joints of meat.
   One weighed 3700 g, the other weighed 4500 g.
   What was the total weight of the meat in kilograms and grams ?

   3700 g + 4500 g = 8200 g
   8200 g = 8 kg 200 g

   The total weight of the meat was 8 kg 200 g.

4   Mrs Foster bought 15 bread rolls.
   The total weight of the bread rolls was 1 kg 200 g.
   What was the weight of one bread roll ?

   First we must change the 1 kg to grams.
   1 kg = 1000 g
   So 1 kg 200 g = 1200 g

   15 rolls weigh 1200 g
   1200 ÷ 15 = 80

   So 1 bread roll weighs 80 g.

Exercise 7.2

1.

500 g

Here is a picture of a dial on a weighing-scale.

1   What is the maximum weight that can be weighed on the scale ?
2   How many graduation marks are there from 100 g to 150 g ?
3   What weight does one graduation mark represent ?
4   What weight does arrow A show ?
5   What weight does arrow B show ?
6   What weight does arrow C show ?

2.   Write these weights in kilograms and grams.
     Boxes have been drawn to help you.
     1   1500 g = ☐ kg ☐ g
     2   4200 g = ☐ kg ☐ g
     3   5740 g = ☐ kg ☐ g

3.   Write these weights in kilograms and grams.
     This time there are no boxes to help you.
     1   3500 g   **2**   4750 g   **3**   6050 g

4.   Write these weights in grams.
     1   1 kg 500 g   **4**   1 kg 80 g
     2   3 kg 700 g   **5**   7 kg 50 g
     3   5 kg 375 g   **6**   10 kg 5 g

5.   How much heavier is 450 g than 250 g ?

6.   Mrs Patel buys a 1 kg bag of flour to bake some cakes.
     She uses 250 g of the flour.
     How much flour is left in the bag ?

7.   A bar of chocolate in its wrapper weighs 235 g.
     The wrapper weighs 6 g.
     What is the weight of the chocolate ?

8. **1** What is the maximum weight that
         can be weighed on this spring
         balance ?
    2 How many graduation marks are
         there from 2 kg to 3 kg ?
    3 What weight does one graduation
         mark represent ?
    4 What weight does arrow *A* show ?
    5 What weight does arrow *B* show ?
    6 What weight does arrow *C* show ?
    7 What weight does arrow *D* show ?

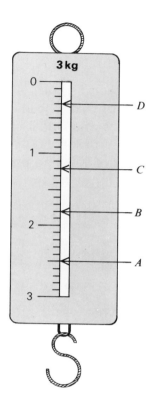

9. **1** What is the maximum weight that
         can be weighed on this scale ?
    2 How many graduation marks are
         there from 7 kg to 8 kg ?
    3 What weight does one graduation
         mark represent ?
    4 What weight does arrow *A* show ?
    5 What weight does arrow *B* show ?
    6 What weight does arrow *C* show ?
    7 What weight does arrow *D* show ?

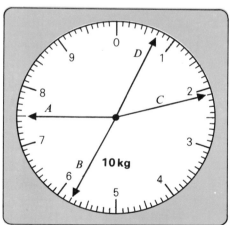

10. Mrs Stein has baked two cakes for the church fair.
     The sponge cake weighed 1400 g.
     The fruit cake weighed 3200 g.
     1 What was the total weight of the cakes in grams ?
     2 What was the total weight of the cakes in kilograms and grams ?
     3 How many grams heavier was the fruit cake than the sponge cake ?

11. Mr Evans bought the following items from the supermarket.
     The weight of each item is given below.

     A tub of margarine, 500 g
     A packet of cereal, 600 g
     A tin of baked beans, 450 g
     A piece of cheddar cheese, 420 g
     A jar of pickle, 600 g
     A box of washing powder, 3 kg

     1   What was the total weight of the shopping, in grams ?
     2   What was the total weight of the shopping, in kilograms and grams ?

12. Mr Jones posted 3 parcels. Each parcel weighed 1500 g.
     1   What was the total weight of the parcels in grams ?
     2   What was the total weight of the parcels in kilograms and grams ?

13. George loads his van with 5 boxes.
     Each box weighs 80 kg.
     The van is allowed to carry 500 kg.
     1   What is the total weight of the boxes ?
     2   How much more weight is the van allowed to carry ?

14. The chef at a hotel bought 12 kg of bread rolls for a party.
     Each bread roll weighed 60 g.
     1   What is 12 kg in grams ?
     2   How many bread rolls did the chef buy ?

15. The hardware store sells hammers, which are packed in wooden boxes.
     Each box contains 10 hammers.
     One hammer weighs 3 kg.
     The total weight of the wooden box and the ten hammers is 35 kg.
     What is the weight of the box ?

Capacity

Examples

1   What is 3000 ml in litres ?

           1 litre = 1000 ml
   So 3000 ml = 3 litres

2   What is $2\frac{1}{2}$ litres in millilitres ?

        1 litre = 1000 ml
  So $\frac{1}{2}$ litre = 500 ml
    $2\frac{1}{2}$ litres = 2000 ml + 500 ml = 2500 ml

    $2\frac{1}{2}$ litres = 2500 ml

3   Mrs Wyatt bought a 500 ml bottle of cooking oil.
After she had used 125 ml what amount remained in the bottle ?

500 ml − 125 ml = 375 ml
There was 375 ml left in the bottle.

4   How many drinks, each of 200 ml, can be poured from a 3-litre bottle of lemonade ?

3 litres = 3000 ml
3000 ÷ 200 = 15
15 drinks can be poured from the bottle.

Exercise 7.3

1. **1**   What is the maximum volume that this beaker can measure ?
    2   How many graduation marks are there from 100 ml to 200 ml ?
    3   What volume does each graduation mark represent ?
    4   What is the volume of liquid in the beaker ?

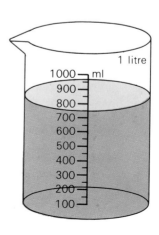

2. **1** What is the maximum volume that
           this beaker can measure ?
    2 How many graduation marks are
           there from 100 ml to 200 ml ?
    3 What volume does each graduation
           mark represent ?
    4 What is the volume of liquid in the
           beaker ?

3. **1** What is the maximum volume that
           this measuring cylinder can measure ?
    2 How many graduation marks are
           there from 10 ml to 20 ml ?
    3 What volume does each graduation
           mark represent ?
    4 What volume does arrow *A* show ?
    5 What volume does arrow *B* show ?
    6 What volume does arrow *C* show ?
    7 What volume does arrow *D* show ?

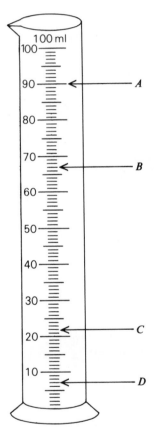

4. **1** What is 4000 ml in litres ?
    2 What is 7000 ml in litres ?
    3 What is 10 000 ml in litres ?
    4 What is 500 ml in litres ?

5. **1** What is 5 litres in millilitres ?
    2 What is 8 litres in millilitres ?
    3 What is $3\frac{1}{2}$ litres in millilitres ?
    4 What is $5\frac{1}{2}$ litres in millilitres ?

6. Write these volumes to the nearest litre.
   1   1200 ml   4   2764 ml   7   10 520 ml
   2   3900 ml   5   1505 ml   8   12 499 ml
   3   1784 ml   6   4750 ml

7. Carl added 200 ml of water to 30 ml of orange squash.
   What was the total volume of his drink ?

8. The capacities of the coffee cup, tea cup, mug and tumbler are shown below.

   coffee cup   **tea-cup**   **mug**   **tumbler**
   250 ml   **300 ml**   **580 ml**   **840 ml**

   1   What is the total capacity of all four items ?
       Give your answer in millilitres.
   2   What is the total capacity in litres ?
   3   How much more does the tea-cup hold than the coffee cup ?
   4   How much more does the tumbler hold than the mug ?
   5   How many coffee cups could be filled from a 1-litre coffee pot ?

9. Brenda filled her car with petrol. The capacity of the fuel tank is 36 litres. On a
   journey the car used 29 litres of petrol. How much fuel was left in the tank ?

10. The Clarke family took a 2-litre bottle of lemonade on a picnic. How much
    lemonade was left in the bottle after drinks of 350 ml, 350 ml, 200 ml and 300 ml
    were poured ?

11. An oil can holds 250 ml of oil.
    It is filled from an oil drum which holds 20 litres of oil.
    How many times is it possible to refill the oil can with oil from the oil drum ?

12. A milk bottle holds 568 ml of milk.
    There are 20 bottles in a crate.
    1   How many millilitres of milk are there in a crate full of milk bottles ?
    2   What is this amount of milk to the nearest litre ?

13.   A bucket holds 4 litres of water.
       How many buckets full of water are needed to fill a tank which has a capacity of
       144 litres ?

14.   A tea urn holds 20 litres of tea.
       A tea cup holds 330 ml.
       1   How many cups could be **filled** from the urn ?
       2   Would there be any tea left in the urn ?
       3   If so, how much ?

Time

The units for time are not based on the number 10.
It would be very difficult to change from our present system.

60 seconds = 1 minute	1 year = 12 months
60 minutes = 1 hour	1 year = 365 days
24 hours = 1 day	1 leap year = 366 days
7 days = 1 week	
52 weeks = 1 year	

Clocks

There are two main types of clock.
1   Clocks which have hands.
2   Digital clocks.
We also use special types of time-recording instruments, for example, stopclocks,
stopwatches, hourglasses, etc.

Recording time

There are two methods of recording time.

1.   **The 12-hour clock**

       Morning times are denoted by am.
       Afternoon times are denoted by pm.
       You must remember to include the am or pm or confusion could occur.

2. **The 24-hour clock**

24-hour clock notation is often used on timetables for trains, buses, etc.

Some digital clocks use the 24-hour clock notation, e.g. clocks on video recorders, cookers, etc.

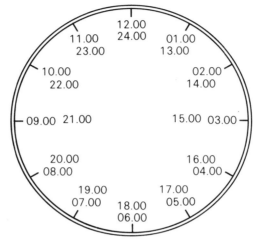

Each time consists of 4 figures.
The first two figures give the number of hours past midnight.
The second two figures give the number of minutes past the hour.
The hours and minutes can be separated by a dot. On timetables times can be printed as 4-figure numbers.

Examples

	12-hour clock	24-hour clock
Breakfast time	8.00 am	08.00
Morning break	10.45 am	10.45
Noon	12.00 pm	12.00
Tea time	5.30 pm	17.30
Midnight	12.00 am	00.00

Tea is at seventeen thirty hours.
Breakfast is at eight hundred hours.

Using a calculator

Hours and minutes, or minutes and seconds, are not based on the number 10. You will have to do the calculations for the different units separately.

Examples

1   Michael records two television programmes on the same videotape. The first lasts
for 1 hour 25 minutes and the second lasts for 1 hour 45 minutes. What was the
total length of the two programmes ?

     1 h 25 min
+ 1 h 45 min
    3 h 10 min
    1

First use your calculator to add 25 and 45.
This gives 70 minutes.
70 minutes = 1 h 10 min
Write the 10 min in the minutes column and carry the 1 h to the hours column.
Add up the hours column.
The two programmes last for 3 hours and 10 minutes.

2   A football team trains for 4 hours a day.
They spend 2 hours 15 minutes being coached and practising on the pitch. The
remaining time is spent in the gym working on fitness. How long do they spend in
the gym ?

   3   6 0
   4 h 00 min
− 2 h 15 min
   1 h 45 min

You cannot take 15 from 0.
Borrow 1 hour from the hours column and change it to 60 minutes in the minutes
column.
Work out the minutes and hours columns.

They spend 1 hour 45 minutes in the gym.

You may use a method of subtraction that is different to this one. Use the method
which you find easiest.

3   How many minutes are there from 16.50 to 17.25?

This question can be answered by adding on.
From 16.50 to 17.00 there are 10 minutes.
From 17.00 to 17.25 there are 25 minutes.
So from 16.50 to 17.25 there are 10 + 25 = 35 minutes.

4   What time does the stopwatch show ?

There are two readings to take.
First the minutes, in the small circle.
Each graduation mark is equal to 1 minute.
The minute hand is between 5 and 6.
You always take the lower number,
(except when the hand is between 30 and 1,
when the reading is 0 minutes).
So we read 5 minutes.

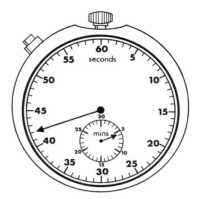

Then you read the number of seconds.
Each graduation is equal to 1 second.
The second hand is pointing to 42 seconds.

So the stopwatch shows 5 minutes 42 seconds.

Exercise 7.4

1.   Write the times shown on these clocks. Use 12-hour clock notation. Remember
to write am or pm.

   1   School starts

   2   Supper time

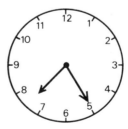

   3   School finishes

   4   Afternoon tea

2.   Write these times in 24-hour clock notation.
     1   3.00 am   **5**   11.23 am
     2   4.00 pm   **6**   half-past three in the afternoon
     3   6.20 am   **7**   quarter to eleven in the morning
     4   5.15 pm   **8**   half-past twelve at night

3.   Write these times using 12-hour clock notation.
     1   16.00   **5**   00.15
     2   02.00   **6**   09.24
     3   19.30   **7**   quarter-past five in the afternoon
     4   13.20   **8**   five minutes to six in the morning

4.   What time does each of these stopwatches show ?
     1   **2**   **3**

5.   How many minutes are there in

     1   2 hours   **3**   a quarter of an hour
     2 $1\frac{1}{2}$ hours   **4**   a day ?

6.   How many seconds are there in

     1   3 minutes   **3** $\frac{1}{2}$ hour
     2 $2\frac{1}{2}$ minutes   **4**   1 hour ?

7.   Alan has a 90-minute blank cassette tape.
     He tapes a radio programme which lasts for 25 minutes.
     How much blank tape is left ?

8.   Anne travels on a train for 2 hours and 30 minutes. Then she drives for
     45 minutes. What is the total time that Anne was travelling for ?

9.   A train left Manchester at 3.20 pm and arrived in Southport at 4.15 pm.
     How long did the journey take ?

10. Victoria had a 4-hour blank video tape. She used it to tape a programme which lasted for 1 hour 25 minutes. How much blank tape did Victoria have left ?

11. A film started at 21.15 and finished at 23.05. How long did the film last ?

Exercise 7.5   Applications and Activities

1. 1 tonne = 1000 kg
    5 tonnes 350 kg = 5000 kg + 350 kg = 5350 kg
    So 5 tonnes 350 kg = 5350 kg.
    Write these weights in kilograms.

    1   6 tonnes   **4**   12 tonnes 175 kg
    2   5 tonnes 260 kg   **5** $\frac{1}{2}$ tonne
    3   7 tonnes 830 kg   **6**   1 tonne 10 kg

2. **A lorry and its load**
    The total weight of a loaded lorry is called its **gross weight**. The weight of the lorry without its load is called its **tare weight**.

    Weight of the load = gross weight − tare weight

    Lorries are weighed on weighbridges.
    Copy and complete this table for lorries and their loads.
    The first line has been done for you.

	Cargo	Gross weight	Tare weight	Weight of load
	Potatoes	15 tonnes 800 kg	5 tonnes 300 kg	10 tonnes 500 kg
1	Wheat	32 tonnes 400 kg	12 tonnes 200 kg	
2	Sand	25 tonnes 650 kg	6 tonnes 300 kg	
3	Gravel	23 tonnes 100 kg	6 tonnes 300 kg	
4	Coal		14 tonnes 200 kg	22 tonnes 500 kg
5	Furniture		4 tonnes 620 kg	2 tonnes 730 kg
6	Petrol	32 tonnes 800 kg		12 tonnes 300 kg
7	Sugar	37 tonnes 370 kg		15 tonnes 480 kg
8	Straw	21 tonnes 235 kg	8 tonnes 465 kg	

3.

    1   Estimate the length of the curvy line.

    2   Decide how you could measure the length of this line, and then measure it as accurately as you can.

4.   **Capacity**

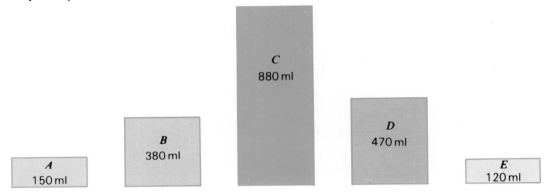

Each of the five containers holds water.

The capacity of each container is written on the side.

    1   What is the total capacity of the five containers in millilitres ?

    2   What is the total capacity of the five containers in litres ?

    3   How much more water does D hold than A ?

    4   Which container holds the least amount of water ?

    5   Which **two** containers could be **emptied** to fill another container which has a capacity of $\frac{1}{2}$ litre ?

    6   Which **two** containers could be **emptied** to fill a 1 litre container ?

    7   Which **three** containers could be emptied to fill a 1 litre container ?

5.   **Measuring Time**

You can make an instrument to measure an amount of time.

One example is to use sand pouring through a funnel. Find the amount of sand needed to pour through the funnel in exactly one minute.

You can think of other types of instruments to make, such as using water or a burning candle.

Use your instrument for measuring time in a practical way.

6. **Television programmes**

1   How long did the early evening news last for ?

2   How long did the late news last for ?

3   Which programme lasted 40 minutes ?

4   What time did the Local News start (in 12-hour clock notation) ?

5   What time did the television channel close (in 12-hour clock notation) ?

6   The film was in two parts. What was the total length of the film ?

Monday	
News	18.05
Local News	18.40
Chat Show	19.00
Soap	19.30
Comedy	20.05
Film (part one)	20.45
News	22.00
Film (part two)	22.35
Weather	23.55
Close	00.05

PUZZLES

15.   Ali, Barny, Chris, Dale and Eric are sat on a park bench.

Ali is not sat on the far right.
Barny is not sat on the far left.
Chris is not sat at either end.
Dale is sat on the right of Barny.
Eric is not sat next to Chris.
Chris is not sat next to Barny.

Who is sat at the far right ?

16.   Copy the diagram on the right.
Place the numbers 1 to 8 in the circles so that the numbers along each side of the square add up to the same total.

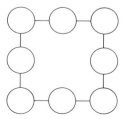

Miscellaneous Section A

Aural Practice

Exercises A1 and A2 are **aural exercises**.
You have practised reading questions and writing down the answers.
To do an aural exercise someone should **read** the questions to you.
You have to **listen** to the question, work out what you are required to do, and write the answer down. If possible try to do the working in your head. Should you get stuck use pencil and paper to help you.

A teacher or friend should read the questions to you.
Try to do the 15 questions in 10 minutes or less.

Exercise A1

1. Write the number thirty-six in figures.

2. Which compass direction is opposite to East ?

3. Which number is five more than 19 ?

4. How many centimetres are equal to 2 metres ?

5. What is the name given to an angle which is less than 90° ?

6. How many weeks are 35 days equal to ?

7. How many degrees make a full-turn ?

8. What is the cost of 3 apples, if one apple costs 20 pence ?

9. What is the next even number after 58 ?

10. How many kilograms is 5000 g equal to ?

11. Work out 100×15.

12. Write 14.30 hours in the 12-hour clock system.

13. How many millilitres are there in $1\frac{1}{2}$ litres ?

14. Write down the smallest number that can be made using all the digits four, seven and one.

15. Add together 250 g and 130 g.

Exercise A2

1. Write down the number which is one less than 60.

2. What is 14 × 10 ?

3. Which number is 15 less than 40 ?

4. How many degrees make a right-angle ?

5. If today was 13th August what would the date be in 2 week's time ?

6. Which compass direction is exactly half-way between South and West ?

7. What time is 30 minutes after 5.50 pm ?

8. A taxi can carry 5 people. How many such taxis are needed to carry 30 guests to a wedding ?

9. What type of angle is the smaller angle between the hands of a clock at 2 pm ?

10. How many metres make 3 kilometres ?

11. Write 6.30 pm in the 24-hour clock system.

12. How much blank tape is left on a 90-minute tape after a programme lasting 75 minutes is taped ?

13. Write down the next 5 odd numbers after 11.

14. A measuring beaker has 5 graduation marks from 1 litre to 2 litres. How many millilitres does 1 graduation mark represent ?

15. What is 64 divided by 2 ?

Exercise A3 Revision

1. This abacus chart shows the numbers
276 and 138.
   1 What is 276 + 138 ?
   2 What is 276 − 138 ?

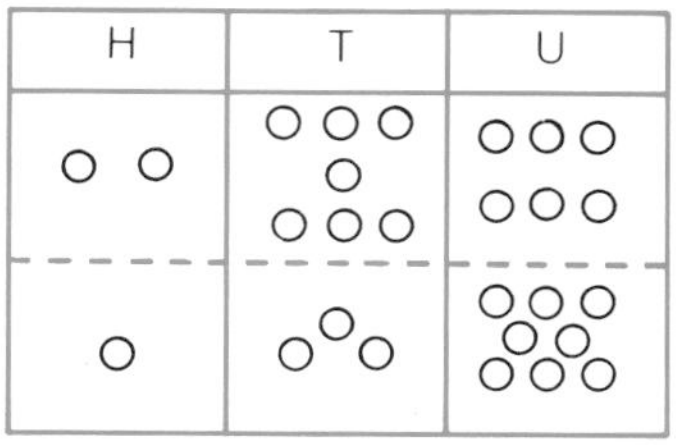

2. Find the numbers which could replace the asterisk to make these sums correct.

1
```
   1 5
 + 2 *
 ─────
   3 9
```
2
```
   5 *
 − 2 5
 ─────
   2 5
```
3
```
   4 * 6
 + 2 3 5
 ───────
   7 1 1
```
4
```
   4 7 3
 − 1 * 7
 ───────
   2 9 6
```

3. Look at this list of angles.
124°, 5°, 72°, 194°, 276°, 358°, 87°, 91°, 184°, 130°.

   1 List the acute angles.
   2 List the obtuse angles.
   3 List the reflex angles.

4. Mrs Green adds 800 g of sugar to 2200 g of flour.
   1 What is the total weight of the mixture, in grams ?
   2 What is the total weight of the mixture, in kilograms ?

5. Work these out without using a calculator.
   1 47 × 10   **4** 72 ÷ 2
   2 23 × 100   **5** 72 ÷ 4
   3 37 × 6   **6** 96 ÷ 6

6. **1** Name the point where the lines *AB* and *PQ* intersect.
   2 Which two lines intersect at the point *Y* ?
   3 How many points of intersection are there in the diagram ?

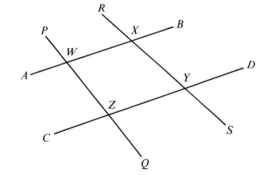

7. The caretaker set out desks ready for the school exams.
   He set out 15 rows of desks.
   There were 9 desks in each row.
   How many desks did he set out altogether ?

8. How many 300 ml mugs can be filled with water from an urn which holds 12 litres of water ?

9. Aslam wrote to his pen-friend. He said in his letter that there were 24 days to go to his birthday which was on the 21st of April. On what date did Aslam write the letter ?

10.

A ─────────────────────────────────── B

    1   What is the length of the line *AB*, to the nearest centimetre ?
    2   What is the length of the line, to the nearest millimetre ?

11.   Mr Sutton can plant 8 seeds in a small pot.
    How many small pots will he need to plant all the 55 seeds that are in one
    packet ?

12.   What are the coordinates of the points
    A, *B*, *C* and *D* ?

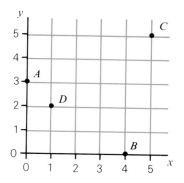

13.   This table shows the number of pints of milk that a milkman delivered to a small
    block of flats during a particular week.
    There was no delivery on Sunday.

	Flat 1	Flat 2	Flat 3	Flat 4	Flat 5	Flat 6	Total
M	2	1	3	0	2	0	
T	2	0	0	1	1	0	
W	2	1	2	2	2	2	
T	2	0	1	0	1	1	
F	2	1	0	1	2	0	
S	3	2	4	2	3	3	
Total							

    1   Copy the table.
    2   Complete the bottom row. This tells you the number of pints of milk
        delivered to each flat during the week.
    3   Complete the column on the right.
    4   What information does the column on the right give ?
    5   What was the total amount of milk delivered to the block of flats during the
        week ?

14. This is part of the timetable for the Ayling to Darenby bus service.

    1 How long does it take the bus to travel from Ayling to Baxton ?

    2 How long does it take the bus to travel from Baxton to Carby ?

    3 How long does the journey take from Ayling to Darenby ?

Ayling	07.45
Baxton	08.10
Carby	08.25
Darenby	08.36

15. Rachel was interested in the different types of window frames that the houses in her street had. She did a survey of the street. These were the types of window frames that Rachel saw.

    UPVC—Hard wearing plastic frames which were double-glazed (U).
    Aluminium—Metal frames which were double-glazed (A).
    Hardwood—Wooden frames which were double-glazed (H).
    Painted—Single glazed, painted frames (P).

    The letter in brackets is the code that Rachel used to record her observations.

    This is the data that Rachel collected.

    H   A   U   P   H   H   A   U   P   P
    P   U   H   P   U   H   H   H   U   A
    P   A   P   A   H   H   P   H   H   H
    H   P   A   H

    1 Make and fill in a data collection sheet for Rachel's data.
    2 Which is the most common type of window frame ?
    3 How many houses did Rachel survey ?

Exercise A4   Activities

1. **Sums of consecutive numbers**

   11 = 5 + 6

   11 is equal to the sum of 5 and 6.
   5 and 6 are consecutive numbers.

   21 = 1 + 2 + 3 + 4 + 5 + 6   or   21 = 6 + 7 + 8

   Write sums of consecutive numbers for as many of the numbers from 1 to 100 as you can.
   For some numbers it is impossible to do this.
   Which numbers are they ? Do these numbers form a pattern ?

2. **Number Trail**

A Number Trail can be written for your school or your local area.
You make up questions which other people answer.
It is important that your Number Trail has a starting point and a finishing point.
Questions must be asked which can be answered by making observations along the Trail.

You could ask questions like these.

How many windows are there in the Science Block ?
How many doors are there on the lower corridor ?
How many fence posts are there in the fence at the front of the school ?
How many steps are there in the main staircase ?

There are many examples of numbers that you can notice and use on your trail. The school notice board may have a telephone number on it, the building may have a foundation stone with a date on it, the tuck shop may have a notice giving the times of opening, the canteen may display a price list.

Try to ask interesting questions. Use questions that other people might not think of using.

Make sure that you know the answers to your questions !

3. **Pencil and Paper Pattern Drawing**

You need a sharp pencil.
On a sheet of plain paper, or centimetre-squared paper, draw a square with sides 10 cm long. Mark off points every 2 cm along each side.

Starting with point A, draw straight lines joining A to every point on the two opposite sides, including the opposite corner point. (There are 9 lines altogether.) Then using point B, draw straight lines joining B to every point on the other three sides, including two corner points. (14 lines altogether.) Repeat using C and all the other points in turn. (When you get to the second side, some of the lines have already been drawn.)

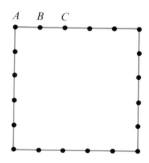

Look for patterns in your drawing. Can you see sets of parallel lines ?
You could invent similar drawings. Perhaps you could draw coloured lines.
Cut out the drawings and arrange them on a poster.

8 Thinking about approximation and

Telephone directory

How many telephone numbers are there in your local telephone directory?
First make a guess at the number of telephone numbers in the directory.
Now count the number of telephone numbers on one page.
Next find the number of pages in the directory.
Multiply the number of telephone numbers on one page by the number of pages in the directory.
Were you surprised by the number of telephone numbers in your local directory?
Why is the answer not an exact one?
Do you really need an accurate answer?

Which container holds the most liquid?

Guess which container is holding the most liquid.
How could you check your guess?
Would it be possible for each container to hold the same amount of liquid?

estimation

Tallest first

Whenever we measure a length we have to round off to a unit. The unit to which we round off depends on the accuracy we require.

For example, the length of this page may be measured to the nearest millimetre, but the distance to the Sun may be measured to the nearest million kilometres.

Look at the following pictures. In each case the height given has been rounded off. Which is the tallest ?

Gustav Eiffel designed the engineering for two of the following constructions. With which two constructions was he linked ?

The Eiffel Tower, Paris,
300 metres high

The Statue of Liberty, New York,
93 metres high

Blackpool Tower,
158 metres high

8 Estimation and Approximation

Approximation

We do not always want to know the exact answer to a question.

How many hairs are on your head ?

How many kilometres is the Earth from the Sun ?

What is the population of London ?

How many litres of water are needed to fill a swimming pool ?

In questions like these, an answer given to the nearest 10, nearest 100 or nearest 1000 is often good enough.

Such an answer is called an **approximation**.

The size of a number

Some numbers are big. Some numbers are small.

The first figure in a number tells us the most about the size of a number. The position and value of this figure tells us what it is worth.

Examples

Which figure tells you the most about the size of each number ?
Say what the figure is worth.

1 64   The 6 tells us the most about this number.
         It is worth 6 tens or 60.

2 19   The 1 tells us the most about this number.
         It is worth 1 ten or 10.

3 415   The 4 tells us the most about this number.
         It is worth 4 hundreds or 400.

4 2948 The 2 tells us the most about this number.
         It is worth 2 thousands or 2000.

Exercise 8.1

Copy each number in questions 1 to 15. Underline the figure which tells you the most about the size of the number. Say what the figure you underlined is worth.

1.	25	5.	17	9. 799
2.	38	6.	135	10. 1435
3.	75	7.	254	11. 3764
4.	91	8.	109	12. 176

13. 31
14. 7890
15. 83

16. The planet Mars takes 687 days to orbit the Sun.
   1 Which figure tells you the most about the length of time it takes Mars to orbit the Sun ?
   2 What is the value of this figure ?

17. Divers used the bathyscaphe Trieste (a vessel for deep-sea diving) to explore the Mariana Trench, which is the deepest part of any ocean.
   They went down 923 metres.
   1 Which figure tells you most about this depth ?
   2 What is the value of this figure ?

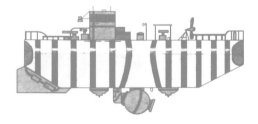

Rounding to the nearest 10

Sometimes we only require an approximate answer to a question.
To get an approximate answer we **round off**.

Look at this diagram. It shows part of a number line.

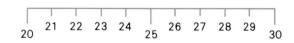

Is 24 nearer to 20 or 30 ?
24 is nearer to 20.
So 24 rounded to the nearest 10 is 20.

Is 27 nearer to 20 or 30 ?
27 is nearer to 30.
So 27 rounded to the nearest 10 is 30.

Is 25 nearer to 20 or 30 ?
25 is exactly half-way between 20 and 30.
If a number is exactly half-way it is usual to round up.
So 25 rounded to the nearest 10 is 30.

Examples

1 Round off 76 to the nearest 10.

76 is nearer to 80 than to 70.
So 76 rounded to the nearest 10 is 80.

2 Round off 152 to the nearest 10.

152 is nearer to 150 than to 160.
So 152 rounded to the nearest 10 is 150.

3 Round off 365 to the nearest 10.

365 is exactly half-way between 360 and 370.
If a number is exactly half-way it is usual to round up to the next ten.
So 365 rounded to the nearest 10 is 370.

Exercise 8.2

Round off each of the following numbers to the nearest 10.

1.	22	5.	86	9.	68	13.	4381
2.	29	6.	124	10.	111	14.	1305
3.	35	7.	436	11.	168	15.	1472
4.	59	8.	275	12.	105		

16.   Death Valley is in California, USA. The highest temperature recorded at Death Valley is 57°C. What is this temperature to the nearest 10°C ?

17.   The top of a tropical rain forest can be 88 metres from the ground. What is this height to the nearest 10 metres ?

Rounding off to the nearest 100

Sometimes we only want to approximate to the nearest 100.
Look at this diagram. It shows part of a number line.

Examples

1   Round off 327 to the nearest 100.

327 is nearer to 300 than to 400.
So 327 rounded to the nearest 100 is 300.

2   Round off 1450 to the nearest 100.

1450 is exactly half-way between 1400 and 1500.
So 1450 rounded to the nearest 100 is 1500.
Remember: If a number is exactly half-way it is usual to round up.

3   Round off 763 to the nearest 100.

763 is nearer to 800 than to 700.
So 763 rounded to the nearest 100 is 800.

Exercise 8.3

Round off each of the following numbers to the nearest 100.

1. 341	5. 697	9. 750	13. 27 842
2. 385	6. 920	10. 4370	14. 39 450
3. 306	7. 1784	11. 950	15. 12 4531
4. 572	8. 3269	12. 14 360	

16.   The Humber Bridge was built in 1981. It is 1410 metres long.
How long is the Humber Bridge to the nearest 100 metres ?

17.   The Andes is the longest range of mountains. It is 7235 kilometres long. What is
the length of the Andes to the nearest 100 kilometres ?

Estimation

Whenever you do a calculation you should always ask yourself the question: Is my answer a sensible one ?
Even if you are using a calculator mistakes can happen.

To check that a calculation is roughly correct you can make an **estimate**.
In making estimates you make use of approximations.

Examples

1   Estimate the answer to the question 24 + 79.

Round off each number to the nearest 10.
We round to the nearest 10 because 24 and 79 are small numbers.

24 rounded to the nearest 10 is 20.
79 rounded to the nearest 10 is 80.

20 + 80 = 100
An estimate of 24 + 79 is 100. (The actual answer is 103.)

2   Give an estimate for 895 − 174.

Round off each number to the nearest 100.
We round to the nearest 100 because 895 and 174 are large numbers.

895 rounded off to the nearest 100 is 900.
174 rounded off to the nearest 100 is 200.

900 − 200 = 700
An estimate of 895 − 174 is 700. (The actual answer is 721.)

3   Is **A**, **B** or **C** the best estimate for 5763 − 4239 ?
   A   20 000   **B**   200   **C**   2000

Do not work the exact value out. Use estimations.
5763 rounded to the nearest 1000 is 6000.
4239 rounded to the nearest 1000 is 4000.
6000 − 4000 = 2000

C is the best estimate.

Exercise 8.4

1. Estimate the answers to the following questions by using approximations to the nearest 10.

   1 34 + 42
   2 59 + 48
   3 32 + 75

   4 65 − 38
   5 94 − 27

2. Estimate the answers to the following questions by using approximations to the nearest 100.

   1 216 + 532
   2 625 + 255
   3 563 − 271

   4 739 − 403
   5 874 − 329

3. Estimate the answers to the following questions by using approximations to the nearest 1000.

   1 1538 + 2413
   2 3750 + 4362
   3 7438 − 2315

   4 8941 − 4376
   5 7495 + 3501

For these questions decide whether **A**, **B** or **C** is the best estimate of the answer.

4. 89 − 38

   A 100   **B** 50   **C** 5

5. 274 + 380 + 119

   A 800   **B** 80   **C** 600

6. 653 − 170 + 119

   A 1000   **B** 60   **C** 600

7. 85 + 147 + 275 + 362

   A 600   **B** 900   **C** 1200

Rounding to the nearest whole number

Sometimes we do not get exact answers to problems.
Use your calculator to work out 84 ÷ 35

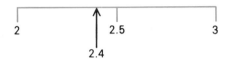

The answer is 2.4. The diagram shows the position of 2.4 on the number line.
2.4 is nearer to 2 than 3.
So 84 ÷ 35 = 2, **to the nearest whole number**.

Examples

1   Work out 260 ÷ 80. Give your answer to the nearest whole number.

260 ÷ 80 = 3.25
3.25 is nearer to 3 than to 4.

So 260 ÷ 80 = 3, to the nearest whole number.

2   Work out 98 ÷ 35. Give your answer to the nearest whole number.

98 ÷ 35 = 2.8
2.8 is nearer to 3 than to 2.

So 98 ÷ 35 = 3, to the nearest whole number.

3   Work out 207 ÷ 46. Give your answer to the nearest whole number.

207 ÷ 46 = 4.5
4.5 is exactly half-way between 4 and 5.
Remember: If a number is half-way it is usual to round up.
So 207 ÷ 46 = 5, to the nearest whole number.

Calculator displays

The result of a division calculation need not be an exact decimal. For example, 74 ÷ 9
gives 8.222... on a calculator display.

You may only require the answer to the nearest whole number. Since 8.222... is nearer
to 8 than to 9, you would give 8 as the answer.

Quick method for rounding to the nearest whole number

Look at the first figure after the decimal point.

If it is a 0 ⎫
1 ⎪
2 ⎬ round
3 ⎪ down
4 ⎭

5 ⎫
6 ⎪
7 ⎬ round
8 ⎪ up
9 ⎭

Exercise 8.5

The following results were displayed after using a calculator to do some calculations.
Round off each number displayed to the nearest whole number.

1.   2.142857...   3.   2.5555555...   5.   4.9090909...
2.   1.2222222...   4.   1.0909090...   6.   1.4516129...

Use your calculator to work these questions out.
Give each answer to the nearest whole number.

7.   249 ÷ 16   9.   1347 ÷ 13   11.   1278 ÷ 7
8.   592 ÷ 41   10.   4522 ÷ 11   12.   1246 ÷ 30

Exercise 8.6   Applications and Activities

1.   **Tall buildings**

This table shows some of the tallest buildings in the world.

Building	Height	
Sears Tower	443 metres	
World Trade Center	411 metres	
Empire State Building	381 metres	
Standard Oil Building	346 metres	
John Hancock Building	343 metres	
Chrysler Building	319 metres	
Bank of China	315 metres	

Copy the table.
In the last column write the height of each building to the nearest 10 metres.

2. **Football attendances**

    The table below shows the number of people who watched some League Division One matches on a particular Saturday.

Game	Attendance	
Aston Villa v Tottenham	32638	
Crystal Palace v Derby	14752	
Liverpool v Sunderland	37582	
Luton v Norwich	8604	
Man. City v Wimbledon	21089	
Notts Forest v Man. United	23859	
Q.P.R. v Coventry	9510	

    Copy the table.
    In the third column of your table write the number of people who watched each match, to the nearest 100.

    If there were football matches played last week, make a table, like the one in the question, to show the number of people who watched. (The numbers are shown in newspapers.) You could choose the division in which your local team plays. Or in a similar way you could find the number of people who watched another sport.

3. **Estimating measurements**

    You are more likely to have to estimate a measurement than to have to find its actual value.

    Length

    The height of a door is approximately 2 m.
    What is the approximate length of your foot ?

    Using these two measurements you can estimate the length of other shapes and objects.

Item	Estimate	Actual measurement
exercise book		
length of classroom		
breadth of classroom		
height of classroom		
length of corridor		
length of field		

Make estimates of the lengths and enter your estimates in the second column and the actual measurements in the third column.
You can include many other lengths in your table, such as the height of a friend.

Weight

A large packet of breakfast cereal weighs 500 g.
A bag of sugar weighs 2 kg.

Get used to feeling the different weights of objects by picking them up and comparing them with objects you know the weight of.

Make a table, like the one you made for estimating length, and estimate the weights of different objects. Try to estimate the weights of objects which are light as well as objects which are heavy.

After you have made your estimates weigh the objects, using a suitable device (kitchen scales, spring balance, bathroom scales, etc). Take care to read the scales accurately.

Capacity

Look at the capacity of several containers such as bottles of lemonade.
Measure 1 litre of water using a jug or a measuring beaker.

Estimate the capacity of different containers such as bottles, cups, teaspoons, tablespoons, etc.
Find the capacity of each item by using a suitable measuring device (measuring cylinder, beaker, etc).
Make a table to show your results.
Can you find two different-shaped containers which have the same capacity ?

Time

You can estimate one minute by counting ''1 and 2 and 3 and... up to 60''.
Try using this method several times.
Do not look at a clock or a watch when you are counting.

PUZZLE

17.   87*7 divides by 9 exactly.
The figure in the tens column is missing.
What should it be ?

9 Thinking about displaying information

Information from graphs and diagrams

Graphs, diagrams and maps are used to display information. Some are very colourful and are interesting to look at. Some examples are shown below.

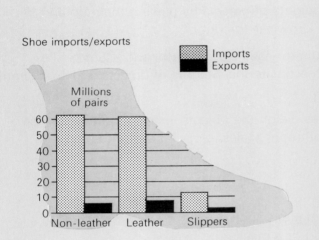

Shoe imports/exports

Imports
Exports

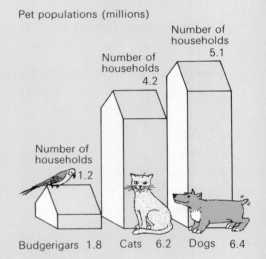

Pet populations (millions)

Why do we use graphs, diagrams and maps to display information ?
Where have you seen diagrams used to display information ?

Languages

A language is a group of words. The words are put together by people so that they can talk to one another. There are many different languages used in the world today.

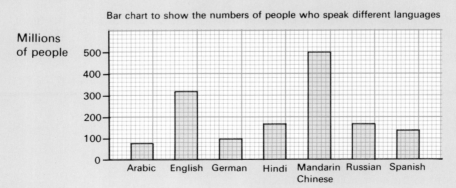

Bar chart to show the numbers of people who speak different languages

Weather maps

How many times a day do you see a weather map on the television ? Weather maps display information using symbols and numbers. Try to list 3 symbols that are used on a weather map. What do the symbols stand for ?
Make a list of the different places where you might see a weather map.

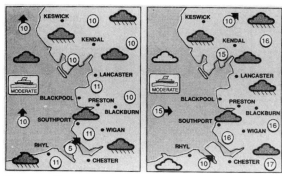

Two weather maps

Population

According to the Census of 1811 the population of London was 1 009 546.
Other cities in the world grew rapidly. Tokyo was the first city to have a population of more than 10 million people.
The pictogram shows the population of some of the most populated cities in the world. The population has been estimated to the nearest million for each city.
Why can we not give an exact number of people for each city ?

		represents 1 million people
Tokyo	13	
Shangai	12	
Sao Paulo	14	
Rio de Janeiro	9	
Paris	9	
New York	9	
Mexico City	18	
Calcutta	9	
Buenos Aires	10	
Beijing	9	

Displaying Information

In chapter 4 you looked at how data can be collected.
You used a data collection sheet to record the data.

If you **listen** to someone telling you about data they collected for a survey you would probably not remember much.

If you **looked** at the data collected for a survey you might remember a little more.

If you saw a **picture** of the data you would remember a lot more.

In this chapter you are going to look at various ways of displaying data.

Block graphs

A **block graph** is a very simple method of displaying data.
Blocks or squares are put together in groups.
One block represents one person or one object in the group.
You can draw designs or patterns in the blocks to make a bright display.
You can draw these graphs on squared paper or graph paper.

Example

Harold and Debbie asked people in their form what type of milk they put on their breakfast cereal. This is the data collection sheet they used.

Type of milk	Tally	Total
Full-cream	ЦНТ	5
Semi-skimmed	ЦНТ III	8
Skimmed	III	3
Did not have cereal	IIII	4

Draw a block graph to show the data collected by Harold and Debbie.

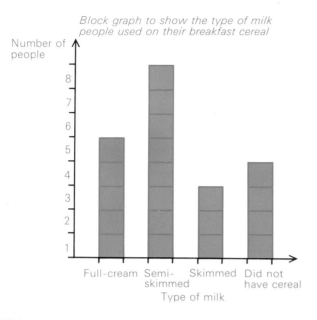

Block graph to show the type of milk people used on their breakfast cereal

Things to include on a graph

1 The horizontal line must be labelled.

2 The vertical line must be labelled.

Each of these lines is called an **axis**. The plural of axis is **axes**.

3 The different sets on the horizontal axis must be labelled.

4 The numbers of people or objects must be clearly labelled on the vertical axis.

5 The graph must have a title.

Sometimes a block graph is drawn sideways.

Exercise 9.1

1. Mr and Mrs Davies are organising a day out for the children who live in their street.
    The children decided what they would like on their sandwiches.
    Francis and Jason made a block graph to represent the choices. (The graph is on the next page.)
    1   What is the most popular type of sandwich ?
    2   Which is the least popular type of sandwich ?
    3   Which type of sandwich was chosen by 4 children ?
    4   How many children went on the day out ?

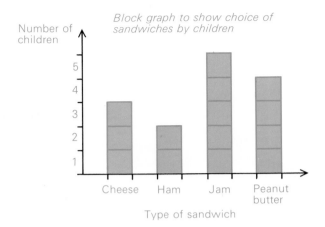

Block graph to show choice of sandwiches by children

Number of children (vertical axis)

Type of sandwich (horizontal axis): Cheese, Ham, Jam, Peanut butter

2. Alison and Mahoud were going on the trip organised by Mr and Mrs Davies.
    They collected data on the types of drink that people liked.
    This is the data collection sheet they made.

Type of drink	Tally	Total
Orange squash	I I I	
Lemonade	⅃⅄⊤ I	
Coke	I \ I I	
Orange juice	I	

1   Copy and complete the data collection sheet.
2   Draw a block graph to show the data.

3. Mr and Mrs Davies wanted the children to
    organise as much of the day out as possible.
    Sally and Stuart asked the children where they
    would like to go.
    They displayed the replies on a block graph.

    1   How many children wanted to go to the
        Lake District ?
    2   How many more children wanted to go to
        the sea-side than to a theme park ?
    3   Where do you think the children went for
        their day out ?

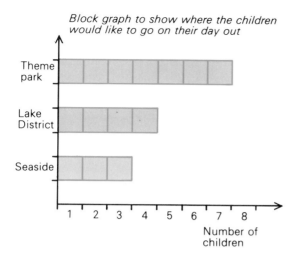

Block graph to show where the children would like to go on their day out

Pictograms

A **pictogram** uses symbols or pictures to represent data.
A symbol can be used to represent a group of objects or people.

For example: ⋎ could represent 5 people.
Parts of this symbol can be used to represent less than 5 people.

Example

This pictogram shows the number of pupils in class 7G who had a school meal during one week.

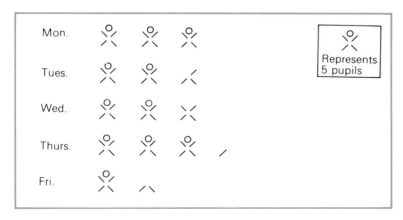

Notice that: ╱ represents 1 person,   ╱╲ represents 3 people,

╱╲ represents 2 people,   ╳ represents 4 people.

Look at the pictogram on the previous page.

1   How many pupils had school lunch on Monday ?

15   This is 3 complete symbols.

2   How many pupils had a school meal on Wednesday ?

14   There are 2 complete symbols which represent 10 pupils, and ✕ which represents 4 pupils, giving a total of 14 pupils.

3   What was the total number of meals taken by class 7G during the week ?

Monday	15
Tuesday	13
Wednesday	14
Thursday	16
Friday	7
Total	65

Exercise 9.2

1.   *Pictogram to show the number of books read*

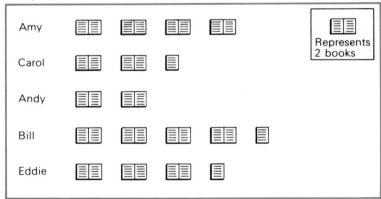

The pictogram shows the number of books read by 5 children in a month.

▤▤ represents 2 books.

1   What does ▤ represent ?

2   Who read the most books ?

3   How many books did Andy read ?

4   How many books did Bill read ?

5   How many more books did Eddie read than Andy ?

6   What was the total number of books read by the 5 children during the month ?

2.   Mr Thomas is a local builder.
      This pictogram shows the number of houses he built during the years 1988–1991.

Pictogram to show the number of houses built

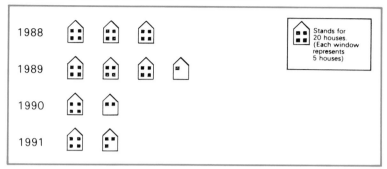

      1   How many new houses does a house with 2 windows represent ?
      2   In which year were the most houses built ?
      3   How many houses were built in 1988 ?
      4   How many houses were built in 1990 ?
      5   What was the total number of houses built during the 4 years ?

3.   Paula and Chris wanted to show how many cars used a particular road. They
      wanted to see if there was more traffic at certain times during the morning.
      A pictogram was used to display the data.

Pictogram to show the number of cars counted between 8 am and 12 pm

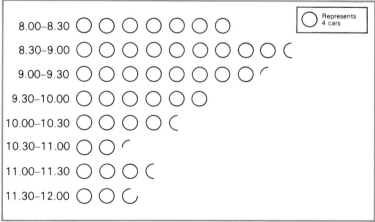

      1   For how long did Paula and Chris collect data ?
      2   Which was the busiest half-hour ?
      3   Why do you think there were so many cars between 8.00 am and 9.00 am ?
      4   How many cars were counted between 9.30 am and 10.00 am ?
      5   How many cars were counted between 10.30 am and 11.00 am ?
      6   How many cars were counted between 11.30 am and 12.00 pm ?
      7   How many cars did they count altogether during the survey ?

4. Melissa and Barbara live on a farm.
They did a survey on the number of sheep kept by farmers in the district.

Farmer	Jenkins	Wyatt	Ford	Taylor	Whittle
Number of sheep	27	23	31	20	14

Use 🐑 to represent 5 sheep.

1 Draw symbols to show how you can represent 1, 2, 3 and 4 sheep.
2 Draw a pictogram to display the data.
3 How many sheep did the girls count altogether ?

Bar charts

Bar charts are easier to draw than block graphs or pictograms.
The height of each bar tells you the number of objects or people in each group.

Examples

1 Mr Bright drew a bar chart to show the number of pupils present in his form. All the pupils were present on Wednesday.

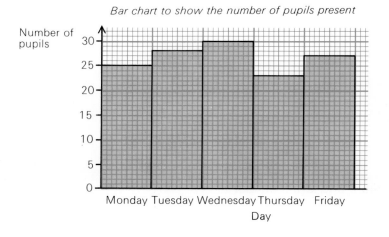

Bar chart to show the number of pupils present

1 How many pupils were present on Monday ?

There were 25 present on Monday.

2 How many pupils were present on Tuesday ?

There are 5 small squares between 25 and 30.
So 1 small square represents 1 pupil.
There were 28 present on Tuesday.

3 How many pupils were absent on Thursday ?

All the pupils were present on Wednesday, so there are 30 pupils in the class.
On Thursday 23 pupils were present, so 7 were absent.

2 Barry counted the number of different types of trees in a field near his home.
His findings are shown in the table below.

Tree	Apple	Pear	Chestnut	Cherry	Almond
Number	12	3	2	5	8

Draw a bar chart to show the numbers of different types of trees that Barry counted.

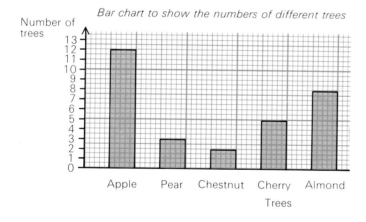

Notice that gaps can be left between the bars.

In this graph the order of the bars is not important. They are shown here in the same order as Barry listed them. They could have been arranged in a different order, perhaps putting them in order of size of bars with the smallest bar (Chestnut) first and the largest one last. They could have been arranged with the largest one (Apple) first, going down in size. They could be have been arranged with the trees in alphabetical order, with Almond first and Pear last.

In the previous graph the bars are already arranged in the sensible order Monday to Friday and it would not be appropriate to rearrange them.

Exercise 9.3

1. This bar chart shows the number of pints of milk delivered to Mr Lloyd's house last week.

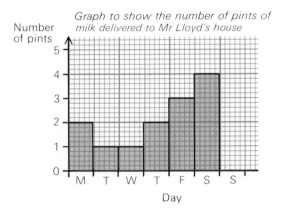

Graph to show the number of pints of milk delivered to Mr Lloyd's house

Number of pints

Day

1 How many pints were delivered on Thursday ?
2 On which day was the most milk delivered ?
3 On which day was there no milk delivered ?
4 How many more pints of milk were delivered on Monday than on Tuesday ?
5 What was the total amount of milk delivered to Mr Lloyd's house last week ?

2. Tom and Elaine did a survey of how pupils travelled to school.
    They collected the replies to their survey on a data collection sheet.
    1 Copy and complete this data collection sheet.

	Tally	No. of pupils
Car	ⅢⅢ I	6
Bus	ⅠⅠⅠ	
Walk		9
Train	ⅠⅠⅠⅠ	
Bike		6

2 Draw a bar chart to show how the pupils travelled to school.
3 How many pupils were surveyed ?

3. Peter kept a record of the number of hours he spent watching television.

Day	M	T	W	T	F	S	S
Number of hours	2	1	3	2	4	5	5

1 Draw a bar chart to show this data.

2 What was the total number of hours that Peter spent watching television ?

4. This graph shows the number of hours sunshine recorded each day.

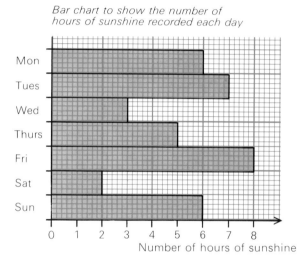

Bar chart to show the number of
hours of sunshine recorded each day

1 Which day had the least sunshine ?

2 Which day had 5 hours of sunshine ?

3 Which days had more than 5 hours of sunshine ?

4 What was the total number of hours of sunshine recorded for the week ?

Exercise 9.4 Applications and Activities

1. **Chips or baked potatoes ?**

Rachel is studying the eating habits of people in her year.
The school canteen serves chips or baked potatoes with meals.

Rachel thinks that eating baked potatoes is better for your health than eating chips. She also thinks that girls eat a more healthy diet than boys.

Rachel designed a data collection sheet and used it to collect data one lunch-time.

ЦНТ I I ЦНТ	ЦНТ ЦНТ I ЦНТ ЦНТ	Baked potatoes
ЦНТ ЦНТ I I I ЦНТ ЦНТ	ЦНТ I I I ЦНТ	Chips
Boys	Girls	

The data collection sheet shows that 12 boys had baked potatoes with their lunch.

1 How many girls had baked potatoes ?
2 How many boys had chips ?
3 How many girls had chips ?
4 How many boys were surveyed ?
5 How many girls were surveyed ?
6 How many people had baked potatoes with their lunch ?
7 How many people had chips with their lunch ?
8 How many people were surveyed altogether ?
9 Draw a pictogram to show the choices of the girls.
10 Draw a pictogram to show the choices of the boys.

Comment on the results of Rachel's survey.
You could do a survey in your own school.

2. **Paper production**

The world uses a lot of paper every year.
This table shows the top producers of paper in the world.

Country	Millions of tonnes
China	6
France	5
Japan	16
USA	54
West Germany	8

You could use a symbol like one of these to represent 5 million tonnes of paper, or you could design your own symbol.

 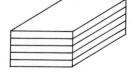

1   How would you show 3 million tonnes using symbols ?
2   Draw a pictogram to show the amount of paper produced.
3   Make a collection of different types or uses of paper. For example newspaper, graph paper, carbon paper, wrapping paper, cardboard packaging.
     See how many different examples you can find.
     Make a display of your collection, together with your pictogram.
4   What is meant by re-cycling ? Find examples of re-cycled paper to include in your display.

3.   **Hobbies, pastimes and sports**

Design a data collection sheet that you can use to survey the hobbies, pastimes and sports that a group of people enjoy.

You can survey people in your class, or you may wish to extend your survey to other groups of people, such as another class, a year group or older people.

Draw a bar chart to show your data.

What do you think the results of a similar survey taken 50 years ago would have shown ?

Make a poster to show the results of your survey.
Include details of how you carried out your survey. You could use pictures, newspaper and magazine cuttings, etc. to show the different hobbies, pastimes and sports that people enjoy. See if you can find pictures of old and modern-day activities.

10 Thinking about negative numbers

The number line

Which is the bigger number, −1 000 000 or 1 ?

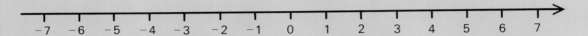

The number line above can be used to show the position of a number.

Geographers use sea-level as their base-line (zero level). Look at maps and see how colour is used to distinguish between places which are below sea-level and places which are above sea-level.

Negative numbers are also used in temperature, where 0°C (the freezing point of water) is used as the base-line.

Can you think of examples from the world of finance, or sport, where negative numbers are used ?

World time zones

How are negative numbers used on this world time zone map ?

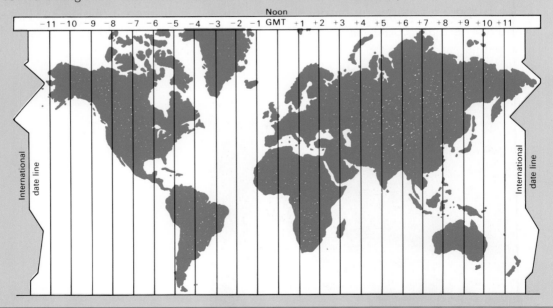

Mercury

Mercury is used in thermometers and barometers.
It is a strange metallic element.
The melting point of mercury is approximately −38°C.
In its liquid form it does not wet glass.
Why do you think mercury is used in thermometers?

Absolute zero

The lowest possible temperature which could exist is −273.16°C, and is called *absolute zero*.
It is impossible to cool anything down to this temperature.

A barometer on the wall of a hotel

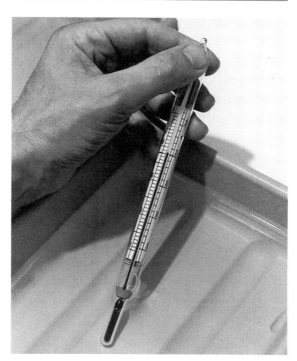

A thermometer

Using negative numbers in tables

To show if a record or team is moving up or down a table the signs + and − are used.
+ means that an upward movement has taken place.
− means that a downward movement has taken place.

For example, in a pop record chart +2 could mean that a record is 2 places higher in the chart than it was the previous week. −3 could mean that a record is 3 places lower than it was the previous week.
Using this system what could 0 be used to show?

10 Negative Numbers

The number ladder

Numbers can be shown on a number line or a number ladder.
The ladder continues upwards.
It also continues downwards.

The numbers below 0 are called **negative numbers**.
The numbers above 0 are called **positive numbers**.

−2 is bigger than −5 because it is higher up the ladder.

−2 is 3 bigger than −5. This is because −2 is 3 rungs higher up the ladder than −5.

Examples

1   Compare 3 and −4. Which is the bigger number and by how many ?

3 is 7 bigger than −4, because 3 is 7 rungs above −4.

2   Aled saves some of his pocket-money each week. He is saving for a computer game priced at £32. So far he has saved £24.
He worked out 24 − 32 on his calculator and the display showed −8.
What does this mean ?

Aled has taken away the cost of the game from the amount of money that he has saved.
−8 means that he is still £8 short, and so he must save another £8 before he can buy the game.

Has your calculator got a $\boxed{^+/_-}$ button ?
If so, to enter a negative amount such as −5, press $\boxed{5}$ then the $\boxed{^+/_-}$ button.
Some calculators work differently. If you are not sure how yours works then ask your teacher to help you.

Exercise 10.1

1. Say which is the bigger number and by how many.
   Use a number ladder to help you if necessary.

   1 −3 and 2   **4** −5 and 6   **7** −6 and −2
   2 0 and 4   **5** 3 and −3   **8** −1 and 1
   3 −1 and −2   **6** −10 and 0

2. On one day last year the temperature recorded at Warmington was −9°C. The temperature recorded at Alvington was −13°C.
   1 Which place recorded the lower temperature ?
   2 What was the difference in the temperatures ?

3. Fred measured the width of his doorway and it was 76 cm. He had a box which was 85 cm long, 74 cm wide and 1.5 m high.
   1 Fred worked out 76 − 85 on his calculator. What information did the answer give Fred ?
   2 He next worked out 76 − 74 on his calculator. What information did this answer give Fred ?

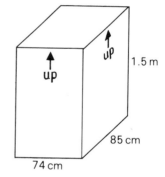

4. A bird's nest was 18 m above the level of the water. The bird dived 23 m from its nest, straight downwards, to catch a fish.
   1 Work out 18 − 23 on your calculator.
   2 What does your answer mean ?

5.   Andrea measured her height, and her brother's height, both in centimetres. On her calculator she entered her brother's height and took away her own height. She got the answer − 7. What does this mean ?

6.   Hackington Ladies Football Team scored 15 goals in their first five games. They had 18 goals scored against them.
     Goal difference = Number of goals scored by a team − number of goals scored against the team.

     1   Find the goal difference for Hackington Ladies, by working out 15 − 18 on your calculator.
     2   What does your answer mean ?

7.   Weston Football Club scored 45 goals last season.
     Their goal difference was 5.
     How many goals did the teams playing against them score ?

8.   West End Hockey Club scored 30 goals. Their goal difference is − 8.
     1   Did opposing teams score more or less than 30 goals ?
     2   How many goals did opposing teams score against West End ?

9.   Four football teams finished the season with 25 points.
     One of the teams will be relegated. (This means moved to the division below.)
     The team with the worst (lowest) goal difference goes down.
     The goals scored by each team and the goals scored against them are shown in this table.

Team	Goals For	Goals Against
Rovers	17	25
City	36	32
United	24	33
Town	12	18

     1   Work out the goal difference for each team.
     2   Which team is to be relegated ?

Temperature

Quite often in our country the temperature goes below 0°C or freezing point.

Temperatures are measured using a thermometer.
This thermometer reads −5°C.

The thermometer is marked in degrees Fahrenheit and degrees Celsius.

You must say which scale you are reading from. There is a big difference between −5°C and −5°F.

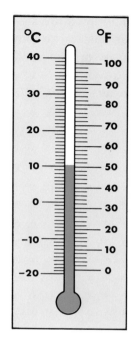

Exercise 10.2

1.   This thermometer is marked in degrees Fahrenheit and degrees Celsius.
     What temperature does the thermometer show
     1   in degrees Fahrenheit,
     2   in degrees Celsius ?

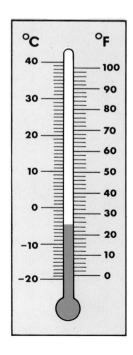

2. The diagram shows a thermometer with a Celsius scale. The temperature recorded by the arrow at *A* is 55°C.
Write down the temperatures recorded by the arrows at *B, C, D, E, F, G, H, I* and *J*.

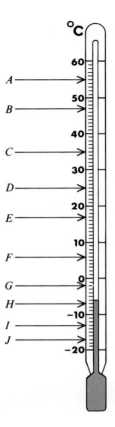

3. Use a strip of graph paper to make a number scale as shown. The numbers represent the readings on a thermometer.

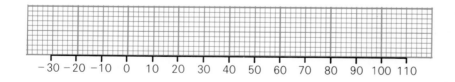

Draw arrows to record the following temperatures.
Label each arrow.

A 100°C.   The temperature at which water boils.
B −20°C.   Lowest temperature recorded in Australia.
C 58°C.   Highest temperature recorded in Africa.
D 14°C.   Highest temperature recorded in Antarctica.
E −18°C.   Maximum temperature in a deep freezer.
F 37°C.   Body temperature.

4.

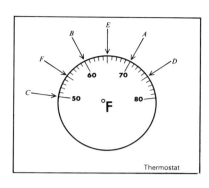

Thermostat

This is a central heating thermostat.
When the room reaches a set temperature the
thermostat switches the heat off. After the
temperature drops a little the thermostat
switches the heat back on again.

The ideal temperature for a living room is 70°F.
This is shown by the arrow labelled *A* on the
diagram.

Give the letter of the arrow which points to these room temperatures.
1 Bathroom 65°F.
2 Bedrooms 55°F.
3 Dining-room 70°F.
4 Hall 60°F.
5 Kitchen 60°F.
6 Toilet 60°F.
7 Which rooms have the highest temperature ?
8 Which rooms have the lowest temperature ?
9 What is the difference in temperature between the warmest and coolest
rooms ?

5.   This thermostat is used to control a freezer.
Arrow *A* is pointing to −15°C.
1 Write down the temperatures recorded by the arrows at *B*, *C*, *D*, *E* and *F*.
2 Which of the temperatures *A* to *F* is the highest ?
3 Which of the temperatures *A* to *F* is the lowest ?

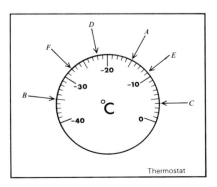

Thermostat

Exercise 10.3   Applications and Activities

1. **The Lift**

This bank has floors below ground-level as well as floors above ground-level.

1   How many floors does the bank have ?

The control panel in the lift is unusual. The $\boxed{+}$ button tells the lift to go up and the $\boxed{-}$ button tells the lift to go down.

2   Where would the lift travel to if you get in the lift on FLOOR 1 and press the $\boxed{+}$ and then the $\boxed{2}$ buttons ?

3   Where would the lift travel to if you get in the lift on FLOOR 3 and press the $\boxed{-}$ and then the $\boxed{5}$ buttons ?

4   If you were on FLOOR -3 which two buttons would you press to get to FLOOR 1 ?

Which two buttons would you press to get from

5   FLOOR -1 to FLOOR -3 ?
6   FLOOR -2 to FLOOR 2 ?
7   FLOOR 1 to FLOOR -3 ?
8   FLOOR 3 to the Ground Floor ?
9   FLOOR -2 to the Ground Floor ?
10   FLOOR 3 to FLOOR -3 ?

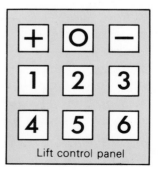

Lift control panel

2. **Maximum and minimum temperatures**

A class did a project on temperature.
They collected the maximum and minimum temperatures for each day during a week in winter.

A maximum and minimum thermometer was used to find the temperatures.
The readings the class obtained are shown in the table below.

Day	Mon	Tues	Wed	Thurs	Fri
Max. Temp. °C	5	6	3	−1	1
Min. Temp. °C	2	1	−5	−8	−6

What was the difference between the maximum and minimum temperatures on
1   Monday,
2   Tuesday,
3   Wednesday,
4   Thursday,
5   Friday ?
6   On which day did the biggest difference between the maximum and minimum temperatures occur ?

3. **The Ladder Game**

This is a game for two people.

Make a larger copy of the ladder on a big
piece of paper.
You need 2 counters, a coin and a die.

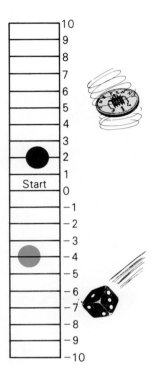

Each player puts their counter on the start
at 0.
When it is your go toss the coin and roll
the die.

If the coin shows HEADS you move up
the ladder.
If the coin shows TAILS you move down
the ladder.
The number on the die tells you how many
rungs to move.

The winner is the first player to get to the
TOP or the BOTTOM of the ladder.

4. **The Handicap Badminton Tournament**

A badminton club organised a handicap badminton tournament. Each player was
given a handicap. The better the players were the more points they had to win.
The idea was to give everyone a fair chance of winning.

The handicap system was as follows.
   1st team players started at -7.
   2nd team players started at -3.
   Adult non-team members started at 0.
   Junior non-team members started at 5.

The first player to get to 15 points won the match.
For example. Sarah is a junior non-team member.
            She started on 5 and had to win 10 points to win the match.

At the semi-final stage of the tournament, only 4 players remained.
In the first semi-final Susan played Sally.
Susan plays for the 2nd team.
Sally is an adult non-team member.
   1   What score did Susan start at ?
   2   How many points did Susan need to win, in order to win the match ?

3   What score did Sally start at ?

4   How many points did Sally need to win, in order to win the match ?

Susan beat Sally. The final score was 15 − 13.

In the second semi-final Hilary played Alison.
Hilary plays for the 1st team.
Alison is a junior non-team member.

5   What score did Hilary start at ?

6   How many points did Hilary need to win, in order to win the match ?

7   What score did Alison start at ?

8   How many points did Alison need to win, in order to win the match ?

Alison beat Hilary. The score was 15 − 11.

9   How many points did Hilary win in the match ?

In the final Susan beat Alison 15 − 9.

10   How many points did Susan win to beat Alison ?

11   How many points did Alison win in the final ?

12   How many more points did Susan win in the final than Alison ?

PUZZLES

18.   How many times during the day does the minute-hand of a clock hide the hour-hand?

19.   What is the least number of weights that Jack needs to be able to weigh all whole numbers of kilograms from 1 kg to 63 kg ?

20.   A gardener has 2 buckets. One holds 10 litres and the other 7 litres. How can he use the two buckets to pour exactly 9 litres of water into a tank ?

21.   There are 9 teams in the Ladies' Netball League. Each team plays each other in two matches. One match is played at home and one match is played away. How many League matches are played in one season ?

22.   How many squares are there in this diagram ?
There are more than 9.

11 Thinking about money

The decimal system

It was decided in 1849 that England needed a decimal system of money. Only in 1971, 122 years later, was the decimal system of money fully introduced.

The only coin that now remains in use from the old system is the florin. The florin was worth two shillings in old money. It is worth 10p in the decimal system we use now.

The florin was introduced in 1849 as the first step towards a decimal system of money.

The old money system

The system that was in use before the decimal system was as follows:

   12 pence = 1 shilling

20 shillings = £1

(So £1 = 240 pence)

The decimal system of money

The decimal system is based on the number 10, which makes calculation easy.   100p = £1

The 'tail' and 'head' of one of the very first florins

Some coins from the old money system. Which is the 'odd' coin out ? Can you name each coin ?

Saving money

There are many places in which you can save money.
Do you use any of the following ?

A bank account

National Savings Account (at the post office)

A building society account

Methods of paying

There are many methods of paying for goods or services. Can you think of any other ways of paying ?

Saving up and paying by cash

Paying by cheque

Paying by credit card

11 Money

Changing pounds to pence

To change pounds to pence multiply by 100.
This is because there are 100 pence in a pound.

$$£1 = 100p$$

Examples

Amount in £'s	Amount in pence
£2	200p
£4.00	400p
£3.56	356p
£2.70	270p
£0.89	89p
£0.08	8p

Notation

The figures before the decimal point (to the left of the decimal point) tell you the number of complete pounds.

The two figures after the decimal point (to the right of the decimal point) tell you the number of pence.

If figures are written after the decimal point there must be exactly **TWO**. Five pounds can be written as £5 or £5.00 **but not** £5.0.

Changing pence to pounds

This is the opposite to changing pounds to pence.

$$100p = £1$$

Examples

Amount in pence	Amount in £'s
7p	£0.07
45p	£0.45
60p	£0.60
300p	£3.00 or £3
517p	£5.17
1860p	£18.60

Exercise 11.1

1. Change the following amounts to pence.
   1 £5
   2 £8.00
   3 £2.47
   4 £3.50
   5 £12.75
   6 £0.72
   7 £0.05
   8 £1.07
   9 £10.06
   10 £51.10

2. Change the following amounts to pounds.
   1 400p
   2 250p
   3 575p
   4 1600p
   5 3750p
   6 11p
   7 6p
   8 208p
   9 1001p
   10 2110p

3. Wendy bought a pencil priced £0.46. How many pence is this ?

4. Richard paid a total of 125p for a Christmas card and a stamp.
   What is this amount, written in £'s ?

Using a calculator

Most calculators do not show amounts of money in the usual way. They show the **number** of pounds, or they show the **number** of pence. You have to translate the information that the calculator shows on its display.

For example. Work out £0.20 × 3. Do this by pressing

$\boxed{0}$ $\boxed{\cdot}$ $\boxed{2}$ $\boxed{0}$ $\boxed{\times}$ $\boxed{3}$ $\boxed{=}$

The calculator displays 0.6

We know that £0.20 is 20p.
We also know that 20p × 3 = 60p.
60p can be written as £0.60
0.6 on the calculator display means £0.60

Points to note when using a calculator

1   If you enter amounts in pence the answer given by the calculator will be in pence.

2   If you enter amounts in pounds the answer given by the calculator will be in pounds.

3   You may have to round answers to the nearest penny.

4   If you enter an amount in pounds and press a key (+, −, × or ÷) you may find that the amount you entered appears to change.
   For example. To enter £0.20 press ⬚0⬚ ⬚·⬚ ⬚2⬚ ⬚0⬚ and then press the ⬚=⬚ key. The display should show 0.2.
   0.20 is the same as 0.2
   The calculator has translated your amount of money into a simple decimal.

Some calculators work differently. If you are unsure of what your calculator does, ask your teacher for help.

Examples

1   What keys would you press to enter £1.07 ?

   You would press the keys ⬚1⬚ ⬚·⬚ ⬚0⬚ ⬚7⬚

2   How would your calculator display £0.10 as an answer ?

   It would show 0.1
   Check this by pressing ⬚0⬚ ⬚·⬚ ⬚1⬚ ⬚0⬚ ⬚=⬚

Exercise 11.2

1.   Which keys would you press on your calculator to enter the following amounts ?

1	£2.58	**5**	£3.04	**8**	£10.04
2	£1.27	**6**	£0.26	**9**	£205.30
3	£5.63	**7**	£0.01	**10**	£101.01
4	£45.39				

2. How would your calculator display the following amounts after the $\boxed{=}$ button has been pressed ?

1	£2.87	**5**	£5.06	**8**	£100.00
2	£0.70	**6**	£0.06	**9**	£105.90
3	£2.55	**7**	£76.00	**10**	£160.10
4	£4.60				

3. The following are answers given on a calculator display. All of the amounts were entered in pounds. How should each amount be correctly written on paper ?

1	0.9	**5**	0.15	**8**	7
2	0.89	**6**	12.8	**9**	4.2
3	1.5	**7**	0.02	**10**	0.1
4	2.36				

Questions involving money

Examples

1 A ticket for the school play costs £1.50. How much would 10 tickets cost ?

Using your calculator, working in £'s,
1.50 × 10 = 15

The answer is also in £'s, so 10 tickets cost £15.

2 Carol bought 3 pencils which cost 45p each and 2 drawing pens which cost £1.95 each.
How much did Carol spend altogether ?
How much change did Carol get from a £10 note ?

The pencils cost 45p each.
So 3 pencils cost 3 × 45p = 135p

The drawing pens cost £1.95 each.
So 2 drawing pens cost 2 × £1.95 = £3.90

The total cost = 135p + £3.90
You cannot do this addition on your calculator because the units are not the same.
So change the 135p to £1.35

£1.35 + £3.90 = £5.25
The change from £10 is given by £10 − £5.25 = £4.75

So Carol spent £5.25 and got £4.75 change.

3 How many 22p stamps can be bought for £10 ?
What change would you get if you paid with a £10 note ?

Number of stamps = £10 ÷ 22p
(The units must be the same so change £10 to 1000p.)
$$= 1000p \div 22p$$
$$= 1000 \div 22$$
$$= 45.4545...$$

You have not got enough money for 46 stamps.
This is an example where you have to **round down**.

45 stamps cost 45 × 22p = 990p or £9.90
Change = 1000p − 990p = 10p or £10 − £9.90 = £0.10 = 10p

You can buy 45 stamps and you will get 10p change.

Exercise 11.3

1. How much change would you get from a £1 coin if you spend the following amounts ?

1	30p	**3**	45p	**5**	87p
2	75p	**4**	36p	**6**	63p

2. How much change would you get from a £5 note if you spend the following amounts ?

1	£2	**3**	£1.25	**5**	£4.26
2	£3.50	**4**	£2.37	**6**	85p

3. Michael buys 3 chocolate bars which cost 23p each.
   1 How much do the chocolate bars cost altogether ?
   2 How much change does Michael get from a £1 coin ?

4. Samantha buys four items from the grocer's.
   Two of the items cost 38p each. The other items cost 25p and £1.50.
   1 How much did the four items cost altogether ?
   2 How much change did Samantha get from a £5 note ?

5. Ernie goes into a secondhand shop and buys a telescope for £9.85 and a book on astronomy for £2.35.
   1 How much do the telescope and book cost altogether ?
   2 How much change did Ernie get from a £20 note ?

6.   Julie collects badges from the places she has visited.
     Whilst on holiday Julie bought 5 badges which cost 90p each and 2 badges
     which cost £1 each. At the end of the holiday she bought another 3 badges for
     £1.25 each.
     1   What was the total amount Julie paid for her badges ?
     2   How much money did Julie have left from her £20 spending money ?

7.   Four friends share a taxi home from town.
     The fare was £5.60.
     How much should each person pay ?

8.   Rohini filled her car up with unleaded petrol.
     The fuel tank held 40 litres of petrol.
     The cost of the petrol was 49.3 pence per litre.
     How much should Rohini pay ?

9.   Gill ordered some goods from a mail order catalogue.
     She ordered a pair of jeans for £35, an electric toaster for £25.50 and a
     computer game for £22.90.
     1   What was the total value of the goods Gill ordered ?
     2   Gill has to pay for the goods over 20 weeks. How much does she have to
             pay every week ?

10. Three friends hire a badminton court at the sports centre.
     The court costs £2.70 for one hour and they each have to pay an admission
     charge of 25p. One of them hires a racket for £1.10 and they buy two shuttles
     which cost 95p each.
     What is the total cost of playing badminton for an hour ?

11. How many 17p stamps can be bought for £5 ?
     What change would you get from a £5 note ?

12. How many books could you buy from a secondhand bookstall for £3 if each
     book costs 40p. How much change would you get from three £1 coins ?

13. A bus driver takes fares from people as they get on the bus.
     At one stop 7 children and 4 adults get on the bus.
     Each child paid 85p and each adult paid £1.20.
     How much money did the driver take at the bus stop ?

14. Sandra is decorating her living-room.
     She buys one tin of emulsion paint costing £8.49, one tin of gloss paint costing
     £7.55, 6 rolls of wallpaper costing £13.40 each and a packet of paste costing
     £2.39.
     1 How much did the decorating materials amount to ?
     2 Sandra paid with five £20 notes. How much change did she get ?

15. Gordon is going to service his car.
     He buys 4 spark plugs costing £2.95 each, an oil filter costing £3.49, a 5 litre
     can of oil for £7.29 and a set of contact breaker points for £1.35.
     1 What was the total cost of the parts ?
     2 How much change did Gordon get if he paid using a £20 note and a £10
            note ?

Exercise 11.4   Applications and Activities

1. **Calculating the change**

    You can calculate your change by **adding on**.
    For example. If you buy something for 32p and pay with a £1 coin, you could
    work out your change like this.

    32p + 2p makes 34p
        + 1p makes 35p
        + 5p makes 40p
        + 10p makes 50p
        + 50p makes £1

    You get a 2p coin, a 1p coin, a 5p coin, a 10p coin and a 50p coin for your
    change. This is a total of 68p.

    Work out the change you would get from a £1 coin if you spend the following
    amounts. Calculate your change by adding on.
    List the coins you could get in your change.

    1 30p   **3** 46p   **5** 7p
    2 25p   **4** 76p

    If you were the shopkeeper, how would you give the change if these amounts
    were spent and a £10 note was handed to you ?

    6 £4   **8** £2.25   **10** £1.28
    7 £7.50   **9** £8.16

2. **School holiday**

Each pupil saved up money to spend on the school holiday. Mr Scott was in charge of the pocket money for 10 pupils. Each week he collected money from the 10 pupils, and he put this money in the bank for safety.
The holiday lasted 5 days. Every day Mr Scott went to the bank and withdrew enough money to give the 10 pupils their pocket money.
He designed a table to make his job easier.

	Name	Total saved	Daily amount	£1	50p	10p	5p	2p	1p
1.	Alex	£10.00	£2.00	2	0	0	0	0	0
2.	Emma	£12.00	£2.40	2	0	4	0	0	0
3.	Gail	£7.30	£1.46	1	0	4	1	0	1
4.	Stuart	£15.00							
5.	Lesley	£14.00							
6.	Bill		£1.50						
7.	Dawn		£1.80						
8.	Lucy	£18.00							
9.	Gary	£8.20							
10.	George	£17.00							

1 Copy the table.
2 Complete the first two columns of the table.
3 Write down in your table the numbers of the coins needed to make up the daily amount of money for each pupil. Use the least number of coins possible. Notice that Mr Scott did not include 20p coins in his table.
4 What was the total number of £1 coins needed each day ?
5 Work out the number of 50p, 10p, 5p, 2p and 1p coins needed each day.
6 How much money did Mr Scott pay out each day ?

3. **Best buy**

In a supermarket you can buy items in single packs, double packs, triple packs and quadruple packs. Sometimes even more items are packed together and sold in one large pack.

It is not always the case that the more you buy the less you have to pay for each item.

For example. Toilet rolls are sold at £1.26 for a double pack and £1.91 for a triple pack. Which is the best buy ?

Find the cost for 1 toilet roll in each case.
£1.26 for 2 rolls. So 1 roll = £1.26 ÷ 2 = £0.63 or 63p
£1.91 for 3 rolls. So 1 roll = £1.91 ÷ 3 = 0.6366... or 63.666...p which is 64p to the nearest penny.

The best buy is the double pack for £1.26

Find the best buy for each of these items.
In each case work out the cost of 1 item. Round off to the nearest penny where necessary.
1   Cakes. 75p for 3 or £1.20 for 5.
2   Orange juice. £2.76 for 4 cartons or 67p per carton.
3   Baked beans. £1.12 for 4 tins or £2.76 for 10 tins.
4   Pop. £1.04 for 4 cans or £1.55 for 6 cans.
5   Crisps. £1.08 for 6 packets or £1.20 for 6 packets plus a free packet.

4.   **Raffle tickets**

Class 7 sold raffle tickets at the school fete.
Tickets were sold for 30 pence each.
1   What was the cost of 5 raffle tickets ?
2   How many tickets could a person buy with a £1 coin ?
     How much change would they get ?
3   How many tickets could be bought with a £5 note ?
     How much change would be given ?
4   Class 7 sold 1850 tickets. How much money did they collect from selling the tickets ?

The tickets had cost the class £15 and £75 was spent on prizes. The first three tickets drawn would win a prize.
5   What was the total amount paid for the prizes and printing the raffle tickets ?
6   How much profit did the raffle make ?
7   Why is 30p not a very convenient amount to sell tickets for ?
8   If you were holding a raffle, say what price you would sell the tickets for, and explain why you decided on that price.

5.   **Sporting Chance**

Make a booklet which describes a sport or hobby that you do, or that you would like to do. Your sport or hobby may be stamp collecting, skateboarding, mountain bike riding, horse riding, etc. You may wish to choose an unusual sport or hobby such as scuba diving, visiting railway museums, gliding, mountaineering, etc. The choice of sport or hobby is yours.

As well as describing a sport or hobby, your booket should give details of the various costs involved.

Include the cost of any equipment,
            the cost of any protective or special clothing,
            the cost of hiring a hall, court, pool, etc,
            the cost of membership fees that must be paid,
            the cost of any insurance,
            the cost of travelling to and from meetings, training sessions, etc,
            the cost of magazines, papers, etc.

Try to include pictures in your booklet to make it more interesting.

PUZZLES

23.   A delivery van carried 5 boxes of butter and 1 box of cheese. The boxes weighed 7, 16, 17, 21, 28 and 33 kg.
       At the first hotel he delivered some butter, and he delivered twice as much butter to the second hotel.
       What was the weight of the box which contained the cheese ?

24.   Copy the diagram and draw lines from
       1 to *A*,
       2 to *B*,
       3 to *C*,
       4 to *D*,
       5 to *E*.

       All 5 lines must go through the gap in the fence.
       Lines must not meet, cross over, or go through a letter which is not their final finishing letter.

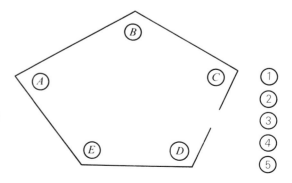

25.   How can Mary measure exactly 4 litres of water if she only has jugs which hold exactly 5 litres and 3 litres of water ?

12   Thinking about shapes

Pinboard shapes

Use a pinboard to make as many different-shaped triangles as you can. The following diagrams show two examples.

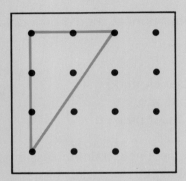 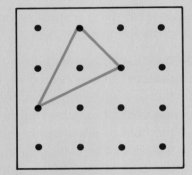

How many different-shaped triangles can you make ?
Try making some four-sided figures.

Rigid structures

Make these two shapes using straws and pipe cleaners.

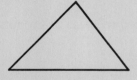

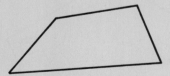

The triangle is a rigid shape. It is because of its strength that it is used in buildings.
You could strengthen the 4-sided shape by putting in another straw to make two triangles.

Part of a boat lifting device.

The first wallpaper

The first ever wallpaper was believed to have been hung in the Master's Lodgings at Christ College, Cambridge.

The wallpaper dated back to about 1509 and was a black and white design. The pattern was symmetrical.

The designer was believed to be Hugo Goes who was a printer in Steingate, York. He used a wooden block, which measured approximately 53 cm by 41 cm, to create his design on the backs of old documents.

Planes of symmetry

If something is symmetrical and is three-dimensional it has planes of symmetry.
Where are the planes of symmetry in the following ?

Tower Bridge, London

The Taj Mahal, Agra, India

The Arc de Triomphe, Paris

A satellite dish

12 Shapes

Shapes

Triangles

A shape with 3 straight sides is called a **triangle**.

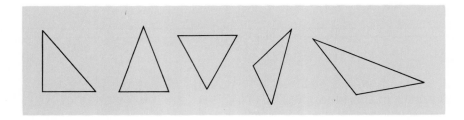

Some other shapes

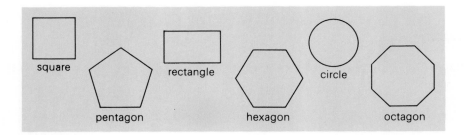

Lines of symmetry

A shape is symmetrical if you can fold it so that one half fits exactly over the other half.
The fold-line is called a **line of symmetry** or an **axis of symmetry**.
If you put a mirror along the line of symmetry and look into it you will see the complete shape.

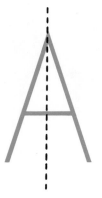

Examples

1   How many lines of symmetry does a
    rectangle have ?

    A rectangle has 2 lines of symmetry.
    Lines of symmetry are shown using
    dotted lines.
    You can check the lines of symmetry by
    using a mirror. Place it along each dotted
    line in turn.

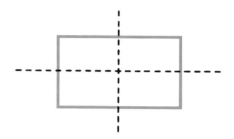

2   How many lines of symmetry does this letter have ?

The letter F has no lines of symmetry.

Planes of symmetry

3-dimensional objects can have a **plane of symmetry**.
A plane of symmetry **slices** through a shape.

Examples

1   How many planes of symmetry does this radiator have ?

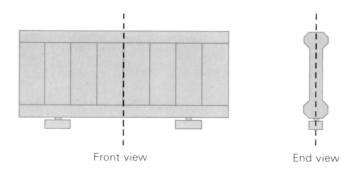

Front view   End view

The radiator has 2 planes of symmetry.

2   How many planes of symmetry does this door-wedge have ?

It has 1 plane of symmetry.

Rotational symmetry

This shape has rotational symmetry of order 4.

If it is turned through 90°, and then 90°, and
then 90° again it is unchanged.
On the 4th turn through 90° the shape is back
at its starting position.

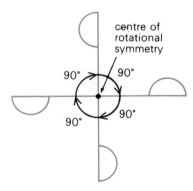

This shape has rotational
symmetry of order 4.

This shape has rotational symmetry of order 3.

If it is turned through 120°, and then 120°,
it is unchanged.
On the 3rd turn through 120° the shape is back
at its starting position.

The point about which the shape turns is called
the **centre of rotational symmetry**.

This shape has rotational
symmetry of order 3

Examples

1 What is the order of rotational symmetry of
this shape ?

The hexagon fits into its own outline
6 times when it is turned through 360°.

The dot shows the centre of rotational
symmetry.

The order of rotational symmetry is 6.

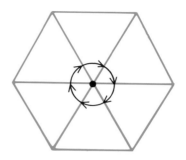

2 What is the order of rotational symmetry of
this letter ?

The order of rotational symmetry is 2.

The dot shows the centre of rotational
symmetry.

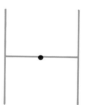

Exercise 12.1

1. Which of these shapes has a line or lines of symmetry ?
    Use a mirror to check if you are not sure.

1   **2**   **3**

4   **5**

2.   Which of these figures have a plane or planes of symmetry ?

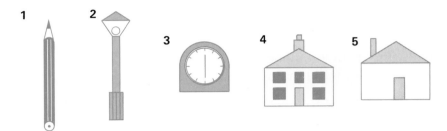

3.   What is the order of rotational symmetry of these figures ?

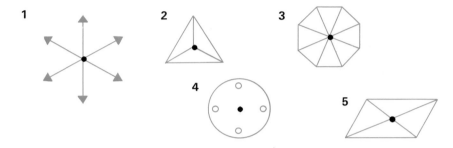

4.   Look at the letters below.

BHJMZ

1   Which letters have exactly **one** line of symmetry ?
2   Which letter has exactly **two** lines of symmetry ?
3   Which letters have no lines of symmetry ?
4   Which letters have rotational symmetry of order 2 ?

Congruent figures

Congruent figures are the same shape and the same size. If two figures are
congruent a tracing of one of the figures will fit exactly over the other figure. It may be
necessary to turn the tracing paper over before obtaining an exact fit.

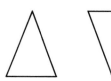

Reminder

An angle between 0° and 90° is called an
acute angle.

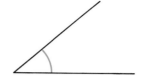

An angle which is equal to 90° is called a
right-angle.

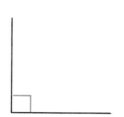

An angle between 90° and 180° is called an
obtuse angle.

Sorting shapes

You can sort shapes in many ways.
For example, you could look at the number of sides,
                          the lengths of sides,
                          the size of angles,
                          the lines of symmetry,
                          the order of rotational symmetry,
                          the shape and the size of a figure.

Example

Look at this set of shapes.

1   Which shapes have 3 sides ?

Shapes *A* and *B*.

A has two straight sides and one curved side.

2   Which shapes have only straight sides ?

Shapes *B*, *C* and *D*.

3   Which shapes have exactly one line of symmetry ?

Shapes *A* and *D*.

If you are not sure about lines of symmetry use a mirror to check.

4   Which shapes have an acute angle ?

Shapes *A*, *B* and *D*.

You will need to check angles carefully.
You **cannot** measure an angle between a straight side and a curved side.

Exercise 12.2

1.   Look at this set of shapes.

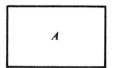   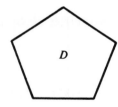

List the shapes which have
1   a curved side
2   three sides
3   four sides
4   more than four sides
5   sides that are **all** the same length
6   one or more right-angles
7   one or more obtuse angles

8   one or more acute angles
9   exactly one line of symmetry
10   an even number of lines of symmetry
11   rotational symmetry of order 2

What is the name given to the following shapes ?
12   *A*
13   *C*
14   *D*
15   *F*

2.   Name pairs of congruent figures in this diagram.

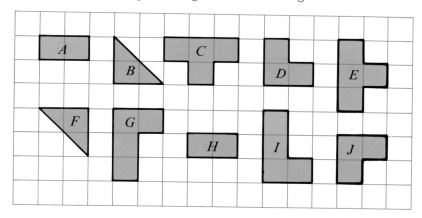

Solid figures

You should know the names of these solid figures.

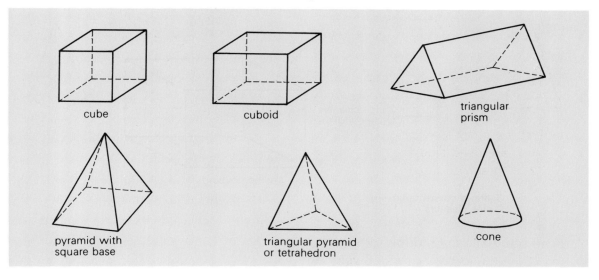

cube

cuboid

triangular prism

pyramid with square base

triangular pyramid or tetrahedron

cone

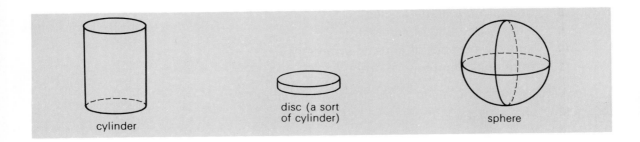

cylinder   disc (a sort
                  of cylinder)   sphere

Naming parts of a solid shape

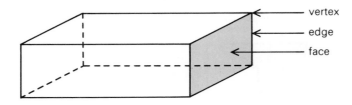

vertex
edge
face

Each surface is called a **face**.
Two faces meet at a line called an **edge**.
A corner or point of a shape is called a **vertex**.
The plural of vertex is **vertices**.
The edges of a shape meet at the vertices.

Skeleton figures

You can make **skeleton figures** using straws and pipe cleaners.
To join three straws together at a vertex you can twist two pipe cleaners together. Take care when you are doing this not to scratch your fingers with the ends of the pipe cleaners.

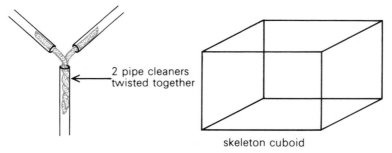

2 pipe cleaners
twisted together

3 straws connected using
2 pipe cleaners

skeleton cuboid

You can see that a cuboid has 12 edges,
                              8 vertices,
                              6 faces.

Plane surfaces and curved surfaces

A **plane surface** is a flat surface.
A **curved surface**, as its name tells us, is not flat but curved.

Exercise 12.3

1.   Name these solid figures.

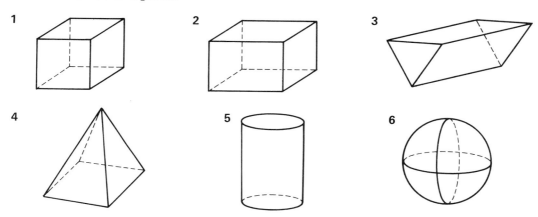

2.   What mathematical name can be given to these objects ?

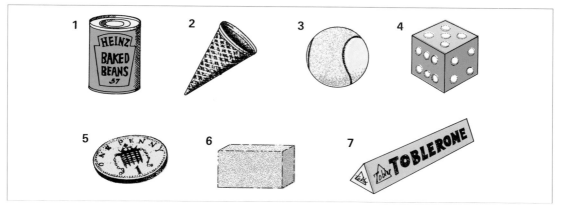

3.   Look at the objects in question 2.
      Name the objects which have
      1   only plane surfaces,
      2   a curved surface,
      3   faces which are squares,
      4   faces which are circles,
      5   faces which are rectangles,
      6   faces which are triangles.

4.   Look at these solid figures. The dotted lines show the edges that cannot be seen
       when you look at the figure from one side.

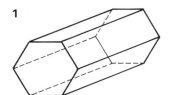

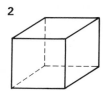

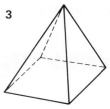

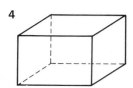

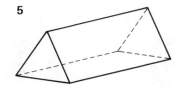

Copy and complete this table. The first line has been done for you.

	Name of figure	Number of edges	Number of vertices	Number of faces
1	Hexagonal prism	18	12	8
2				
3				
4				
5				

5.   This is a model of a **tetrahedron** or
     triangular pyramid.
     It has been made using straws and pipe
     cleaners.
     Each straw is the same length.

     1   How many edges does the
           tetrahedron have ?

     2   How many vertices does a tetrahedron
           have ?

     3   How many faces does a tetrahedron
           have ?

     4   If each straw is 10 cm long, what is
           the total length of the straws needed
           to make the model of the tetrahedron ?

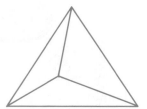

Drawing shapes

Drawing instruments

To make good drawings you must have the correct drawing instruments.
You need a ruler, pencil, set-square and a pair of compasses.
You will need a protractor later.
Once you have obtained your drawing instruments look after them.
You will need them many times when your are doing your maths.

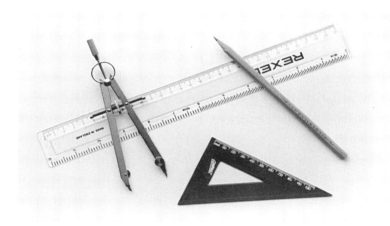

Exercise 12.4

In this exercise you are going to use your drawing instruments to draw some shapes.
Some questions will lead you step by step until you have completed a shape. Other
questions will allow you to practise your drawing skills.

1. **The rectangle**
    You are going to draw a rectangle which measures 7 cm by 4 cm on
    squared paper.
    1 Draw a line 7 cm long.
        Label the line AB.
    2 From B, measure 4 cm along the line
        which is at right-angles to the line
        AB.
        Mark the point C.
        Draw the line BC.

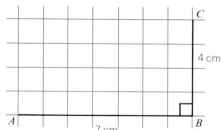

3 From *A*, measure 4 cm along the line which is at right-angles to the line *AB*.
Mark the point *D*.
Draw the line *AD*.
Finally draw the line *DC* to complete the rectangle.

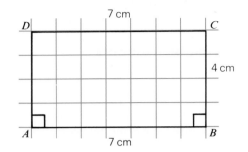

4 Draw the lines *AC* and *BD* (the diagonals of the rectangle).

5 Measure and write down the lengths of *AC* and *BD*.

2. The square

A square is a rectangle in which the length and breadth are the same. In this question you are going to draw a square with side 5 cm on squared paper.

1 Draw a line 5 cm long.
Label the line *PQ*.

2 From *Q*, measure 5 cm along the line which is at right-angles to the line *PQ*.
Mark the point *R*.
Draw the line *QR*.

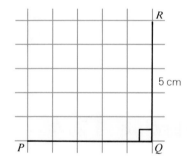

3 From *P*, measure 5 cm along the line which is at right-angles to the line *PQ*.
Mark the point *S*.
Draw the line *PS*.
Finally draw the line *SR* to complete the square.

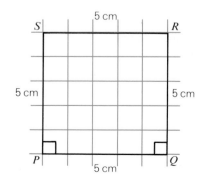

4 Draw the lines *PR* and *QS* (the diagonals of the square).

5 Measure and write down the lengths of *PR* and *QS*.

3. **The triangle**

You are going to draw a triangle with sides 8 cm, 7 cm and 5 cm on squared paper.

1 Draw a line 8 cm long.
Label the line *AB*.

2 Set your compasses to 7 cm.
Take care when you are using compasses. If your compasses need a pencil fixing to them find another pencil to use with your ruler when you draw straight lines.

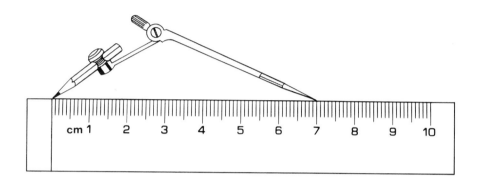

3 Centre at *A*. This means put the compass point at *A*.
Draw a large arc, using the compasses.
An **arc** is part of a circle. The distance from *A* to any point on the arc is 7 cm.

A _____ 8 cm _____ *B*

4   Set your compasses to 5 cm.
Centre at *B*.
Draw an arc to cut the first arc.
Any point on the second arc will be 5 cm from *B*.

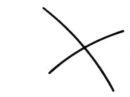

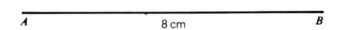

A   8 cm   *B*

5   Mark the point where the two arcs intersect with a dot.
Label the point *C*.
The point where the arcs intersect is 7 cm from *A* and 5 cm from *B*.

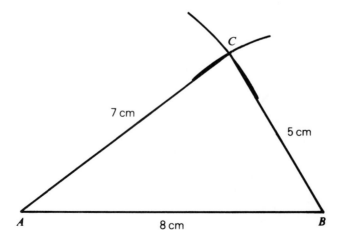

Draw the lines *AC* and *BC*. Write the lengths of the sides on the diagram.
You have now drawn a triangle with sides 8 cm, 7 cm and 5 cm.

4.   **The circle**

You have already drawn part of a circle in question 3.
A part of a circle is called an **arc**.
In this question you are going to draw two circles.
One circle will have a radius of 5 cm.
The other circle will have a radius of 3 cm.
Both circles will have the same centre.

1   Draw a small cross with a pencil and label it O.
The middle of the cross will be the centre of the circles.

2   Set your compasses to 5 cm.
This is the **radius** of the circle.
3   Draw the circle.

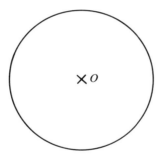

4   Set your compasses to 3 cm.
This is the radius of the second circle.
5   Using the same centre O, draw the second circle.

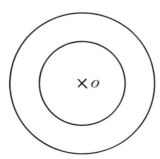

Two circles which have the same centre are said to be **concentric**.

5.   This is a diagram of a rectangle with a triangle added to each end.
      The lengths of the sides are shown on the diagram.
      1   Use your drawing instruments to draw the shape on squared paper.
             Draw the rectangle first and then the triangles.
      2   Measure the distance from *F* to *C*.

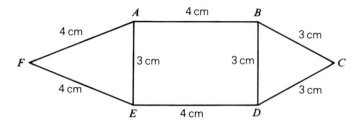

6.   This diagram shows a square inside a circle.
      1   Use your drawing instruments to draw
             the square on squared paper.
      2   Draw the diagonals of the square *AC*
             and *BD*.
      3   Draw the circle. The centre of the
             circle is where the diagonals of the
             square cross.

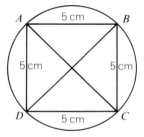

Making three-dimensional shapes

The net of a solid figure

This is a pyramid with a square base.
If you cut along the four edges which lead to
the top vertex you can make the shape flat.

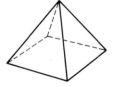

This is called the **net** of the pyramid.
A **net** is a shape which can be folded to make a
three-dimensional shape.

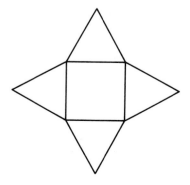

This is also a net of a pyramid.
It was made by cutting along different edges of
the pyramid.

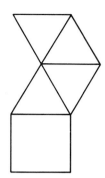

You can use your drawing instruments to draw the nets of shapes.
The net of a shape must be accurate.
A good net makes a good three-dimensional shape.

Exercise 12.5

1.   This is a net of a cube. It could be cut out and folded to make a cube.

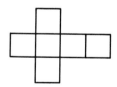

      Which of the following diagrams could be used as a net of a cube ?

1
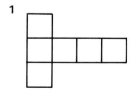

2
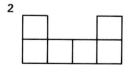

3
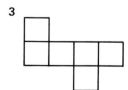

4
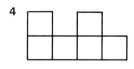

5
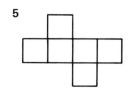

6
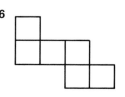

2.   What solid figure is this the net of ?

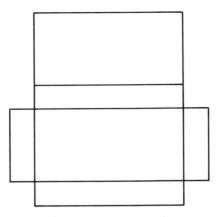

3.   This is a **triangular prism**.

   1   How many triangular faces does the
           prism have ?

   2   How many rectangular faces does the
           prism have ?

   3   What is the length and breadth of
           each of these rectangular faces ?

   4   Use your drawing instruments to draw
           a net of the prism on squared paper,
           drawing the rectangles first.

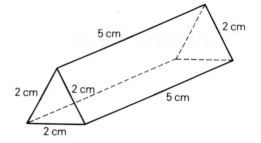

4.   This is a net of a **hexagonal prism**.

   1   How many faces does the prism have ?
   2   How many edges does the prism have ?
   3   How many vertices does the prism have ?

Exercise 12.6   Applications and Activities

1. **Making three-dimensional shapes**

In Exercise 12.5 you looked at the nets of some three-dimensional figures. You are now going to use nets to make three-dimensional figures using paper.

The cube

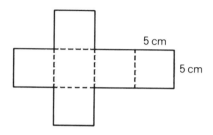

The net of a cube is made of 6 squares.
Before we can make the cube we have to add some **tabs** to the net. The **tabs** allow us to glue two faces together to form an edge.

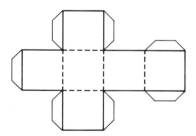

Put tabs on every other edge of the net going round in order.
This rule for putting tabs on a net works for all three-dimensional figures.

1   Draw the net of the cube. Centimetre squared paper makes the task easier.
2   Draw the tabs on the net.
3   Cut the net out carefully.
4   Draw along the dotted lines with a biro. This is called **scoring** the line.
     It makes the paper easier to bend.
     Score along the edges of every tab. Bend the paper along the scored lines.
5   Glue one tab at a time. Take your time glueing the cube together.

Before glueing your cube together you can turn the net over and draw designs on each face, or you could write numbers on each face to make a die.

The cuboid

The net for a cuboid is shown below. Tabs have been added to the net.

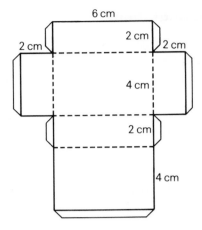

Draw the net on squared paper using the measurements in the diagram. Cut the net out. Score along the dotted lines and along the edges of the tabs. Make the cuboid.

The triangular prism

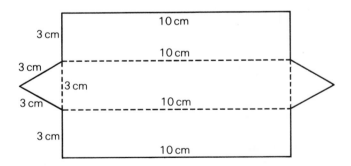

This is the net for a triangular prism.
1   Use your drawing instruments to draw the net on squared paper.
2   Add tabs to the net.
3   Cut the net out and score along the necessary lines to make the paper bend easily.
4   Make the figure.

2. **Letters of the alphabet**

Look at the letters of the alphabet below.

A   B   C   D   E   F   G   H   I   J   K   L   M
N   O   P   Q   R   S   T   U   V   W   X   Y   Z

1   Which letters have exactly **one** line of symmetry ?
2   Which letters have exactly **two** lines of symmetry ?
3   Which letters have no lines of symmetry ?
4   Copy the letters.
    Use a dotted line to show each line of symmetry.
5   Which letters have rotational symmetry of order 2 ?
6   Are there any letters which have rotational symmetry of order more than two ?
7   On the same letters you used in **4** mark a dot to show the centre of rotational symmetry.

3. **Collecting three-dimensional shapes**

If you go to a supermarket you will see items packed in many different shaped packets, cartons and boxes.
Make a collection of empty boxes, cartons, tins, etc.
See how many different-shaped containers you can find.
Try to give mathematical names to the containers you find.
Why do you think different-shaped containers are used ?

Put your collection on display for others to see.

PUZZLES

26. Draw 5 straight lines so as to make the greatest number of triangles.

27. Patrick said he had 5 times as many marbles as his younger brother, Sean.
     Sean said that Patrick had 24 more marbles than he had.
     Their father said that both statements were correct.
     How many marbles did each boy have ?

28. If you were given 1p per week pocket money when you were 1 year old, 2p per week when you 2 years old, 4p per week when you were 3 years old, how much would you get per week when you were 11, if the amount was doubled each year ?

13 Thinking about decimals and

Parts of a metre

The centimetre

1 metre can be divided into 100 parts.
Each part is called a **centimetre**.

> 1 metre (m) = 100 centimetres (cm)

Centi comes from the Latin word *centum* which means hundred.
Its value is one-hundredth.
So a centimetre is one-hundredth of a metre. This can be written using decimals.

1 centimetre (cm) = 0.01 metre (m)

The millimetre

1 metre can be divided into 1000 parts.
Each part is called a **millimetre**.

> 1 metre (m) = 1000 millimetres (mm)

Milli comes from the Latin word *mille*
which means thousand.
Its value is one-thousandth.
So a millimetre is one-thousandth of
a metre. This can be written using
decimals.

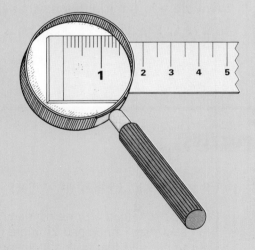

1 millimetre (mm) = 0.001 metre (m)

10 millimetres are equal to 1 centimetre, so

1 millimetre (mm) = 0.1 centimetre (cm)

Can you think of other words which start with *cent*, *centi* or *milli* ?

measurement

Different measuring instruments

People use different instruments to measure distances. Some instruments are designed specially for a particular job. How many different types of measuring instruments can you think of ?
Here are some people using different measuring instruments.
What are they measuring ?

An archaeologist using a steel tape

An archaeologist using a tape measure

A mechanic using a dipstick

A mechanic using feeler gauges

An engineer using a micrometer

13 Decimals and Measurement

Changing millimetres to centimetres

$$10\,mm = 1\,cm$$

A millimetre is one-tenth of a centimetre.

We can write this using decimals.

$$1\,mm = 0.1\,cm$$

Examples

$$6\,mm = 0.6\,cm$$
$$13\,mm = 1.3\,cm$$
$$50\,mm = 5\,cm$$
$$300\,mm = 30\,cm$$
$$517\,mm = 51.7\,cm$$

Exercise 13.1

1. Find the length of each line. Measure to the nearest millimetre, giving answers in centimetres, using decimals.

   1 _____

   2 _____

   3 _____

   4 _____

2.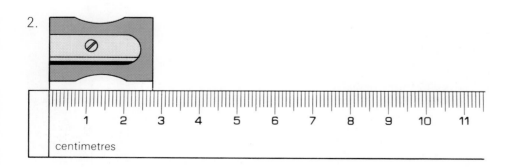

   What is the length of the pencil sharpener, in centimetres ?

3.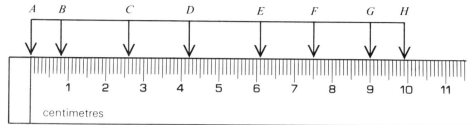

The length of the line from A to H is 9.9 cm.
What is the length of the line from

1	A to F	**5**	A to B	**8**	E to F
2	A to E	**6**	G to H	**9**	C to D
3	A to D	**7**	F to G	**10**	B to H ?
4	A to C				

4. **1** What is the length of XY ?
    2 What is the length of YZ ?
    3 What is the length of ZX ?
    4 Find the perimeter of the shape.
    (Measure all lengths to the nearest
    millimetre, giving the answers in
    centimetres, using decimals.)

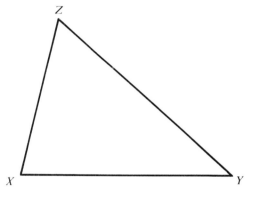

5. Which would be the most suitable metric unit and measuring instrument to
    measure the things listed below ?
    Copy and complete the table. The first one has been done for you.

	Item to be measured	Suitable unit	Measuring instrument
1	Length of textbook	cm	ruler
2	Length of classroom		
3	Length of corridor		
4	Length of your little finger		
5	Length of the field		
6	Distance you can throw a tennis ball		
7	Height of your desk		
8	Length of your desk		
9	Your height		
10	Thickness of your textbook		

Changing metres to centimetres

1 m = 100 cm

A centimetre is one-hundredth of a metre.

We can write this using decimals.

1 cm = 0.01 m

To change metres to centimetres multiply by 100.

Examples

1 Write 2.56 m in metres and centimetres.

2.56 m is 2 metres and 56 hundredths of a metre.
56 hundredths of a metre is 56 cm.

So 2.56 m = 2 m and 56 cm.

2 Write 4.05 m in metres and centimetres.

4.05 m = 4 m and 5 cm.
Note: 5 hundredths of a metre = 5 cm.

3 Change 1.76 m to centimetres.

1.76 × 100 = 176

So 1.76 m = 176 cm

Or you could say that 1.76 m = 1 m and 76 cm
                                    = 100 cm and 76 cm
                                    = 176 cm

Multiplying by 100 is much quicker.
Remember: When you multiply by 100 all figures move 2 places to the left.

4 Change 4.1 m to centimetres.

4.1 × 100 = 410
Note: 4.1 m is the same as 4.10 m.

So 4.1 m = 410 cm.

Exercise 13.2

1. Write each of these distances in metres and centimetres.
    Boxes have been put in to help you.
    1   2.45 m = ☐ m and ☐ cm
    2   15.21 m = ☐ m and ☐ cm
    3   5.07 m = ☐ m and ☐ cm

2. Write each of these distances in metres and centimetres.
    This time there are no boxes to help you.
    1   4.18 m   **3**   2.3 m   **5**   7.09 m
    2   12.07 m   **4**   9.73 m   **6**   29.83 m

3. Change the following distances to centimetres.
    1   1.58 m   **5**   2 m   **8**   6.03 m
    2   3.26 m   **6**   0.4 m   **9**   126.4 m
    3   12.81 m   **7**   3.3 m   **10** 0.03 m
    4   5.09 m

4. Robert is 1.47 m tall.
    How tall is Robert in metres and centimetres ?

5. The height of a shelf in a bookcase is 0.7 m.
    What is this height in centimetres ?

6. The height of a door is 1.98 m.
    What is the height of the door in metres and centimetres ?

7. A room measures 5.4 m by 2.37 m.
    1   What is the length of the room in metres and centimetres ?
    2   What is the width of the room in metres and centimetres ?

Changing centimetres to metres

100 cm = 1 m
To change centimetres to metres divide by 100.

Examples

1   Write 342 cm in metres and centimetres.

342 cm = 3 m and 42 cm.

2   Write 230 cm in metres and centimetres.

230 cm = 2 m and 30 cm.

3   Change 153 cm to metres.

153 ÷ 100 = 1.53

So 153 cm = 1.53 m
Remember: When you divide by 100 all figures move 2 places to the right.

4   Change 40 cm to metres.

40 ÷ 100 = 0.4

So 40 cm = 0.4 m.

Exercise 13.3

1.   Write each of these distances in metres and centimetres.
     Boxes have been put in to help you.
     1   348 cm = ☐ m and ☐ cm
     2   37 cm = ☐ m and ☐ cm
     3   906 cm = ☐ m and ☐ cm

2.   Write each of these distances in metres and centimetres.
     This time there are no boxes to help you.

1	525 cm	**3**	52 cm	**5**	2735 cm
2	120 cm	**4**	7 cm	**6**	1506 cm

3.   Change the following distances to metres.

1	356 cm	**5**	1362 cm	**8**	15 cm
2	504 cm	**6**	1470 cm	**9**	1050 cm
3	260 cm	**7**	100 cm	**10**	4 cm
4	90 cm				

4.   The length of a piece of dress material is 270 cm.
      What is the length of the material, written in metres ?

5.   A large jigsaw puzzle measured 145 cm long and 75 cm wide.
      1   What was the length of the jigsaw puzzle, in metres ?
      2   What was the width of the jigsaw puzzle, in metres ?

6.   Carole measured the height of her garden wall. It was 240 cm high. How high
      was the wall, in metres ?

7.   Ben measured the length and width of his drive at home.
      The length of the drive was 1550 cm.
      The width of the drive was 450 cm.
      1   What was the length of the drive in metres ?
      2   What was the width of the drive in metres ?

Using a tape measure

We use a ruler to measure short distances.
To measure longer distances we use a tape measure.
For example. We could use a tape measure to record the lengths of competitors'
throws in the javelin event.

When you are measuring longer distances you do not need to be as accurate as when
you measure short distances.

A good tape measure will have a clear scale which is easy to read.
Long tape measures are numbered every 10 centimetres.
10 cm = 0.1 m
0.1 m is a tenth of a metre.
The tape measure will also be marked every centimetre.
This makes it easy to take measurements to the nearest centimetre.

Remember: 100 cm = 1 m
                10 cm = 0.1 m
                 1 cm = 0.01 m

Examples

This diagram shows part of a tape measure.

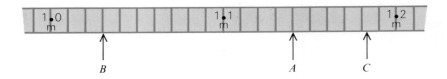

1   What measurement is arrow *A* pointing to ?

A is between 1.1 m and 1.2 m.
So the distance is going to be 1.1 m plus a bit more.
Between 1.1 m and 1.2 m the tape is divided into 10 equal sections.
Each part is a centimetre or 0.01 m.
A is 4 parts or 4 centimetres past 1.1 m.

So *A* is pointing to 1.14 m.

2   Where is arrow *B* pointing to ?

B is 3 centimetres past 1.0 m.

So *B* is pointing to 1.03 m

3   Where is arrow *C* pointing to ?

C is between 8 cm and 9 cm past 1.1 m. It is nearer to 8 than to 9.

So *C* is pointing to 1.18 m.
This is called measuring to the nearest centimetre.

Whenever you are measuring you have to measure to the nearest appropriate unit.
Different measurements require different levels of accuracy. This was explained in
Chapter 7.

Exercise 13.4

1. This diagram shows part of a tape measure.

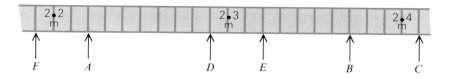

   What measurements do the following arrows show ? Give your answers in metres.

   1 *A*   **4** *D*
   2 *B*   **5** *E*
   3 *C*   **6** *F*

2. This diagram shows part of a tape measure.

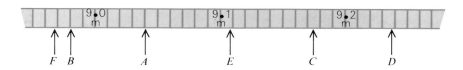

   What measurements do these arrows show ? Give your answers in metres. You
   may have to give some measurements to the nearest centimetre.

   1 *A*   **4** *D*
   2 *B*   **5** *E*
   3 *C*   **6** *F*

3. This diagram shows part of a tape measure.

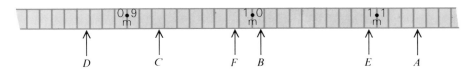

   What measurements do these arrows show ? Give your answers in metres. You
   may have to give some measurements to the nearest centimetre.

   1 *A*   **4** *D*
   2 *B*   **5** *E*
   3 *C*   **6** *F*

4. Write your answers to Question 3 in centimetres.

Addition and subtraction problems

When adding or subtracting decimals without a calculator remember to:
1 Keep your figures in tidy columns.
2 Keep the decimal points in a column.
Even if you are using a calculator:
3 Make sure the units that you are using are the same.

Examples

1 Two cars are parked in a driveway.
One car is 3.25 m long and the other car is 4.3 m long.
There is a gap of 84 cm between the cars.
What is the total length of driveway that the two cars take up ?

Total length = 3.25 m + 84 cm + 4.3 m
All of the units are not the same.
Change 84 cm to 0.84 m.
You can now set your sum out in columns if you are not using a calculator.

$$\begin{array}{r} 3.25\,\text{m} \\ 0.84\,\text{m} \\ +\ 4.30\,\text{m} \\ \hline 8.39\,\text{m} \end{array}$$ You can put a 0 after the 3 in 4.3 if it helps to keep your columns tidy.

The cars take up 8.39 m of driveway.

2 What is the distance from *A* to *B* on this tape measure ?

B is pointing to 2.51 m
A is pointing to 2.29 m

The distance from *A* to *B* is 2.51 m − 2.29 m

$$\begin{array}{r} 2.51 \\ -\ 2.29 \\ \hline 0.22 \end{array}$$

The distance from *A* to *B* is 0.22 m

3   Henry has a piece of timber 2 m long.
He cuts 45 cm off to make part of a shelf.
How much timber does Henry have left ? Give the answer in metres.

Your have to work out 2 m − 45 cm.
Change the 45 cm to 0.45 m.

Now 2 m − 0.45 m = 1.55 m

Henry has 1.55 m of timber left.

With many problems you can change all of the measurements to centimetres and change back to metres after you have done the calculations. If you are using a calculator you should be able to work all in metres or all in centimetres.

Exercise 13.5

1.   Helen has two pieces of cotton thread.
The red piece is 80 cm long and the blue piece is 75 cm long.
   1   What is the total length of the two pieces of thread, in centimetres ?
   2   What is this total length in metres ?

2.   Graham has three model boats. They are 15 cm long, 30 cm long and 45 cm long. He placed the three models end to end, in a straight line, so that there were no gaps between the boats.
   1   What was the total length of the line, in centimetres ?
   2   What is this length in metres ?

3.   Isabelle had a piece of ribbon 1.25 m long.
She cut off 50 cm to give to her friend.
   1   Write 1.25 m in centimetres.
   2   How much ribbon did Isabelle have left ? Give your answer in centimetres.

4.   John is 1.39 m tall. His father is 1.83 m tall.
   1   How many centimetres taller than John is his father ?
   2   What is this difference in height in metres ?

5.   A giraffe is 4.3 m tall. An elephant is 2.4 m tall.
How much taller is the giraffe than the elephant ?

6. Sandy hit a golf ball 253.7 m. Nick hit a
    golf ball 247.6 m.
    How much further did Sandy hit his ball
    than Nick ?

7. The council replaced the lamp posts in a street.
    The old lamp posts were 4.65 m tall.
    The new lamp posts were 5.9 m tall.
    How much taller are the new lamp posts ?

8. Sam has two pieces of string.
    One piece is 3.27 m long. The other piece is 5.42 m long.
    What is the total length of the string ?

9. The height of a door is 1.98 m.
    The distance between the top of the door
    and the ceiling is 46 cm.
    1 What is the height of the room in
          centimetres ?
    2 What is the height of the room in
          metres ?

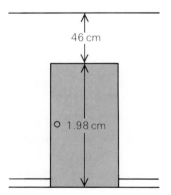

46 cm

0 1.98 cm

10. Amanda has a piece of timber 3.5 m long.
    She has to cut off various lengths for a job she is doing.
    1 Amanda first cut off 45 cm. What length was left ?
    2 Next she cut off 1.76 m. What length now remains ?
    3 Amanda now requires a piece of timber 1.35 m long.
          Is the piece she has left long enough ?

11.   This diagram shows part of a tape measure.

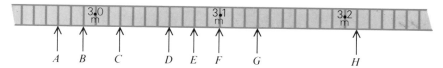

What is the distance between these points on the tape measure ?

1 C and D **5** A and D **8** A and F
2 C and F **6** E and G **9** D and H
3 G and H **7** B and G **10** A and H
4 A and B

12.   Anthea buys 3.25 m of red material, 4.6 m of blue material and 5.45 m of white material. What is the total length of the material that Anthea bought ?

13.   Jackie can reach 1.76 m up a wall.
       She stands on a stool 44 cm high.
       1   How high up the wall can Jackie now reach, in centimetres ?
       2   What is this height in metres ?

Multiplication and division problems

Sometimes when you are doing problems involving multiplication and division the decimals cause confusion. If this happens change units in order to use whole numbers. You can always change units again once you have finished doing the calculations.

If you are working with a calculator you should be able to manage.

Examples

1   A piece of string, 80 cm long, was divided into 5 equal pieces.
       How long was each piece ?

       Method 1 (working in centimetres)

       80 cm ÷ 5 = 16 cm

       So each piece of string would be 16 centimetres long.

       Method 2 (working in metres)

       80 cm = 0.8 m
       0.8 m ÷ 5 = 0.16 m

       So each piece of string would be 0.16 metres long.

       Remember: The units of the number displayed on your calculator will be the same
                   as the units of the number you entered into your calculator.

2   A piece of fencing is 230 cm long. What is the total length of four pieces of the fencing ? Answer in metres.

230 cm × 4 = 920 cm
920 cm = 9.2 m

The total length of the fencing is 9.2 m

You could change the 230 cm to 2.3 m and then multiply by 4.
2.3 m × 4 = 9.2 m, the same result as before.

Exercise 13.6

1.   25 books each 5 cm thick are placed in a pile.
   1   What is the height of the pile, in centimetres ?
   2   What is the height of the pile, in metres ?

2.   An old wall is 4.5 m long. The wall is 18 bricks long.
   1   What is the length of the wall, in centimetres ?
   2   What is the length of one brick, in centimetres ?

3.   5 children wanted to play conkers.
   They each needed a piece of string 45 cm long.
   1   What is the total length of string needed, in centimetres ?
   2   What is this length in metres ?

4.   15 cars each 3.28 m long are parked bumper to bumper.
   What is the total length needed for the cars ? Answer in metres.

5.   George is making shelves to store his books on.
   He needs 3 long shelves which measure 1.25 m and 4 shorter shelves which measure 95 cm.
   1   What is the total length of the 3 long shelves ? Give your answer in centimetres.
   2   What is the total length of the 4 shorter shelves ? Give your answer in centimetres.
   3   What is the total length of the 7 shelves, in centimetres ?
   4   What is the total length of the 7 shelves, in metres ?

6.   A freight train is pulling 26 trucks.
   Each truck is 7.8 m long.
   What is the total length of the trucks ?

7. A climber has a rope 64 m long. He cuts the rope into 10 equal lengths.
    1 How many metres long will each piece be ?
    2 What is each length in centimetres ?

8. A length of wire 25 m long is cut into 4 equal lengths.
    1 How many metres long will each piece be ?
    2 How many centimetres long will each piece be ?

9. A filing cabinet is 1.5 m tall.
    It has four drawers. There is a gap of
    6 cm between the bottom of the lowest
    drawer and the floor. This allows the
    bottom drawer to open without hitting
    the floor.
    1 What is the total height of the filing
          cabinet in centimetres ?
    2 What is the height of the four
          drawers ?
    3 What is the height of 1 drawer ?

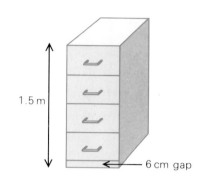

10. A kangaroo covers 27 m in 6 jumps.
    1 How far does the kangaroo travel in one jump ? Give your answer in
          centimetres.
    2 What is this distance in metres ?

11. Some students made a stack of drinks cans.
    Each can was 12 cm high.
    The stack was 60 cans high.
    1 What was the height of the stack in centimetres ?
    2 What was the height of the stack in metres ?

12. Flex for kettles is 70 cm long and it is cut from a roll which is 10 m long
    1 How many 70 cm lengths of flex can be cut from the roll ?
    2 How much flex would be left on the roll at the end ?

13. A bike travels 125 cm each time the wheels make a complete turn.
    1 How far does the bike travel when the wheels make 20 turns ?
          Give your answer in centimetres.
    2 What is this distance in metres ?

14. Amul covered 100 m in exactly 125 paces.
    What was the length, in centimetres, of 1 pace, assuming that all paces were the
    same length ?

Exercise 13.7   Applications and Activities

1.   This plan shows a car parked in a garage.
     The car is 4.36 m long and 2.05 m wide.
     There is a gap of 1.30 m between the front
     of the car and the back wall of the garage,
     and a gap of 0.35 m between the back of
     the car and the doors of the garage.
     The gap between each side of the car and
     the garage wall is 1.25 m.
     1   How long is the garage ?
     2   How wide is the garage ?

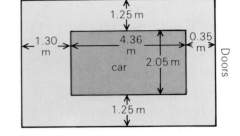

2.   Gillian and Stephen are moving a new
     fridge-freezer into their kitchen.
     The fridge-freezer arrives in a very strong
     box. The measurements of the box are
     shown in the diagram.
     The size of the door is also shown.
     Gillian and Stephen want to move the
     fridge-freezer in its box so that it does not
     get damaged.

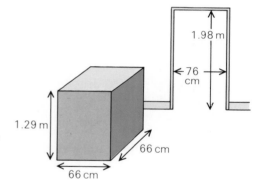

     1   Will the box fit through the door ?
     2   What will be the gap between the top
           of the box and the door frame ?
     3   What will be the total gap between
           the sides of the box and the door
           frame ?
     4   What will be the gap on each side of
           the box if it goes exactly through
           the middle of the doorway ?

3.   A roll of wallpaper is 10 m long and 25 cm wide.
     The wall to be papered is 4.5 m long and 2.3 m high. There are no doors or
     windows in the wall.
     1   How many strips of wallpaper, 25 cm wide, will be needed side by side to
           cover the length of 4.5 m ?
     2   How many strips of wallpaper, 2.3 m long, can you get from one roll of paper ?
     3   How many rolls of paper will be needed to paper the wall ?
     4   If you have saved £50 to buy the paper for the wall, what is the most you
           can afford for one roll of paper ?

4.   **Fencing**

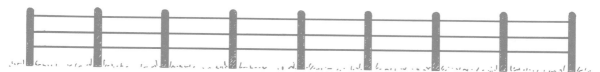

A garden fence has 9 posts. The distance between each post and the next is 2 m. The thickness of each post is 10 cm.

The fence is made using 3 strands of fencing wire. The wire goes through each post and is not slack. 10 cm extra is allowed at each end for fixing the wire to the post.

1   How many 2 m gaps are there between the posts ?

2   What is the total thickness of the 9 posts ?

3   What is the total distance from one end of the fence to the other end of the fence ?

4   What length of wire is needed for 1 strand of the fence ?
Do not forget to include the extra wire at each end.

5   What is the total length of wire required for the fence ?

5.   **Reference Books**

Each quarter (3 months) a reference book about antiques is produced.
Each book is 5 cm thick.
So far 27 reference books have been produced.
These 27 books fit exactly on one of Anne's bookshelves with no gaps between the books.

1   How long is one of Anne's bookshelves, in centimetres ?

2   What is this length in metres ?

3   Each bookshelf has the same length. How many new volumes will Anne be able to fit on one of her bookshelves, if from volume 28 onwards the books are going to be 6 cm thick ?

6.   Make an instrument to measure length. It could be a long piece of tape, measuring in metres, or a shorter type of rule to measure in centimetres up to 1 metre.
Use your measuring instrument in a practical way.

PUZZLE

29.   A bag of potatoes weighs 6 kg and half of its own weight.
How heavy is the bag of potatoes ?

14 Thinking about algebra

What is algebra ?

Algebra is the branch of mathematics which uses letters or symbols to represent or stand for unknown quantities.

A problem can often be written down in the form of an equation.

For example. I think of a number and add 5 to it. The answer I get is 24.
This can be written as an equation. $x + 5 = 24$

x stands for the number I thought of.
This equation can be solved.
If x is replaced by 19 you get a true statement, because $19 + 5 = 24$

You can now work out the answer in terms of the problem.

The number I thought of was 19.

Wind chill factor

The wind has the effect of making the temperature recorded by a thermometer feel lower.
The wind reduces the temperature in the air by about 1°C for every 3 km/hour of windspeed.
For example, a temperature of 12°C, recorded on a day when the windspeed is 30 km/hour, will feel as if it was 2°C.
We can write this as a formula.

Air temperature =

Recorded temperature $- \dfrac{\text{Windspeed}}{3}$

(Temperatures in °C, windspeed in km/hour)
This can be written using symbols.

$$A = T - \frac{W}{3}$$

What do the symbols stand for ?
What would the air temperature be on a day when the recorded temperature was 6°C and the windspeed was 24 km/hour ?

The effect of the wind will make it feel even colder

Patterns using algebra

Patterns can be drawn using algebra.
Draw and number a square, like the
one on the right.

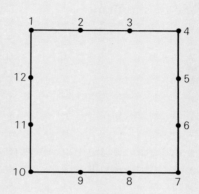

Use $x \rightarrow x + 5$

Start with $x = 1$.

So $1 \rightarrow 1 + 5 = 6$.

Draw a line from 1 to 6.

Now $6 \rightarrow 6 + 5 = 11$

Draw a line from 6 to 11.

Now $11 \rightarrow 11 + 5 = 4$

You get the answer 4 because you keep going round the square.
Draw a line from 11 to 4.

Keep repeating the process until you finish back at 1.

The diagrams below show the first 3 lines.

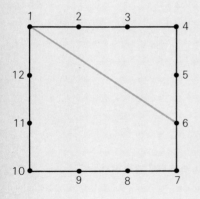 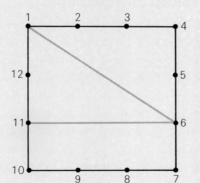 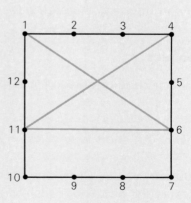

Does it matter where you start from ? Try starting at another number.
Draw another square for $x \rightarrow x + 7$.
Try using a bigger square with more numbers on each side.

14 Algebra

In algebra we use symbols or letters to stand for numbers.
Using symbols or letters saves a lot of time and writing.
So algebra is a type of shorthand.

Equations

Example

I think of a number, I add six to it and the result is 15.
What is the number I thought of ?

We can write this as an equation.

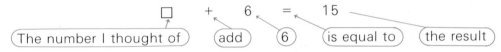

This is much easier to read than a long sentence.
If you replace □ by 9 you get a **true statement**.

9 + 6 = 15

So the number I thought of was 9.
You can now say that you have **solved an equation**.

Examples

1   What should replace □ to make 4 + □ = 12 true ?

   □ = 8

   This is a short way of saying that □ should be replaced by 8.
   □ = 8 because 4 + 8 = 12 is true.
   If you replace □ by any other number you will not get a **true statement**. For
   example, 4 + 9 = 12 is not a true statement.

2   What should replace △ to make 4 = 10 − △ a true statement ?

   △ = 6

   This is because 4 = 10 − 6.

3 What should replace ∗ to make 5 × ∗ = 35 a true statement ?

5 × 7 = 35
So ∗ = 7

4 What should replace △ to make 3 = 12 ÷ △ true ?

3 = 12 ÷ 4
So △ = 4

Exercise 14.1

1. What number should replace □ to make the statement true ?
1	4 + □ = 9	**6**	17 = □ + 9
2	7 + □ = 11	**7**	20 = 5 + □
3	□ + 3 = 12	**8**	23 = 17 + □
4	□ + 5 = 15	**9**	21 + □ = 46
5	10 = □ + 7	**10**	43 = □ + 15

2. What number should replace △ to make the statement true ?
1	9 − △ = 4	**6**	12 = 20 − △
2	12 − △ = 3	**7**	△ − 8 = 7
3	△ − 4 = 6	**8**	29 − △ = 6
4	△ − 6 = 12	**9**	△ − 25 = 32
5	4 = 12 − △	**10**	53 = △ − 28

3. What number should replace ∗ to make the statement true ?
1	5 × ∗ = 10	**6**	36 = 9 × ∗
2	6 × ∗ = 24	**7**	42 = 6 × ∗
3	4 × ∗ = 28	**8**	64 = 8 × ∗
4	∗ × 5 = 40	**9**	9 × ∗ = 72
5	∗ × 3 = 27	**10**	∗ × 6 = 54

4. What number should replace △ to make the statement true ?
1	12 ÷ △ = 3	**6**	7 = 28 ÷ △
2	16 ÷ △ = 2	**7**	6 = 54 ÷ △
3	24 ÷ △ = 8	**8**	9 = △ ÷ 5
4	△ ÷ 4 = 4	**9**	10 = △ ÷ 8
5	△ ÷ 5 = 6	**10**	12 = △ ÷ 1

5.   Here is a mixture of questions. Find the number which should replace the symbol
      to make the statement true ?

      1   □ + 15 = 40   **6**   * + 19 = 46
      2   36 ÷ △ = 3   **7**   △ × 5 = 0
      3   * × 9 = 9   **8**   48 = * − 2
      4   □ − 35 = 65   **9**   9 ÷ □ = 9
      5   14 = △ − 27   **10**   △ − 37 = 43

Functions

A **function** takes numbers and performs mathematical operations such as addition,
subtraction, multiplication and division, on them.

Numbers that are put into the function are called **INPUT**.
Numbers that are produced by a function are called **OUTPUT**.

Several results of operations performed by a function can be shown on an
INPUT − OUTPUT table.

Examples

1   INPUT—function → OUTPUT

      1 ──────────┬────────→ 7
      2 ──────────┤────────→ 8
      3 ──────────┼────────→ 9
      4 ──────────┤────────→ a
     12 ──────────┴────────→ b

The function for this table is 'add 6'.
Find the values of a and b.

$a = 10$
To get this, add 6 to 4 to get 10.

$b = 18$
To get this, add 6 to 12 to get 18.

2   INPUT—function → OUTPUT

2 ——————————→ 5
3 ——————————→ 7
4 ——————————→ 9
5 ——————————→ p
9 ——————————→ q

The function for this table is 'double the number and add 1'.
Find the values of p and q.

p = 11
To get this, double 5 which is 10. Add 1 to 10 to get 11.

q = 19
To get this, double 9 which is 18. Add 1 to 18 to get 19.

Exercise 14.2

1.   The function for this table is 'add 5'.   INPUT—function → OUTPUT
      1   What is the value of a ?
      2   What is the value of b ?   2 ——————————→ 7
                                                        3 ——————————→ 8
                                                        4 ——————————→ 9
                                                        5 ——————————→ a
                                                        9 ——————————→ b

2.   The function for this table is 'take away 4'.   INPUT—function → OUTPUT
      1   What is the value of c ?
      2   What is the value of d ?   12 ——————————→ 8
                                                        11 ——————————→ 7
                                                        10 ——————————→ 6
                                                        8 ——————————→ c
                                                        5 ——————————→ d

3. The function for this table is 'multiply by 3'.

    1 What is the value of e ?
    2 What is the value of f ?
    3 What is the value of g ?

    INPUT—function → OUTPUT

2	6
3	9
5	e
7	21
9	f
10	g

4. The function for this table is 'divide by 6'.

    1 What is the value of h ?
    2 What is the value of i ?
    3 What is the value of j ?
    4 What is the value of k ?

    INPUT—function → OUTPUT

54	9
42	h
36	6
24	i
18	j
12	2
6	k

5. The function for this table is 'double the number and add 3'.

    1 What is the value of m ?
    2 What is the value of n ?
    3 What is the value of p ?

    INPUT—function → OUTPUT

1	5
2	m
3	9
5	n
8	19
10	p

6. The function for this table is 'divide by 2 and add 1'.

    1 What is the value of q ?
    2 What is the value of r ?
    3 What is the value of s ?
    4 What is the value of t ?

    INPUT—function → OUTPUT

24	13
18	q
14	r
10	6
6	s
4	3
2	t

Working backwards

In the last exercise you put numbers into a function (INPUT) and obtained answers (OUTPUT).
Can we find INPUT values if we know what the OUTPUT is ?
To do this we need to be able to work backwards.

Remember:

Operation	Opposite operation
+	−
−	+
×	÷
÷	×

The opposite operation undoes the work of an operation.

Examples

1   What is the opposite of the function 'add 5' ?

The opposite of add is subtract or take away.
So the opposite of the function 'add 5' is 'take away 5'.

2   What is the opposite of the function 'multiply by 3 and take away 2'.

This function multiplies by 3 first then takes away 2.
The opposite function does operations in the reverse order.
So the opposite function is 'add 2 and divide by 3'.

You can check this by putting a value into the function 'multiply by 3 and take away 2'.
When you INPUT 5 the OUTPUT is 13.

INPUT 13 into the opposite function, which is 'add 2 and divide by 3'.
You get 13 + 2 which is 15. 15 divided by 3 = 5.
This is what you started with so the opposite function is correct.

3   I think of a number, double it and add 4. The result is 14.
Draw a flow diagram to show the function.
Then draw a flow diagram to show the opposite function, and use it to find the number I thought of.

? ⟶ ⎡double⎤ ⟶ ⎡add 4⎤ ⟶ 14

The flow diagram starts with the number I thought of (represented by the question mark) and finishes with the result (14).

5 ⟵ ⎡halve⎤ ⟵ 10 ⎡take away 4⎤ ⟵ 14

The flow diagram to show the opposite function includes the working.
Notice that the opposite of doubling is halving. (Doubling is multiplying by 2, halving is dividing by 2.)

The number I thought of was 5.

Exercise 14.3

1.   Write the opposite function of these functions.
   1   add seven
   2   subtract nine
   3   multiply by six
   4   divide by three
   5   multiply by 3 then add 2
   6   multiply by 4 then subtract 3
   7   divide by 2 then add 5
   8   divide by 3 then multiply by 2

2.   The function for this table is 'multiply by 4'.   INPUT—function → OUTPUT
   1   What is the opposite function ?
   2   What is the value of a ?
   3   What is the value of b ?
   4   What is the value of c ?

INPUT	OUTPUT
2	8
3	12
4	16
a	20
b	32
c	40

3.   The function for this table is 'subtract 7'.   INPUT—function → OUTPUT
      1   What is the opposite function ?   8 ——————————→ 1
      2   What is the value of d ? d ——————————→ 3
      3   What is the value of e ?   13 ——————————→ 6
      4   What is the value of f ? e ——————————→ 10
                                                            19 ——————————→ 12
                                                             f ——————————→ 24

4.   The function for this table is 'multiply by 4   INPUT—function → OUTPUT
      and add 5'.   1 ——————————→ 9
      1   What is the opposite function ? g ——————————→ 21
      2   What is the value of g ?   5 ——————————→ 25
      3   What is the value of h ? h ——————————→ 33
      4   What is the value of i ?   8 ——————————→ 37
                                                             i ——————————→ 45

5.   The function for this table is 'add 3 then   INPUT—function → OUTPUT
      divide by 4' j ——————————→ 3
      1   What is the opposite function ?   17 ——————————→ 5
      2   What is the value of j ?   29 ——————————→ 8
      3   What is the value of k ? k ——————————→ 10
      4   What is the value of m ? m ——————————→ 12
                                                            57 ——————————→ 15

6.   I think of a number, double it and add one.
      The result is 11.
      1   Draw a flow diagram to show the function.
      2   Draw a flow diagram to show the opposite function.
      3   Use the diagram in **2** to find the number I thought of.

7.   I think of a number, multiply it by 3 then take away 4. The result is 23.
      1   Draw a flow diagram to show the function.
      2   Draw a flow diagram to show the opposite function.
      3   Use the diagram in **2** to find the number I thought of.

8.   I think of a number, multiply it by 4 and subtract 7.
      1   If the result is 17 what was the number I thought of ?
      2   If the result was 29 what was the number I thought of ?

Finding the function

So far you have found missing INPUTS and missing OUTPUTS.
Now you are going to try to find a missing function.

When you are looking for a function always try simple functions first.

Examples

1 What is the function for this
INPUT—OUTPUT table ?

INPUT	OUTPUT
1 ——————→ 6
2 ——————→ 7
3 ——————→ 8
4 ——————→ 9

The OUTPUT is bigger than the INPUT.
The operations which make a number bigger
are addition and multiplication.

To get from 1 to 6 you must add 5.
So we think the rule is 'add 5'.
You must check that the rule works on other
lines in the table.

$2 + 5 = 7$
$3 + 5 = 8$
$4 + 5 = 9$

The rule works for every line.
So the function is 'add 5'.

2 What is the function for this
INPUT—OUTPUT table ?

INPUT	OUTPUT
2 ——————→ 1
4 ——————→ 2
6 ——————→ 3
8 ——————→ 4
10 ——————→ 5

The OUTPUT is smaller than the INPUT.
The operations which make a number smaller
are subtraction and division.

To get from 2 to 1 you must subtract 1.
But to get from 4 to 2 you must subtract 2.
So the function is not 'subtract 1' or 'subtract 2'.

Try division.
To get from 2 to 1 you must divide by 2.
You must check that the rule works on other lines in the table.

6 ÷ 2 = 3
8 ÷ 2 = 4
10 ÷ 2 = 5

The rule works for every line.
So the function is 'divide by 2'.

This exercise will give you practice in finding the missing functions.

Exercise 14.4

1.   What is the function for this INPUT—OUTPUT table ?

INPUT	OUTPUT
3 ——————→	7
4 ——————→	8
5 ——————→	9
6 ——————→	10
8 ——————→	12

2.   What is the function for this INPUT—OUTPUT table ?

INPUT	OUTPUT
20 ——————→	10
18 ——————→	8
16 ——————→	6
13 ——————→	3
12 ——————→	2

3.   What is the function for this INPUT—OUTPUT table ?

INPUT	OUTPUT
24	8
18	6
12	4
6	2
3	1

4.   What is the function for this INPUT—OUTPUT table ?

INPUT	OUTPUT
1	4
3	12
7	28
9	36
12	48

5.   Find the function for each of these INPUT—OUTPUT tables.
      Each function will have two parts.
      For example the function could be 'double the number and add 6'.

1

INPUT	OUTPUT
1	4
2	7
3	10
4	13
5	16

2

INPUT	OUTPUT
3	9
4	11
5	13
6	15
7	17

3

INPUT	OUTPUT
10	4
8	3
6	2
4	1
2	0

4

INPUT	OUTPUT
1	0
3	6
5	12
7	18
9	24

Exercise 14.5   Applications and Activities

1. To find the perimeter of a rectangle use the function 'add the length and breadth together and double the answer'. (If the length and breadth are measured in centimetres, the function will give the perimeter in centimetres.)
    Use the function to find the perimeter of a rectangle with
    1   length 3 cm and breadth 4 cm
    2   length 6 cm and breadth 4 cm
    3   length 7 cm and breadth 4 cm

2. To find the perimeter of a square use the function 'multiply the length of a side by 4'. (If the length of a side is measured in centimetres, the function will give the perimeter in centimetres.)
    Use the function to find the perimeter of a square with side
    1   3 cm   **2**   4 cm   **3**   7 cm   **4**   10 cm

3. A tool hire company hires out equipment.
    To find the cost of hiring a ladder the function 'daily charge multiplied by the number of days, then add the fixed charge' is used. All amounts are in £'s.
    The daily charge for hiring a ladder is £5 and the fixed charge is £8.
    1   What is the cost of hiring a ladder for 4 days ?
    2   What is the cost of hiring a ladder for 7 days ?
    For how many days was a ladder hired if the total charge was
    3   £18   **4**   £33   **5**   £48 ?

4. $\square + \square = 12$. To make this into a true statement, $\square = 6$.
    Symbols which are the same in a question have the same value.
    What must $\triangle$ be replaced by in order to make $\triangle + \triangle + \triangle = 12$ true ?

5. What number should replace the symbol in each of these ?
    1 $\square + \square = 10$ **6** $\triangle \times \triangle \times \triangle = 8$
    2 $12 - \triangle = \triangle$ **7** $* + * = 12 - *$
    3 $* \times * = 25$ **8** $\square \times \square = 27 \div \square$
    4 $49 \div \triangle = \triangle$ **9** $81 \div \square = \square$
    5 $\square + \square + \square = 24$ **10** $\triangle + \triangle + \triangle = 24 + \triangle$

6. **Finding amounts**

Gail bought 4 tins of baked beans. She also bought a bar of chocolate which cost 20p. The total bill was £1.40. What did a tin of baked beans cost ?

You can use a flow diagram to answer this question but instead, we will show each step of the working in a sentence.

The total bill is £1.40 = 140p
Take away the cost of the chocolate, 140p − 20p = 120p
4 tins of baked beans cost 120p
So 1 tin costs 120p ÷ 4 = 30p

Answer these questions, either by using flow diagrams or by showing each step of the working in sentences.

1   John adds three teaspoonfuls of sugar to a mug which weighs 300 g.
The total weight of the sugar and mug is 324 g.
What was the weight of one teaspoonful of sugar ?

2   Rachel complained that she spent three times longer plus an extra 5 minutes doing her maths homework than her sister.
Rachel worked for 1 hour and 20 minutes.
How long did her sister work for ?

3   Cyril has 4 times as many marbles as Bill.
Bill has 3 times as many marbles as Alf.
Alf has 2 marbles.
How many marbles does Bill have ?
How many marbles does Cyril have ?
How many marbles do the three boys have altogether ?

4   Tom took 3 years away from his own age and multiplied the result by 2.
This gave the age of his brother Nick who is 18.
How old is Tom ?

5   To get her father's age Gloria multiplied her age by 3 and then took away 2 years.
If her father is 34 years old how old is Gloria ?

6   To get the age of his grandson Cedric added two years to his age and divided the answer by six.
If Cedric's grandson is 11 years old how old is Cedric ?

7. **Tables and chairs**

This is a table in the shape of a pentagon.
Each cross represents 1 chair.
The school library has tables like this.
They are placed around the library.

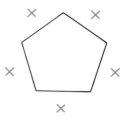

1   How many chairs would you need if you had 2 tables ?
2   How many chairs would you need if you had 3 tables ?
3   Copy and complete this table.

number of tables	number of chairs
1 ⟶	5
2 ⟶	
3 ⟶	
4 ⟶	
8 ⟶	

4   How many tables would you need if you had 35 chairs ?
5   How many tables would you need if you had 60 chairs ?
6   Copy and complete the function which connects the number of tables with the number of chairs.
       'To find the number of chairs multiply...
7   What is the opposite function, which will tell you how you can find the number of tables if you know the number of chairs ?

PUZZLES

30.   Some months of the year have 31 days.
      Some months of the year have 30 days.
      How many months have 28 days ?

31.   How many triangles are there in this diagram ?
      There are more than 9.

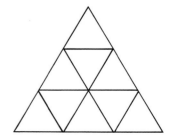

Miscellaneous Section B

Aural Practice

Exercises B1 and B2 are aural exercises.
A teacher or a friend should **read** the questions to you.
Try to complete the 15 questions in 10 minutes or less.

Exercise B1

1. What shape is each face of a cube ?

2. Add together 450 m and 230 m.

3. Samantha draws £60 out of her bank account and the money is paid in £5 notes. How many £5 notes did she get ?

4. John did maths homework for 45 minutes and English homework for 25 minutes. For how long was he doing homework ?

5. What must be multiplied by 4 to get 48 ?

6. How many centimetres are there in 2.6 metres ?

7. Write 450 pence in pounds.

8. What is 29 ÷ 5 to the nearest whole number ?

9. Write 771 to the nearest 100.

10. Mr Clarke owes £5. He earns £25 doing a job and repays his debt. How much money will he have left ?

11. What number do you get if you start with 3, double it and add 4 ?

12. 10 small squares on a graph represent 1 hour. How many minutes does 1 small square represent ?

13. How many degrees higher is a temperature of 3°C than a temperature of −2°C ?

14. What mathematical name can be given to the shape of a tennis ball ?

15. What measurement is exactly half-way between 24 cm and 25 cm ?

Exercise B2

1.   How many pence are there in £4.15 ?

2.   What must be added to 7 to get 15 ?

3.   What number do you get if you start with 12, halve it and add 1 ?

4.   How much change would you get from a £1 coin if you spent 25p ?

5.   Gary has two pieces of string. One piece is 24 cm long and the other piece is 16 cm long. What is the total length of the two pieces ?

6.   Give the answer to 26 ÷ 3 to the nearest whole number.

7.   How many sides does a pentagon have ?

8.   Write 35 mm in centimetres.

9.   How many edges does a cube have ?

10. If 5 small squares on a graph represent £1 what does 1 small square represent ?

11. What is 84 written to the nearest 10 ?

12. Mrs Wright changed the temperature setting on her freezer from −12°C to −20°C. How many degrees lower is the new setting ?

13. I think of a number, double it and add 5. The result is 13. What was the number I thought of ?

14. What measurement is 5 cm less than 2 m, in centimetres ?

15. Lowton is 20 metres below sea-level. Highbury is 30 metres above sea-level. How much higher is Highbury than Lowton ?

Exercise B3   Revision

1.   Here is a number line for 76 + 37.

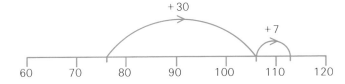

1   What is 76 + 30 ?
2   What is 76 + 37 ?

2. How many lines of symmetry does this
   pentagon have ?

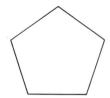

3. Richard puts cans of drinks into packs of four.
   How many 4-can packs can Richard make if he has 75 cans ?

4. This table shows the maximum and minimum temperatures recorded over a
   week.

Day	Mon	Tues	Wed	Thur	Fri	Sat	Sun
Max temp °C	0	3	4	7	3	1	11
Min temp °C	−7	−4	−5	1	−4	−2	3

   1 What were the differences between the maximum and minimum
   temperatures on each day of the week ?
   2 On which day did the smallest difference between the maximum and
   minimum temperature occur ?

5. **1** 236 people watched a local soccer match.
   How many people is this to the nearest 10 ?
   2 Work out 93 ÷ 4 and give the answer to the nearest whole number.
   3 Write 15 724 to the nearest 100.

6. A radio programme started at 8.35 pm and finished at 9.20 pm. Sharon taped the
   programme on a 60-minute blank cassette.
   1 How long did the programme last ?
   2 How much blank tape was left on the casette ?

7. The function for this table is 'multiply
   by 3 and add 5'.
   1 What is the opposite function ?
   2 What is the value of a ?
   3 What is the value of b ?
   4 What is the value of c ?
   5 What is the value of d ?
   6 What is the value of e ?

   INPUT—function → OUTPUT

1	→ 8
4	→ a
7	→ 26
b	→ 32
13	→ c
d	→ 50
24	→ e

8. Manjula wants to make a timing device using candles.
    At the supermarket candles are packed in boxes of 5 and boxes of 4.
    1 The box of 5 candles is priced at £1.62.
           What is the cost of one candle to the nearest penny ?
    2 The box of 4 candles is priced at £1.33.
           What is the cost of one candle to the nearest penny ?
    3 Which box of candles is the better buy ?

9. Look at the diagram on the right.
    It shows some newly planted trees.
    1 Which tree is North of *D* ?
    2 In which direction must you walk in
           order to get from tree *A* to tree *B* ?
    3 In which direction must you walk to
           return from tree *B* to tree *A* ?
    4 What is the direction of tree *A* from
           tree *C* ?

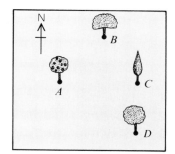

10. Sarah has twice as many stamps in her collection as Bertha.
    Bertha has four times as many stamps as Patricia.
    Patricia has 10 times as many stamps as Esther.
    Esther has 25 stamps.
    1 How many stamps does Patricia have ?
    2 How many stamps does Bertha have ?
    3 How many stamps does Sarah have ?
    4 How many stamps do the four girls have altogether ?

11.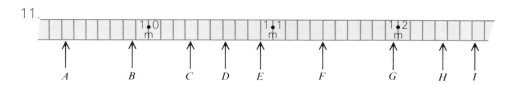

    Give the name of the arrow which is closest to each of these measurements.
    1 1.14 m   **4** 1.20 m   **7** 0.93 m
    2 1.26 m   **5** 1.24 m   **8** 1.04 m
    3 1.06 m   **6** 1.09 m

12. Paul bought a computer game with his birthday money. This cost £7.50. He also
    bought two model kits, costing £4.25 and £3.70.
    1 What was the total cost of the game and the kits ?
    2 What change did Paul get from a £20 note ?

13.   This is a net for a prism whose ends are 7-sided polygons.

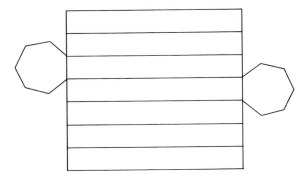

    1   How many faces does the prism have ?

    2   How many edges does the prism have ?

    3   How many vertices does the prism have ?

14.   This pictogram shows the numbers of visitors to seven countries in the world.

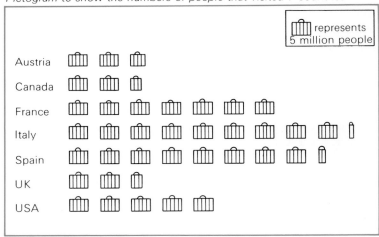

Pictogram to show the numbers of people that visited 7 countries

    1   How many holiday-makers does 🧳 represent ?

    2   Which country had the most visitors ?

    3   Which three of the countries listed had approximately the same number of visitors ?

    4   How many more people visited Spain than the USA ?

15. **1**   Copy the grid on the right on
           squared paper.
     2   Plot the following points in order
           using dots.
           (4, 5) (1, 5) (1, 0) (4, 0) (4, 1)
           (2, 1) (2, 2) (3, 2) (3, 3) (2, 3)
           (2, 4) (4, 4)
     3   Join the points in order and
           complete the figure by joining the
           last point to the first point.
     4   What letter have you made ?

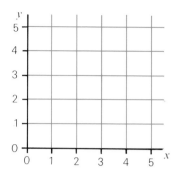

Exercise B4   Activities

1.   **Crossing the road**

     How long do you need to cross a road ?

     Nowadays there are far more cars on the road and it has become more difficult to
     cross the road safely.

     Pelican crossings were put on roads by local authorities to help people to cross
     the road and to reduce the danger to pedestrians.

     However, pelican crossings are not always trouble free.
     If the traffic is stopped for too long a traffic jam builds up.
     If the traffic is not stopped for long enough pedestrians will not have enough
     time to cross the road.

     Work out how long pedestrians should be given to cross the road. Consider
     points such as:
           the width of the road,
           the number of pedestrians crossing the road,
           parents pushing prams,
           elderly people,
           people crossing the road from each direction,
           the number of cars using the road,
           the squence of lights for cars and pedestrians.

     When you press the button at a pelican crossing you sometimes have to wait a
     while for the traffic to be stopped. Why do you think this is ?

2. **Dice Game**

This is a game for two or more players.
You need two ordinary dice, a copy of the
game board and some counters.

1	2	3	4
5	6	7	8
9	10	11	12

When it is your turn you roll the two dice.
Suppose you roll a 5 and a 4. You can do
one of the following.

1   Put a counter on square 5.
2   Put a counter on square 4.
3   Put a counter on square 5 and a
         counter on square 4.
4   Add the two numbers together.
         5 + 4 = 9
         You can put a counter on square 9.
5   Subtract the scores.
         5 − 4 = 1
         You can put a counter on square 1.

A player keeps rolling the dice and putting counters on squares. Only **one**
counter can be put on any square. Once a square has a counter on it you cannot
use that square again.

Your turn ends when you cannot use the scores on the two dice to put a counter
on a square.

When you have finished your turn add up the numbers which have not been
covered with counters. This is your score.
If you cover up all the numbers your score is 0.

Clear the board of counters before the next player starts his turn.
Keep taking turns, adding your later scores to your first score.
The first player to score a total of 200 points is the loser.
Design a game of your own using dice, a game board and counters.

3. **Computer work**

You can use a computer to draw pictures and diagrams.
Most LOGO programs are similar in design but there are slight variations
depending on the computer you have and the version of LOGO that you are
using.

The turtle follows simple commands given by you.
List the type of commands that your turtle can follow.
If you have any trouble ask your teacher for help.

Can you draw these ?

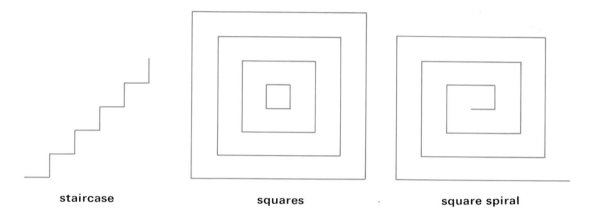

staircase   **squares**   **square spiral**

Design your own patterns.

You can practise using LOGO commands with a partner.
One person acts as a robot and the other person is the controller.
The controller must try to guide the robot by using LOGO commands. Try to
make the robot walk in a square or along a path like one of the above patterns.
Remember that the robot can only follow instructions.

Try to design a maze on squared paper.
Challenge people to write LOGO commands to get from start to finish.

PUZZLES

32.   How many different ways are there of moving
       through the squares from square S to square F ?
       You can only move to the right and up. You
       cannot move to the left or down.

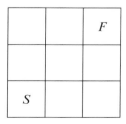

33.   The reflection in a mirror of a clock shows 9.40.
       What is the time really ?

15 Thinking about perimeter, area

Perimeter, area and volume

Perimeter is the **distance** round the outside of a shape.
Area is the amount of **surface** that a shape covers.
Volume is the amount of **space** that an object fills.
In what jobs might people use perimeter, area or volume ?

A tangram square

The 7-piece tangram square has its
origins in China, many years ago.
Copy the diagram on the right.
Use centimetre squared paper glued
to some thin card to make the task
easier.
Cut out the 7 pieces and rearrange
them so as to make pictures like the
ones below. Each picture uses all 7
pieces from the original square, so
each picture must have the same
area.

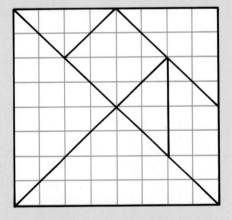

Space creature   Running   Sitting

and volume

The Soma Cube

Make the 7 figures in the picture below using centimetre cubes. How many cubes did you use altogether ?

Try to put the 7 figures together to make a single cube which measures 3 cm long, 3 cm wide and 3 cm high.

There are many different ways of building the cube. Once you have found one way try to find a different way.

Use your 7 pieces to make other interesting figures.
Each figure will have the same volume, 27 cubic centimetres.
This is because the volume of each cube is one cubic centimetre.

15 Perimeter, Area and Volume

Perimeter

Perimeter is the **distance** round the outside of a shape.
The metric units for measuring the perimeter of a shape are:

millimetres (mm)
centimetres (cm)
metres (m)
kilometres (km)

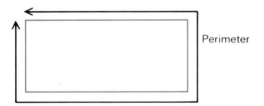

Perimeter

For example. You might want to find the perimeter of the school field. That is the distance round the boundary of the field.
The best unit to use would be the metre (m).

For smaller perimeters you could use millimetres (mm) or centimetres (cm).

For larger perimeters you could use metres (m) or kilometres (km).

Area

Area is the amount of **surface** that a shape covers.
The metric units for area are:

square millimetres (mm^2)
square centimetres (cm^2)
square metres (m^2)
square kilometres (km^2)

The area of a square which measures 1 cm by 1 cm is 1 square centimetre.

1 cm
1cm² 1 cm

For very small areas you could use square millimetres (mm²) or square centimetres (cm²).

For larger areas you could use square metres (m²).

For very large areas you could use square kilometres (km²).

Examples

1 What is the area of this rectangle ?

4 cm

3 cm

You can divide the rectangle up into squares of edge 1 cm.

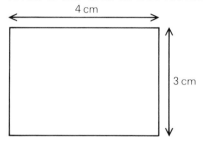

There are 12 squares. Each square has area 1 cm².
So the area of the rectangle is 12 cm².

2 What is the perimeter and area of this shape ?

The perimeter is the total distance round the shape.

Perimeter = (2 + 2 + 4 + 4 + 2 + 2 + 4 + 4) cm
Perimeter = 24 cm

To find the area divide the shape into squares of edge 1 cm, as shown.
There are 20 squares.
Each square has area 1 cm².

So the area of the shape is 20 cm².

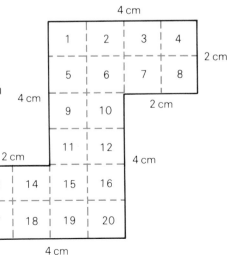

Exercise 15.1

1. This rectangle has been split up into
    squares of edge 1 cm.
    1   How many centimetres long is the
         rectangle ?
    2   How many centimetres wide is the
         rectangle ?
    3   What is the perimeter of the rectangle ?
    4   What is the area of the rectangle ?

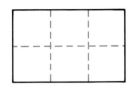

2. The letter **I** has been drawn on centimetre
    squared paper.
    Centimetre squared paper is paper which
    has squares of edge 1 cm.
    The area of each square is 1 cm².

    1   What is the perimeter of the letter ?
    2   What is the area of the letter ?

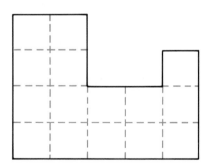

3. This shape has been drawn on centimetre
    squared paper.
    1   What is the perimeter of the shape ?
    2   What is the area of the shape ?

4. Here are some letters which have been drawn on centimetre squared paper.

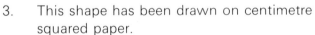

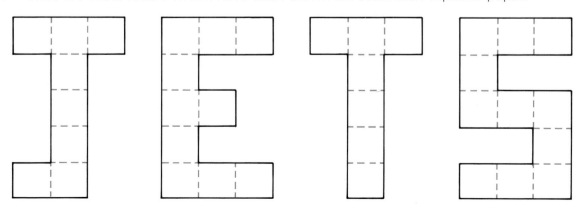

    1   Find the perimeter of each letter.

    2   Which letter has the smallest perimeter ?

    3   Which letter has the greatest perimeter ?

    4   Put the letters in order. Start with the letter which has the smallest perimeter and finish with the letter which has the greatest perimeter.

    5   Find the area of each letter.

    6   Which letter has the smallest area ?

    7   Which letter has the greatest area ?

    8   Put the letters in order. Start with the letter which has the smallest area and work upwards.

5.   Draw a rectangle 5 cm long and 4 cm wide.
Divide your rectangle into squares of edge 1 cm.

    1   What is the perimeter of your rectangle ?

    2   What is the area of your rectangle ?

6.   Draw a square 4 cm by 4 cm.
Divide your square into squares of edge 1 cm.

    1   What is the perimeter of the square which is 4 cm long ?

    2   What is the area of the square which is 4 cm long ?

7.   This table shows the lengths and breadths of some rectangles and squares.
Copy the table.
Find the perimeter and area of each shape.
You can draw the shape if it helps you to answer the question.
The first shape has been completed for you.

	length	breadth	perimeter	area
	8 cm	2 cm	20 cm	16 cm^2
1	5 cm	2 cm		
2	4 cm	3 cm		
3	3 cm	3 cm		
4	5 cm	5 cm		
5	6 cm	5 cm		
6	8 cm	5 cm		
7	9 cm	3 cm		
8	8 cm	7 cm		

8.   Gary has lost some of his work.
He had a rectangle with perimeter 12 cm and area 8 cm^2.
He cannot find the length and breadth of the rectangle.
He remembers that they were both whole numbers.
Can you work out the length and breadth of the rectangle ?

Finding the area of an unusual shape

So far you have found the areas of rectangles and squares.
These shapes had straight sides and a right-angle at each corner.
Other shapes that you looked at could all be split into centimetre squares.
Many shapes do not have straight sides.

To find the area of an irregular shape

We can find the approximate area of an irregular shape by **counting squares**.

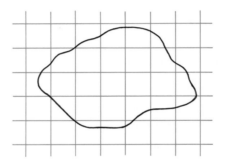

Rules for counting squares

Complete squares

A complete square is counted as 1.

Part squares

 If a **half or more** of the square is shaded the area of the square is counted as 1.

 If **less than half** of the square is shaded the area of the square is counted as 0.

Remember: This method is only **approximate**.
              Sometimes it is difficult to decide if a square should be counted as 1 or 0. You must make your own decision.
              Two people could get different answers to the same question.

Example

This shape has been drawn on centimetre squared paper.
Find the approximate area of the shape.

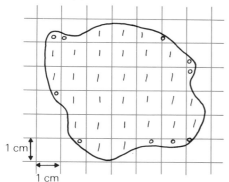

	Total
	3
	6
	6
	6
	6
	2
	Total 29

Work in rows.
Write the number of
squares counted as
1 at the end of each
row.
Add up the row totals
to get the total area.

Each square has area of 1 cm². The approximate area of the shape is 29 cm².

Exercise 15.2

1. This shape has been drawn on centimetre squared paper.
    1 How many squares should be counted
        as 1 in the first row ?
    2 How many squares should be counted
        as 1 in the second row ?
    3 How many squares should be counted
        as 1 in the third row ?

    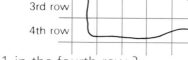

    4 How many squares should be counted as 1 in the fourth row ?
    5 Add up your answers to parts **1** to **4**.
    6 What is the approximate area of the whole shape ?

2. Find the approximate area of this shape.
    It has been drawn on centimetre squared paper.

    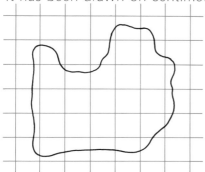

3. Here is a map of Skull Island.
    Each square of the grid represents
    1 kilometre by 1 kilometre.
    1   What is the area of one square of the
          grid ?
    2   Find the approximate area of
          Skull Island.

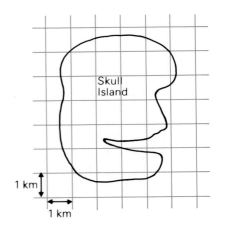

4. This diagram shows a circular roundabout.
    Each square on the grid represents 1 metre
    by 1 metre.
    1   What is the area of one square of the
          grid ?
    2   Find the approximate area of the
          roundabout.

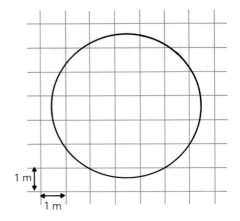

5. This diagram shows the flat end of a
    circular pencil.
    The shaded part is the lead.
    The unshaded part is the wood.
    Each square of the grid represents
    1 millimetre by 1 millimetre.
    1   What is the area of one square of the
          grid ?
    2   What is the approximate area of the
          lead of the pencil ?
    3   What is the approximate area of the
          wood of the pencil ?

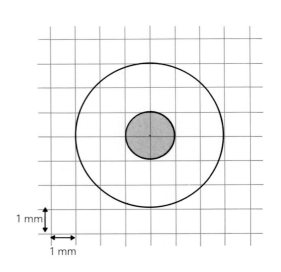

Volume

Volume is the amount of **space** that an object fills.
The metric units for volume are:

> cubic millimetres (mm³)
> cubic centimetres (cm³)
> cubic metres (m³)

Finding the volume of a solid figure

This cube is 1 cm long, 1 cm wide and
1 cm high.
It has a volume of 1 cubic centimetre.

1 cm
1 cm
1 cm
Volume = 1 cm³

Example

What is the volume of this shape ?
It has been made using centimetre cubes. (A centimetre cube is 1 cm long,
1 cm wide and 1 cm high, and has volume 1 cm³.)

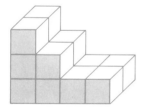

To find the volume of the shape you can either count the number of cubes in each
horizontal layer, or the number of cubes in each vertical layer.

Method 1: Counting horizontal layers

Bottom layer	8 cubes
Middle layer	4 cubes
Top layer	2 cubes
Total	14 cubes

Method 2: Counting vertical layers

1st column	6 cubes	Columns are counted from
2nd column	4 cubes	the left.
3rd column	2 cubes	
4th column	2 cubes	
Total	14 cubes	

Each cube has volume 1 cm³.
So the volume of the shape is 14 cm³.

Exercise 15.3

1. These shapes are made using centimetre cubes.
    Find the volume of each shape by counting the number of cubes.
    Note: Some cubes are hidden by cubes in front of them.

    1   **2**   **3**

    4    **5**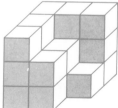

2. This is a cuboid made using centimetre
    cubes.

    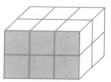

    1 How many cubes are on the bottom
        layer ?
    2 How many cubes are on the top
        layer ?
    3 What is the volume of the cuboid ?

3. This cuboid only has one layer.
    It has been made using centimetre cubes.

    1 How many centimetres long is the
           cuboid ?
    2 How many centimetres wide is the
           cuboid ?
    3 What is the volume of the cuboid,
           in cubic centimetres ?

4. This is another cuboid made using
    centimetre cubes.

    1 What is the length of the cuboid ?
    2 What is the breadth of the cuboid ?
    3 What is the height of the cuboid ?
    4 How many cubes are on the bottom
           layer ?
    5 What is the volume of the cuboid ?

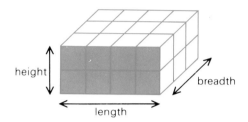

5. This is a larger cuboid made using centimetre cubes.

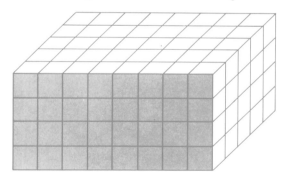

    1 What is the length of the cuboid ?
    2 What is the breadth of the cuboid ?
    3 What is the height of the cuboid ?
    4 How many cubes are on the bottom layer ?
    5 How did you get your answer to part **4** ?
    6 What is the volume of the cuboid ?
    7 How did you get your answer to part **6** ?

6. This shape is 2 cm long, 2 cm wide and
    2 cm high.

    1 What is the name given to this shape ?
    2 What is the volume of this shape ?

7.   Craig has built a cuboid using centimetre cubes.
     It is 3 cm long, 3 cm wide and 2 cm high.
     1   How many centimetre cubes did Craig use to build his cuboid ?
     2   What is the volume of the cuboid that Craig built ?

8.   Alex has built a cube using 27 centimetre cubes.
     1   What is the volume of the cube that Alex built ?
     2   What is the length of one side of the cube ?

9.   Maureen keeps her centimetre cubes in a
     box. The box is in the shape of a cuboid.
     The box is 6 cm long, 5 cm wide and
     3 cm high.

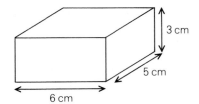

     1   How many cubes will fit along the length of the box ?
     2   How many cubes will fit along the breadth of the box ?
     3   How many cubes will fit in the bottom layer of the box ?
     4   How many layers of cubes will the box hold ?
     5   How many cubes will the box hold ?
     6   What is the volume of the box ?

10. A large cube is 10 cm long, 10 cm wide and 10 cm high.
     How many centimetre cubes are needed to make the large cube ?

Exercise 15.4   Applications and Activities

1.   A silicon chip used in a computer is a rectangle.
     It measures 8 mm by 6 mm.
     1   What is the perimeter of the silicon chip ?
     2   What is the area of the silicon chip ?

2.

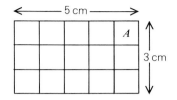

   1   What is the perimeter of the rectangle ?
   2   What is the area of the rectangle ?

   Square *A* which measures 1 cm by 1 cm is cut off.

   3   What is the perimeter of the new shape ?
   4   What is the area of the new shape ?

3.   **The area of your foot**
   Take one shoe off and stand on a large sheet of centimetre squared paper.
   Draw round your foot. If you cannot do this ask a friend to do the drawing.

   Find the approximate area of your foot by counting squares.

   Find the area of your other foot. Are your feet nearly the same in area ?

   If someone else takes the same size of shoe as you do, compare the areas of your feet with the areas of their feet.

PUZZLE

34.   Take a 5 × 5 grid.
   Cut it into 4 pieces by cutting along the sides
   of squares.
   The four pieces should fit together to make
   two squares. One is 4 × 4.
   The other is 3 × 3.

16 Thinking about fractions and

Take half

This triangular cake has been cut into 4 pieces.
Each piece is the same size and is
equal to a quarter of the whole cake.

Two quarters are equal to a half.
How many different ways are there of taking
half of the cake if it is cut into 4 quarters?

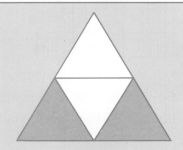

Road signs

The road traffic signs used to warn
a motorist of a steep hill have
changed in recent years.
An old sign might warn a motorist
of a hill using two figures, e.g. 1
in 4. Most of these signs have now
been replaced by signs which give
the steepness of a hill as a
percentage, e.g. 14%.
How can a motorist tell from the
sign whether the road goes uphill
or downhill?
Are there any signs for hills near
where you live?

An old sign warning motorists of a hill

The biggest half

Is there such a thing as the biggest
half?
Is one half of the world bigger
than the other half?
Are there more people in one half
of the class than in the other half?
Is one half of a football match
longer than the other half?
For a true half both amounts should
be exactly equal. In everyday
speech we sometimes talk about
an amount being a half when it is
not. Can you think of any examples?

The new signs warning motorists of a hill caused
confusion at first.

percentages

The Earth

Percentages are often used to compare quantities. They are far easier to use than fractions for such purposes.

70% of the Earth's surface is salt water.

The total of the Earth's surface is 100%, so 30% of the Earth's surface is not salt water.

Saltwater is 96% pure water and 3% common salt.

The other 1% is made up of small amounts of different chemicals.

A hot desert

A volcanic island

Deserts

34% of the Earth's land surface is desert.

34% is approximately $\frac{1}{3}$.

So approximately $\frac{2}{3}$ of the Earth's land surface is not desert.

16% of the Earth's land surface is cold deserts. These are mainly in Greenland, Antarctica and northern Russia.

18% of the Earth's land surface is hot deserts or other deserts, such as volcanic islands.

Do you think that it is better to give the above figures in percentages or fractions? Explain your answer.

16 Fractions and Percentages

You probably started using fractions at a very early age.
Sharing sweets with a friend and having half each.
Getting half-way through an exercise book.
Half-time in a match.
Having quarter of an hour for morning break.

Parts of a whole

Examples

1   What fraction of the square is shaded ?

1 part of the square is shaded.
The square is divided into 2 **equal** parts.

So $\frac{1}{2}$ (a half) of the square is shaded.

2   What fraction of the circle is shaded ?

1 part is shaded.
The circle is divided into 4 **equal** parts.

So $\frac{1}{4}$ (a quarter) of the circle is shaded and
$\frac{3}{4}$ (three-quarters) of the circle is not shaded.

3   Brian said that $\frac{1}{4}$ of the rectangle was

shaded. Was Brian correct ?

No. The rectangle is not divided into 4 equal
parts.

4   What fraction of the hexagon is shaded ?

5 parts are shaded.
The hexagon is divided into 6 equal parts.
So $\frac{5}{6}$ (five-sixths) of the hexagon is shaded
and $\frac{1}{6}$ (one-sixth) of the hexagon is not
shaded.

In a fraction, the bottom number is called the **denominator**.
It tells us how many smaller equal parts the whole unit is divided into.
The top number is called the **numerator**.
It tells us how many of the smaller parts we are counting.

Exercise 16.1

1. What fraction of each of these diagrams is shaded ?

1   **2**    **3**

4   **5**

2. What fraction of each of these diagrams is shaded ?

1   **2**   **3**

4   **5**   **6**

7    **8**

9    **10**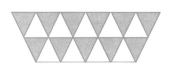

3. Copy this rectangle.
    1 How many equal parts is the rectangle
          divided into ?
    2 Shade $\frac{7}{12}$ of the rectangle.
    3 What fraction of your diagram is not
          shaded ?

4. Copy this diagram.
    1 How many equal parts is the shape
          divided into ?
    2 Shade $\frac{5}{8}$ of your diagram.
    3 What fraction is not shaded ?

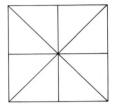

Equivalent fractions

This square is divided into 2 equal parts.
So $\frac{1}{2}$ of the square is shaded.

The same square can be divided into 4
equal parts.
So $\frac{2}{4}$ of the square is shaded.

The same amount of the square is shaded in each diagram.
So $\frac{1}{2} = \frac{2}{4}$

If two fractions are equal they are called **equivalent fractions**.
To make an equivalent fraction multiply (or divide) the numerator and the denominator
by the same number.

For example. $\frac{2}{5} = \dfrac{2 \times 3}{5 \times 3} = \frac{6}{15}$

So $\frac{2}{5} = \frac{6}{15}$

Fractions in their simplest form

Would you prefer $\frac{12}{18}$ of a cake or $\frac{2}{3}$ of a cake ?

They are both the same amounts of cake.

$\frac{2}{3}$ is in its simplest form.

$\frac{12}{18}$ is not in its simplest form.

To get a fraction into its simplest form

Is there any number which will divide into the top number (numerator) and also into the bottom number (denominator) ?

If the answer to this question is 'no' the fraction is in its simplest form.

However, if the answer is 'yes' the fraction is not in its simplest form.

The fraction $\frac{12}{18}$ is not in its simplest form because 12 and 18 can both be divided by 2.

$$\frac{12 \div 2}{18 \div 2} = \frac{6}{9}$$

$\frac{6}{9}$ is still not in its simplest form because 6 and 9 can both be divided by 3.

$$\frac{6 \div 3}{9 \div 3} = \frac{2}{3}$$

$\frac{2}{3}$ is in its simplest form because no whole number (other than 1) will divide into 2 and 3.

You could have found the simplest form more quickly by dividing 12 and 18 by 6.

$$\frac{12 \div 6}{18 \div 6} = \frac{2}{3}$$

Some calculators can change fractions into their simplest form.
It is important that you can do it as well.

Examples

1   Write $\frac{25}{30}$ in its simplest form.

25 and 30 can both be divided by 5.

$$\frac{25 \div 5}{30 \div 5} = \frac{5}{6}$$

So $\frac{25}{30} = \frac{5}{6}$ in its simplest form.

2   Copy and complete the following.

$\frac{3}{5} = \frac{}{20}$

5 has been multiplied by 4 to get 20.

To get an equivalent fraction you must multiply or divide the numerator and denominator by the same number.

So you also multiply 3 by 4, getting 12,

$\frac{3}{5} = \frac{12}{20}$

This is because $\dfrac{3 \times 4}{5 \times 4} = \frac{12}{20}$

3   Copy and complete the following equivalent fractions.

$\frac{2}{3} = \frac{}{6} = \frac{8}{} = \frac{}{24}$

$\frac{2}{3} = \frac{4}{6} = \frac{8}{12} = \frac{16}{24}$

All the fractions in the line are equal to each other.

Exercise 16.2

1.   Copy and complete the following.

1 $\dfrac{6}{8} = \dfrac{6 \div 2}{8 \div 2} = \dfrac{}{4}$

2 $\dfrac{10}{15} = \dfrac{10 \div }{15 \div 5} = \dfrac{}{2}$

3 $\dfrac{16}{20} = \dfrac{16 \div 4}{20 \div } = \dfrac{}{-}$

2.   Write each of these fractions in its simplest form.

1	$\frac{2}{4}$	**6**	$\frac{6}{9}$	**11**	$\frac{20}{30}$
2	$\frac{3}{9}$	**7**	$\frac{6}{8}$	**12**	$\frac{15}{20}$
3	$\frac{4}{16}$	**8**	$\frac{10}{12}$	**13**	$\frac{32}{36}$
4	$\frac{3}{12}$	**9**	$\frac{8}{10}$	**14**	$\frac{40}{60}$
5	$\frac{5}{10}$	**10**	$\frac{8}{12}$	**15**	$\frac{70}{80}$

3. Write each of these fractions in its simplest form.
    Remember: You may take more than one step to find the simplest form of a
                fraction.

    1 $\frac{36}{42}$ **5** $\frac{56}{64}$ **8** $\frac{32}{48}$

    2 $\frac{45}{55}$ **6** $\frac{16}{96}$ **9** $\frac{27}{72}$

    3 $\frac{30}{66}$ **7** $\frac{75}{100}$ **10** $\frac{63}{84}$

    4 $\frac{27}{63}$

4. Copy and complete these equivalent fractions.

    1 $\frac{1}{2} = \frac{}{4}$ **4** $\frac{}{6} = \frac{10}{12}$

    2 $\frac{2}{5} = \frac{6}{}$ **5** $\frac{4}{} = \frac{12}{21}$

    3 $\frac{5}{8} = \frac{20}{}$

5. Copy and complete these sets of equivalent fractions.

    1 $\frac{1}{3} = \frac{}{6} = \frac{3}{} = \frac{}{12}$

    2 $\frac{}{7} = \frac{8}{14} = \frac{}{28} = \frac{20}{}$

    3 $\frac{40}{60} = \frac{}{30} = \frac{10}{} = \frac{}{3}$

Finding fractions of a number

What is $\frac{1}{2}$ of 10 ?

$\frac{1}{2}$ of 10 = 5.

To find a half of something divide by 2.

Examples

1 Find $\frac{1}{2}$ of 24.

$24 \div 2 = 12$
So $\frac{1}{2}$ of 24 = 12

2 Find $\frac{1}{3}$ of 18.

To find $\frac{1}{3}$ of something divide by 3.
$18 \div 3 = 6$
So $\frac{1}{3}$ of 18 = 6

3 Four people shared equally the winnings from a lottery.
They won £60.
How much did each person get ?

There are 4 people so each person got $\frac{1}{4}$ of the winnings.
$60 \div 4 = 15$

Each person got £15.
You would possibly not consider using fractions to do this question. There are
often different ways of looking at the same question.

4 Find $\frac{2}{3}$ of 12.

First find $\frac{1}{3}$ of 12.
$12 \div 3 = 4$
So $\frac{1}{3}$ of 12 = 4
and $\frac{2}{3}$ of 12 = 2 × 4 = 8

5 Find $\frac{3}{4}$ of 24

$\frac{1}{4}$ of 24 = 6   (because 24 ÷ 4 = 6)
$\frac{3}{4}$ of 24 = 18   (because 6 × 3 = 18)

6 Find $\frac{3}{8}$ of 40 metres.

$\frac{1}{8}$ of 40 m = 5 m   (because 40 ÷ 8 = 5)
$\frac{3}{8}$ of 40 m = 15 m   (because 3 × 5 = 15)

Exercise 16.3

1.   Work these out.
   1 $\frac{1}{2}$ of 14   **6** $\frac{1}{7}$ of 35
   2 $\frac{1}{3}$ of 9   **7** $\frac{1}{5}$ of 30
   3 $\frac{1}{5}$ of 20   **8** $\frac{1}{10}$ of 60
   4 $\frac{1}{4}$ of 12   **9** $\frac{1}{8}$ of 32
   5 $\frac{1}{6}$ of 18   **10** $\frac{1}{9}$ of 27

2. **1**   What is $\frac{1}{3}$ of 30 ?
    2   What is $\frac{2}{3}$ of 30 ?

3. **1**   What is $\frac{1}{4}$ of 28 ?

    2   What is $\frac{3}{4}$ of 28 ?

4. **1**   What is $\frac{1}{5}$ of 30 ?

    2   What is $\frac{2}{5}$ of 30 ?

    3   What is $\frac{3}{5}$ of 30 ?

    4   What is $\frac{4}{5}$ of 30 ?

5. Work these out. Remember to include the units in your answer.

    1 $\frac{2}{3}$ of £15   **6** $\frac{5}{9}$ of 27 kg

    2 $\frac{3}{4}$ of 20 m   **7** $\frac{3}{7}$ of 28 cm

    3 $\frac{3}{5}$ of 25 mm   **8** $\frac{5}{6}$ of 42 miles

    4 $\frac{4}{5}$ of 40 tonnes   **9** $\frac{6}{7}$ of £21

    5 $\frac{3}{8}$ of 16 km   **10** $\frac{7}{10}$ of 80 km

Percentages

'Per cent' means **out of 100**.
The sign for 'per cent' is %.

53% means 53 out of 100.
53% can be written as a fraction.
53% $= \frac{53}{100}$

Percentages are a useful way of comparing test marks.
Colin got 47% for his half-term geography test.
He scored 54% in the end of term test.
From this we can easily tell that Colin did better in the end of term test.

Examples

1 Write 45 out of 100 as a percentage.

   45 out of 100 can be written as $\frac{45}{100}$.

   $\frac{45}{100} = 45\%$

2   6 people out of 100 questioned had their birthday in November. Write this as a percentage.

$\frac{6}{100}$ = 6%

So 6% of the people questioned had their birthday in November.

3   Write 35 out of 50 as a percentage.

Per cent means out of 100.

35 out of 50 is the same as $\frac{35}{50}$.

To be a percentage the bottom number must be 100.
Multiply top and bottom of the fraction by 2. This makes an equivalent fraction.

$$\frac{35 \times 2}{50 \times 2} = \frac{70}{100} = 70\%$$

So 35 out of 50 = 70%

4   7 pupils in a class of 25 take sandwiches for lunch.
Write this as a percentage.

$$\frac{7}{25} = \frac{7 \times 4}{25 \times 4} = \frac{28}{100} = 28\%$$

28% of the pupils take sandwiches.

Exercise 16.4

1.   Write these as percentages

1	40 out of 100	**6**	6 out of 100
2	50 out of 100	**7**	39 out of 100
3	80 out of 100	**8**	75 out of 100
4	35 out of 100	**9**	1 out of 100
5	47 out of 100	**10**	100 out of 100

2.   15 out of 100 trains arrived at the station late.
Write this as a percentage.

3.   63 out of every 100 households have central heating.
Write this as a percentage.

4.   72 out of every 100 fans at a football match supported the home team. Write this
      as a percentage.

5.   11 out of every 50 pupils questioned travelled to school by car.
      1   Write 11 out of 50 as a fraction.
      2   What must 50 be multiplied by to get 100 ?
      3   Write 11 out of 50 as a percentage.

6.   Sarah got 7 out of 10 for her French homework.
      1   Write 7 out of 10 as a fraction.
      2   What must 10 be multiplied by to get 100 ?
      3   Write 7 out of 10 as a percentage.

7.   Write these as percentages.
      1   30 out of 50   **6**   12 out of 25
      2   45 out of 50   **7**   10 out of 25
      3   8 out of 10   **8**   13 out of 20
      4   2 out of 10   **9**   4 out of 5
      5   10 out of 20   **10**   3 out of 4

Understanding percentages

75% of children questioned said that they liked ice-cream.
What does this mean ?

$75\% = \frac{75}{100}$

You can write $\frac{75}{100}$ in its simplest form.

$$\frac{75}{100} = \frac{75 \div 5}{100 \div 5} = \frac{15 \div 5}{20 \div 5} = \frac{3}{4}$$

75% means 3 out of 4.
This tells us that 3 out of every 4 of the children questioned liked ice-cream.

So 1 out of 4 of the children did not like ice-cream.

$\frac{1}{4} = \frac{25}{100} = 25\%$

25% of the children did not like ice-cream.
We only have the two answers 'like' and 'not like'.
The percentage of 'likes' + the percentage of 'not likes' = 100%

Examples

1   What does 5% mean ?

5% $= \frac{5}{100}$

This can be written in its simplest form.

$$\frac{5}{100} = \frac{5 \div 5}{100 \div 5} = \frac{1}{20}$$

So 5% means $\frac{1}{20}$ or 1 in 20.

2   80% of the children in a class walk to school. What percentage of the children do not walk to school ?

There are only two possibilities. They are 'walk' and 'not walk'.
So the percentages must add up to 100%.

$100 - 80 = 20$

So 20% of the children do not walk.

3   In a class of 25 pupils there are 15 girls.
What percentage of the class are boys ?

15 out of 25 are girls.
So $25 - 15 = 10$ are boys.
10 out of 25 are boys.

$$\frac{10}{25} = \frac{10 \times 4}{25 \times 4} = \frac{40}{100} = 40\%$$

40% of the class are boys.

Exercise 16.5

1.   Write down each of these percentages as a fraction. Then write the fraction in its simplest form.

1	50%	**5**	75%	**8**	12%
2	25%	**6**	45%	**9**	2%
3	20%	**7**	5%	**10**	28%
4	60%				

2.   60% of the traffic on a motorway was cars.
     What percentage of the traffic was not cars ?

3.   28% of a class had pets at home.
     What percentage of the class did not have pets at home ?

4.   A packet of seeds produced either red or white flowers.
     15 out of 20 seeds produced white flowers.
     What percentage of the seeds produced red flowers ?

5.   7 out of 10 people had tracksuits.
     What percentage did not have tracksuits ?

6.   24 out of 40 pupils chose to play football in a Games lesson.
     What percentage did not choose football ?

Exercise 16.6   Applications and Activities

1.   This square has been divided into triangles.
     Each triangle is the same shape and size.
     Some of the triangles have been shaded.

     1   How many triangles has the square
             been divided into ?
     2   How many triangles have been
             shaded ?
     3   What fraction of the square has been
             shaded ?
     4   What is this fraction as a percentage ?
     5   What percentage of the square is not
             shaded ?

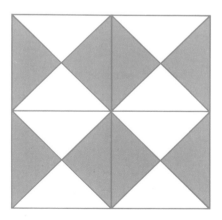

2.   George says that he needs 8 hours sleep a day.
     There are 24 hours in a day.
     1   What fraction of the day does George need to sleep for ?
     2   How many hours of the day is George awake for ?
     3   What fraction of the day is George awake for ?

3.   Sarah spends $\frac{1}{6}$ of her day eating and doing housework,

$\frac{5}{12}$ of her day working or travelling,

$\frac{1}{8}$ of her day relaxing at home.

Sarah spends the remaining hours of the day sleeping.

1   How many hours does Sarah spend eating and doing housework ?
2   How many hours does Sarah spend working or travelling ?
3   How many hours does Sarah spend relaxing at home ?
4   How many hours does Sarah spend sleeping ?
5   What fraction of the day does Sarah spend sleeping ?

4.   Claire, Freda and Louise were trying to compare the marks they had been given for the same history test.
They each had a different teacher for history.
Claire's mark was 75%, Freda's mark was $\frac{16}{20}$ and Louise's mark was $\frac{35}{50}$.

1   What must you multiply 20 by to get 100 ?
2   What is Freda's mark as a percentage ?
3   What is Louise's mark as a percentage ?
4   Which girl obtained the best mark ?

5.   **The air we breathe**

The air we breathe is made up of many gases.

Approximately 78% of the Earth's atmosphere is nitrogen and approximately $\frac{1}{5}$ is oxygen.

1   Write the amount of oxygen in the air as a percentage.
2   Write the amount of nitrogen in the air as a fraction in its simplest form.
3   Add together the percentages of nitrogen and oxygen present in the air.

You should have found that your answer to part **3** was less than 100%, as a small proportion of the air is made up of other gases.
For example, ozone forms a very small part of the atmosphere.

In fact ozone forms only about $\frac{1}{2000}$ of the atmosphere.

Try to find out about other gases that exist in the atmosphere and why they are important for our survival.

6. **Hydro-Electric Power**

Hydro-Electric Power or H.E.P. uses water to drive turbines which generate
electricity. The water power required to drive the turbines comes from waterfalls,
rivers and reservoirs.

One quarter of the world's electricity is generated by H.E.P. This table shows the
amount of electricity generated by H.E.P. for some countries.

Country	Percentage by H.E.P.
Norway	100
Brazil	95
Canada	70
France	50
Japan	30
USA	20

1   One quarter of the world's electricity is produced by H.E.P.
        Write this as a percentage.

For the following countries, write as fractions the proportion of electricity generated
by H.E.P. Then write the fractions in their simplest terms.

2   USA
3   Japan
4   France
5   Canada
6   Brazil

Write a statement about how electricity is generated in Norway.

Try to find out more about H.E.P. and its advantages and disadvantages over other
ways of producing electricity.

17 Thinking about more statistics

Using statistics to estimate the cost

Before having your bathroom re-plumbed it is a good idea to ask for an estimate. It is important to know what the plumber will charge you for the time he spends doing the work. To give an estimate the plumber could look up, in his files, the times taken to complete similar jobs.

For example, if for 7 similar jobs he had done before he took 8, 12, 17, 10, 13, 15 and 9 hours, he could give the following information.

$$\text{The mean time} = \frac{\text{the sum of the times}}{\text{the number of jobs}}$$

$$= \frac{8 + 12 + 17 + 10 + 13 + 15 + 9}{7} \text{ hours}$$

$$= \frac{84}{7} \text{ hours}$$

$$= 12 \text{ hours}$$

A plumber at work

If he charged £15 per hour for his labour it would come to 12 × £15 = £180. He then includes this in his estimated cost for the job.

Why is it a good idea for the customer to ask for an estimate ?

At work

How might the mean of a set of data be used by these people ?

Bridge construction engineers

A car mechanic servicing a car

What statistics could be used in these situations ?

Competitors in the London marathon

Traffic on a busy road

Classifying bridges

Why are different types of bridges used ?
Look at bridges in the area where you live or when you are travelling to different parts of the country (or world).
Keep a record, using a data collection sheet, of the types of bridges you see. Which type of bridge do you see most often ?
Perhaps you might like to make a model of one of the types of bridge.

A suspension bridge, the Severn Bridge

A cantilever bridge, the Forth Railway Bridge

An arch bridge over the River Dovey

A beam bridge over a motorway

17 More Statistics

Line-graphs (time-series graphs)

These graphs always have time on the horizontal axis and the quantity that is being recorded on the vertical axis.

Points are plotted as dots or crosses and then joined, in order, using a ruler and a pencil.

This line-graph shows the number of pupils absent from class 7G during one week.

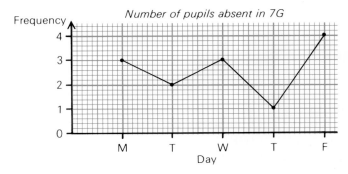

The lines joining the points help to show the changes (increases and decreases) from one reading to the next reading.
Points along the lines have no meaning on this line-graph.

Example

This graph shows the amount of petrol in the fuel tank of a car. The amount of petrol in the tank was recorded every hour. The car stopped once to refill with petrol.

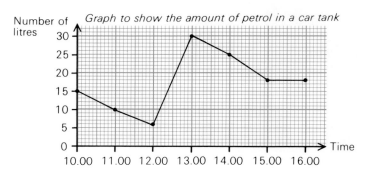

1   Describe what happens to the amount of petrol in the tank between 10.00 and 12.00.

The amount of petrol in the tank went down from 15 litres to 6 litres. At 11.00 the tank held 10 litres of petrol.

2   What happened to the amount of petrol in the tank from 12.00 to 13.00 ?

There was 6 litres in the tank at 12.00 and 30 litres in at 13.00, so the tank was refilled.
We cannot say exactly when the tank was filled. It could have been done at any time between 12.00 and 13.00.

3   Say what the car was doing between 15.00 and 16.00.

The car did not travel anywhere.
We can tell this because no petrol was used.

4   Can you tell how much petrol was in the tank at 10.30 ?

The amount of petrol in the tank at 10.00 was 15 litres and the amount of petrol in the tank at 11.00 was 10 litres. We can only approximate the amount of petrol in the tank at 10.30.
There was approximately 13 litres of petrol in the tank.

We can only approximate using this type of graph.
To find the amount of petrol in the tank at any given time you would have to take an actual measurement. A car uses different amounts of petrol at different speeds.

Exercise 17.1

1.   A large office has a drinks machine.
     Brenda noticed when people took drinks during the day.
     She took a reading of the amount of water in the machine each hour.
     She drew this graph to show the readings she has taken.

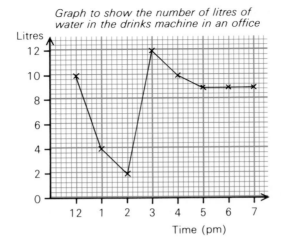

*Graph to show the number of litres of
water in the drinks machine in an office*

1   How much water was in the machine at 1 o'clock ?
2   Estimate the amount of water in the machine at 12.30 pm.
3   Estimate the amount of water in the machine at 1.30 pm.
4   Why do you think that the level of water in the machine dropped a lot
    between 12 o'clock and 1 o'clock ?
5   What do you think happened between 2 o'clock and 3 o'clock ?
6   The level of water did not drop after 5 o'clock.
    Give an explanation for this.

2.   Elizabeth and Emma counted the number of cars which passed the school each
     morning break.
     They made a data collection sheet to record the number of cars.

Day	Tally	Frequency
Monday	ⅢⅢ ⅢⅢ ⅢⅢ ⅢⅢ Ⅲ	28
Tuesday	ⅢⅢ ⅢⅢ ⅢⅢ Ⅲ	
Wednesday	ⅢⅢ ⅢⅢ ⅢⅢ ⅢⅢ ⅢⅢ ⅢⅢ	30
Thursday	ⅢⅢ ⅠⅠ	
Friday	ⅢⅢ ⅢⅢ ⅢⅢ ⅢⅢ ⅠⅠ	

1   How many cars did the girls count on Tuesday ?
2   How many cars did they count on Thursday ?
3   How many cars did they count on Friday ?
4   Draw a line-graph to show the data.
    Remember to label the axes and to give your graph a title.

3.   Sally drew a line-graph to show how much homework she did each day.

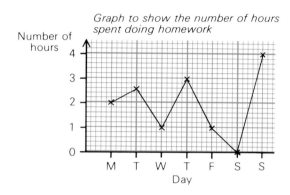

Graph to show the number of hours spent doing homework

1   How long did Sally spend doing homework on Thursday ?
2   On which day did Sally do no homework ?
3   How long did Sally spend doing homework on Tuesday ?
4   On which two days did Sally spend the same amount of time doing homework ?
5   Copy and complete this table.

Time spent doing homework

Day	Number of hours
Monday Tuesday Wednesday Thursday Friday Saturday Sunday	

6   What was the total number of hours Sally spent doing homework during the week ?

4. Mr and Mrs Roberts save as much money as they can each month. They like to use their savings to pay for family holidays and Christmas presents.
The graph below shows the amount of money they saved each month.

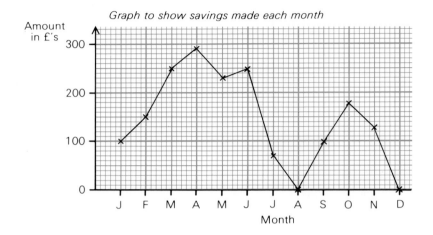

Graph to show savings made each month

1 How much money does one small square on the vertical axis represent ?

2 How much money did they save in February ?

3 How much money did they save in April ?

4 Copy and complete this table showing how much money Mr and Mrs Roberts saved each month.

Month	Amount saved
January	£100
February	
March	
April	
May	
June	
July	
August	
September	
October	
November	
December	

5 What was the total amount they saved during the year ?

6 In which month do you think the Roberts family went on holiday ?

7 Suggest a reason why they did not make any savings in December.

Frequency distributions

Example

Tim rolled a die 50 times and recorded the scores.
The record he made appears below.

1	4	5	3	4	2	1	6	5	1
3	1	3	2	1	4	2	3	4	6
6	5	6	3	6	5	1	5	6	1
6	1	4	3	2	1	4	6	5	2
1	3	2	1	6	2	5	3	1	1

Copy and complete this data collection sheet for the 50 rolls of the die. The tally marks have been put in for you.

Score	Tally	f
1	LHT LHT III	
2	LHT II	
3	LHT III	
4	LHT I	
5	HHT II	
6	LHT IIII	
	Total	

f is short for **frequency**.
Frequency is the number of times that something happens, or that an item is counted.
The last column of the data collection sheet shows the frequency of each happening or item, and a complete list of frequencies is called a **frequency distribution**.

Bar-line graphs

A graph called a **bar-line graph** can be used to show a frequency distribution. It is very similar to a bar chart, with each bar having the thickness of a line. The gaps between the bar-lines tell us that values between those labelled on the horizontal axis have no meaning (e.g. you cannot roll 3.5 on a die).

Example

A bar-line graph can be drawn to show the frequency distribution that Tim obtained when he rolled a die 50 times.

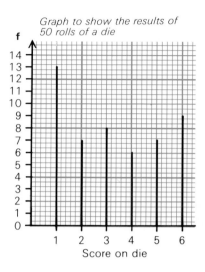

Graph to show the results of 50 rolls of a die

Exercise 17.2

1.   A class of 30 children were given a difficult spellings test. The test was marked out of 10, and the results appear below.

4	7	8	9	10	4	6	8	5	6
5	4	2	3	5	6	8	7	4	9
7	6	3	9	10	8	7	6	4	5

1   Use a data collection sheet to find the frequency distribution of the test marks.

2   Draw a bar-line graph to show the frequency distribution of the marks.

2.   For a technology project Asif chose to do a project on the number and type of electrical appliances (food mixers, cookers, dishwashers, etc.) that can be found in a kitchen.

Part of his project included asking 60 people to complete a questionnaire. One of the questions was, 'How many electrical appliances do you have in your kitchen ?' The replies to this question are listed below.

1	2	4	5	3	2	4	1	3	2
2	1	3	2	3	4	3	5	4	6
8	2	3	7	1	2	5	4	6	4
1	4	4	1	3	4	2	4	5	3
5	5	7	2	6	2	7	3	4	2
3	5	4	3	5	2	4	6	5	4

1   What is the highest number of electrical appliances that was recorded ?

2   Design a data collection sheet and complete it to find the frequency distribution for Asif's data.

3   Draw a bar-line graph to show the frequency distribution of the numbers of electrical appliances.

Using groups

Miss Wright wanted to draw a graph to show the tables test marks for class 7E. The test was marked out of 20.
To display the data she would have to draw a bar chart or a bar-line graph with 20 different columns. Such a graph would not be very useful.

It would be better to put the marks into **groups**.
These groups are sometimes called **classes**.

The test marks obtained by class 7E are shown below.

2	9	14	18	7	4	10	12	14	17
19	20	1	8	12	13	12	8	9	18
18	15	17	14	16	11	9	7	14	19

Miss Wright decided to put the marks into the following groups:
     1–5   Must practise their tables.
     6–10   Some practice required.
    11–15   Good effort.
    16–20   Very good.
Notice that she put the same number of marks, 5, in each group.

Next, Miss Wright made a **frequency table**.

Mark	Tally	Frequency
1–5	III	3
6–10	JHT III	8
11–15	JHT JHT	10
16–20	JHT IIII	9
	Total	30

Frequency diagrams

Using the table Miss Wright was able to draw a frequency diagram.
This is similar to a bar chart with no gaps between the bars.

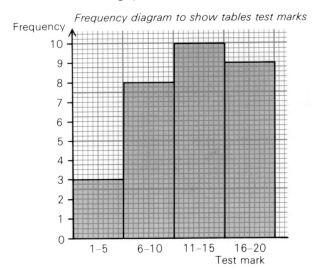

Frequency diagram to show tables test marks

The frequency diagram is easy to draw.
From this diagram we can see that 3 people scored 1 to 5 marks, 8 people scored from 6 to 10 marks, and so on.
We cannot say how many people scored a particular mark, for example, we cannot say how many people scored exactly 10 marks.

This type of diagram is used in newspapers and shown on television.
It is used whenever it is convenient to group data together.
This is often done when the range of the data is large.

When you are putting the data into classes, put the same number of items in each class.

Exercise 17.3

1. Damian and Sasha did a survey on garden peas.
    They wanted to study the different numbers of peas that could be found in a pod.
    After they had collected their data Damian and Sasha drew a graph.

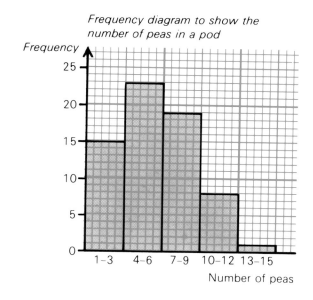

Frequency diagram to show the number of peas in a pod

1   How many pods containing 7, 8 or 9 peas were counted ?
2   How many pea pods did Damian and Sasha study altogether ?

2. Tracey is a member of a stamp-collecting club.
    The club was set up to encourage people to start collecting stamps.
    Tracey did a survey to find out how many stamps each club member had
    collected since their last meeting.
    This is the list of replies that Tracey obtained.

2	12	24	15	37	29	31	42	53	62
8	21	32	41	36	42	39	27	36	52
36	21	35	24	16	18	23	14	9	63
24	51	43	11	7	24	38	51	22	16

1   Tracey decided to put her data into classes.
     Copy this frequency table.
     Complete the table using the data that Tracey collected.

Number of stamps	Tally	Frequency
1–10		
11–20		
21–30		
31–40		
41–50		
51–60		
61–70		
	Total	

2   Draw a frequency diagram to show the data.
     Remember to label the axes and to give the graph a title.

In earlier chapters you collected data and drew graphs to represent data.
You are now going to study a set of data in more detail.
It is useful to find the range of a set of data, and an average value of the data.
You can use these values to compare one set of data with another set.

The range of a set of data

These are the marks obtained by 10 children in a spellings test.
7   3   4   8   9   6   9   5   6   7
The highest mark is 9.
The lowest mark is 3.
The difference between these is called the **range**.
Range = highest value − lowest value
      = 9 − 3
      = 6

The mean of a set of data

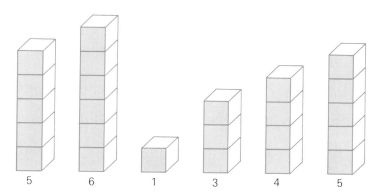

5   6   1   3   4   5

The piles of cubes represent the number of books bought by a group of 6 people during the last two months.
1 cube represents 1 book.

The total number of books bought was 5 + 6 + 1 + 3 + 4 + 5 = 24

We can divide the 24 books equally among the 6 people.
This gives a type of average, called the **mean**.

Mean = total number of books ÷ number of people
     = 24 ÷ 6
     = 4

We can use the cubes to show the mean number of books bought by each person.

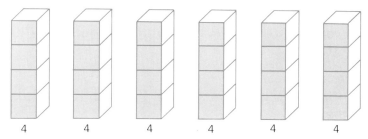

4   4   4   4   4   4

The **mean** number of books is the number of books that each person would have bought, had they all bought the same number.

To find the mean, find the sum of the items and divide by the number of items.

Mean = $\dfrac{\text{sum of the items}}{\text{number of items}}$

Examples

1   This table shows the number of letters a company received during one week.

Monday	Tuesday	Wednesday	Thursday	Friday
15	8	10	6	12

Find the range and mean for this data.

Range = highest number − lowest number
        = 15 − 6
        = 9

Mean = $\dfrac{\text{total number of letters}}{\text{number of days}}$

$= \dfrac{51}{5}$

$= 10.2$

$$\begin{array}{r} 15 \\ 8 \\ 10 \\ 6 \\ 12 \\ \hline \text{Total} = 51 \end{array}$$

2   The ages of 6 children are 5 years, 8 years, 12 years, 4 years, 15 years and 16 years. Find the range and the mean of their ages.

Range = highest age − lowest age
        = 16 years − 4 years
        = 12 years

So the range of the ages is 12 years.

Mean age = $\dfrac{\text{sum of the ages}}{\text{number of children}}$

$= \dfrac{5 + 8 + 12 + 4 + 15 + 16}{6}$ years

$= \dfrac{60}{6}$ years

$= 10$ years

So the mean age of the children is 10 years.

3   Tom keeps a record of his tables test marks.
His class has a tables test nearly every day.
Each test contains 10 questions.

Week 1	7	6	5	8	4
Week 2	8	3	7	8	

What is Tom's mean score for each week ?

$$\text{The mean score for week 1} = \frac{\text{total number of marks}}{\text{number of tests}}$$

$$= \frac{7 + 6 + 5 + 8 + 4}{5}$$

$$= \frac{30}{5}$$

$$= 6$$

$$\text{The mean score for week 2} = \frac{\text{total number of marks}}{\text{number of tests}}$$

$$= \frac{8 + 3 + 7 + 8}{4}$$

$$= \frac{26}{4}$$

$$= 6.5$$

Tom will feel happy that his average mark for week 2 is higher than his average mark for week 1.
(If an average is not an exact whole number, give it as a decimal.)

Exercise 17.4

1.   Dilip scored 7, 4, 3, 6, 2 and 8 marks in the six rounds of a general knowledge quiz.
   1   What was the range of Dilip's marks ?
   2   What was Dilip's mean score for the 6 rounds of the quiz ?

2. Gloria scored 17, 16, 12 and 7 baskets in her last four basketball matches.
    1 What is the range of the number of baskets ?
    2 How many baskets did Gloria score altogether ?
    3 What is the average number of baskets scored by Gloria in each game ?

3. Find the range of each of these sets of data.
    Remember to include the units in your answer.
    1 £2, £9, £3, £15, £6.
    2 7 m, 10 m, 5 m, 6 m, 12 m.
    3 4 years, 7 years, 6 years, 8 years.
    4 10 miles, 7 miles, 4 miles, 6 miles.
    5 50 kg, 51 kg, 49 kg, 48 kg, 50 kg, 53 kg, 49 kg.
    6 25p, 30p, 26p, 19p, 27p.
    7 15 cm, 17 cm, 16 cm, 16 cm, 15 cm, 17 cm.
    8 126 litres, 115 litres, 119 litres, 113 litres.

4. Find the mean for each set of data.
    1 12 cm, 17 cm, 12 cm, 18 cm, 11 cm.
    2 42 kg, 38 kg, 32 kg, 50 kg, 39 kg, 36 kg.
    3 £5, £4, £7, £9, £8, £10, £3, £6, £8, £5.
    4 7 miles, 3 miles, 9 miles, 3 miles.
    5 6 litres, 9 litres, 4 litres, 4 litres, 3 litres, 2 litres, 7 litres.
    6 4 years, 7 years, 8 years, 11 years, 5 years, 4 years.

5. The cost of stamps for 5 letters was
    27p   17p   22p   £1.95   64p
    1 What is the range of the costs ?
    2 What was the average cost of posting a letter ?

6. Helen's class were running the 400 metres, in PE.
    The times of the best 8 runners were, in seconds,
    85, 80, 82, 78, 76, 84, 87, 92.
    1 What is the range of these times ?
    2 What is the average of these eight times ?

7. A group of children had an average of 1.5 pets each.
    Among them they had a total of 54 pets.
    How many children were in the group ?

8.   Sabrina kept a record of the marks she was given for her homework. Each
      homework was marked out of 20.

January	14	10	16	9	17	14	11			
February	18	13	11	16	9					
March	11	12	10	16	17	18	12	11	14	12
April	11	16	14	13	19	15	8	12		

What was the range of Sabrina's marks in
1   January ?
2   February ?
3   March ?
4   April ?

What was the mean mark obtained by Sabrina in
5   January ?
6   February ?
7   March ?
8   April ?
9   In which month did Sabrina obtain her best average mark ?

Exercise 17.5   Applications and Activities

1.   **Testing statements**

      People often make statements without really looking at the facts.
      You can use the work from this and earlier chapters to test statements.

      Using mathematics you can say whether statements are true or false.

      Keith made this statement.
      'People rarely spend more than 15 pence in the lower school tuck shop.'

      Kathryn did not think that Keith's statement was correct.
      Rather than argue she decided to collect some data.

When the tuck shop opened at morning break Kathryn made a note of how much people spent. This was the data Kathryn collected.

10p	5p	8p	20p	25p	30p	45p	10p	12p	9p
8p	12p	10p	8p	9p	7p	25p	36p	40p	8p
18p	20p	15p	12p	35p	24p	10p	3p	6p	7p
35p	25p	21p	18p	7p	9p	10p	12p	15p	40p
25p	15p	10p	13p	8p	9p	24p	27p	15p	30p

The lower school tuck shop was open for 20 minutes.
There are a total of 120 pupils in the lower school.

1   How many pupils were served at the tuck shop ?

2   The tuck shop was open for 20 minutes.
How many seconds is this ?

3   There was only one person serving.
What was the average time taken to serve a pupil ?

4   Kathryn decided to draw a graph to show the data that she had collected.
Copy this frequency table.
Complete the table using Kathryn's data.

Amount spent in pence	Tally	Frequency
1–5		
6–10		
11–15		
16–20		
21–25		
26–30		
31–35		
36–40		
41–45		

5   Draw a frequency diagram to display the data.
Remember to label the axes and to give the graph a title.

6   What was the lowest amount of money spent at the tuck shop ?

7   What was the highest amount of money spent by a pupil ?

8   What was the range of the amounts of money spent ?

9   What was the total amount of money spent at the tuck shop ?
        You may find it easier to add up the ten columns separately.
        Then add your answers together.

10   What was the average amount of money spent by each pupil, to the nearest
        penny ?

11   Look back at Keith's statement. Use the data to decide whether you agree with
        it, and give your reasons.

You could conduct a survey of your own to test statements made by someone.

2.   **Tossing coins**

In this experiment you are going to toss 2 coins 40 times and record the result of
each toss.
The coins can land both showing heads,
                        one showing heads and one showing tails,
                        both showing tails.

Guess which of the three results you think will occur most often.

Make a data collection sheet to record your results with tally marks, and find the
frequency distribution of the results. Show your results on a bar-line graph.
Was your guess a good one ?

You may like to try a similar experiment using three or more coins.

PUZZLES

35.   Start with 17 straws in this pattern.
      Take away 5 straws to leave 3 squares only.

36.   What is the smallest whole number which when multiplied by 7 has an answer whose digits
      are all 1's ?

37.   The 59 guests at a wedding are taken to the reception by a taxi firm. A mini-bus can carry
      9 people and a car can carry 4 people. How many vehicles of each type are needed so that
      all the people are taken to the reception at the same time and there are no empty seats ?

Miscellaneous Section C

Aural Practice

Exercises C1 and C2 are aural exercises.
A teacher or a friend should **read** the questions to you.
Try to do the 15 questions in 10 minutes or less.

Exercise C1

1. Write down the number which is 20 less than 43.

2. A rectangle is 10 cm long and 1 cm wide. What is the perimeter of the rectangle ?

3. Write 9.30 pm in the 24-hour clock system.

4. How much change is left from £5 when £3.80 is spent ?

5. Gill scored 70 out of 100 in a test. Write this as a percentage.

6. What fraction of a minute is 15 seconds ?

7. Which compass direction is opposite to South-East ?

8. What is one-fifth of 15 ?

9. What is the average of the three numbers 10, 5 and 6 ?

10. How many cubes with edges of 1 cm are needed to make a cube which measures 2 cm long, 2 cm wide and 2 cm high ?

11. What is the next number in the pattern 30, 26, 22, 18 ?

12. The average age of 5 people is 9 years. What is the total of their ages ?

13. What is the fraction five-tenths written in its simplest form ?

14. What number is 2 less than 1000 ?

15. Write 27 mm in centimetres.

Exercise C2

1.   What is left when 25 is taken from 70 ?

2.   Write down the next number in the pattern 2, 5, 8, 11.

3.   A rectangle is 3 cm long and 2 cm wide. What is the perimeter of the rectangle ?

4.   How many minutes are there from five minutes to nine to ten minutes past nine ?

5.   Write 245 to the neast 100.

6.   What is one-third of 12 ?

7.   How much is $\frac{3}{4}$ of £32 ?

8.   What fraction of an hour is 10 minutes ?

9.   Work out 23 + 18.

10. How many minutes are there in three-quarters of an hour ?

11. What number do you get when you start with 20, halve it and add 4 ?

12. How many days are there in 6 weeks ?

13. In which direction will you be facing if you face North and turn through 90 degrees in a clockwise direction ?

14. Which number is 5 less than 1 ?

15. 9 families have a total of 27 children. What is the average number of children per family ?

Exercise C3   Revision

1.   Write the number three thousand and seventy-six in figures.

2.   A cuboid has been made using centimetre cubes.
     (Each cube measures 1 cm long, 1 cm wide and 1 cm high.)
     The cuboid is 7 cubes long, 4 cubes wide and 3 cubes high.
     1   How many cubes are on the bottom layer of the cuboid ?
     2   What numbers did you multiply together to find the answer to part **1** ?
     3   What is the volume of the cuboid ?
     4   What numbers did you multiply together to find the answer to part **3** ?

3.   These patterns have been made using matchsticks.

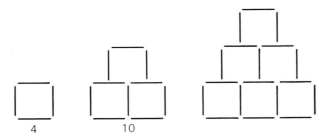

    4   10

There are 4 matchsticks in the first pattern.
There are 10 matchsticks in the second pattern.
1   How many matchsticks are there in the third pattern ?
2   Draw the fourth pattern.
3   How many matchsticks are there in the fourth pattern ?
4   Draw the fifth pattern.
5   How many matchsticks are there in the fifth pattern ?
6   Write the first 10 numbers in the number pattern.
      The pattern starts 4, 10, . . .

4.   This is a thermometer in a freezer.
1   What is the reading on the thermometer
      in degrees Fahrenheit ?
2   What is the reading on the thermometer
      in degrees Celsius ?

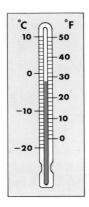

5.   Margaret can reach a height of 1.72 m up a wall.
      If she stands on a stool she can reach further up the wall.
      The stool Margaret stands on is 45 cm high.
1   How far up the wall can Margaret now reach ?
2   The ceiling of the room is 2.35 m from the floor.
      How much taller would the stool have to be so that Margaret could touch
      the ceiling ?

6.   What fraction of each of these shapes has been shaded ?

1

2

3

4
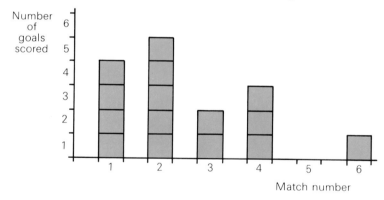

7.   This block graph shows the number of goals scored by Axton Juniors in their first six matches of the season.

Block graph to show the number of goals scored

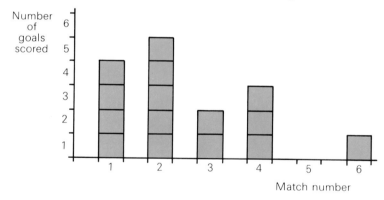

   1   How many goals did the team score in their fifth match ?
   2   In which match did they score the most goals ?
   3   What was the total number of goals scored by Axton Juniors in their first six matches of the season ?

8.   What is the order of rotational symmetry of this figure ?

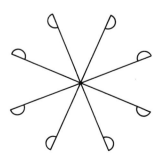

9. **1** How many pencils costing 15p can you buy for £2 ?
    2 What change would you get from £2 ?

10. 20 pupils made a guess at the number of daffodils which grew on the front lawn of the school.
     Their guesses were as follows.

43	37	41	54	47	59	36	32	45	31
54	50	47	53	42	38	37	34	40	36

1 What was the range of the answers given ?
2 Make a frequency table for the data.
       Use the groups 31–35, 36–40, 41–45 and so on.
3 Draw a frequency diagram to show the data.
4 The total of the guesses is 856. What is the mean of the 20 guesses ?

11. The letter F has been drawn on squared
     paper with squares of side 1 cm.
     1 What is the perimeter of the letter ?
     2 What is the area of the letter ?

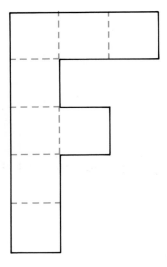

12. The numbers 1 to 10 are written on tiles and placed in a bag.
     You can choose from three winning rules.

     Rule 1—the number on the tile will divide exactly into 15.
     Rule 2—the number on the tile will divide exactly into 36.
     Rule 3—the number on the tile will divide exactly into 100.

     A tile is drawn at random.
     1 How many winning tiles are there for Rule 1 ?
     2 How many winning tiles are there for Rule 2 ?
     3 How many winning tiles are there for Rule 3 ?
     4 Which Rule gives you the best chance of winning ?

13.   Copy this number pattern.

$$9 \times 9 = 81$$
$$99 \times 99 = 9801$$
$$999 \times 999 = 998001$$
...

Write the next four lines in the pattern.

14.   A packet of seeds produced either purple or white flowers.
        Out of 10 seeds 5 seeds produced purple flowers, 1 seed did not grow and the
        remaining seeds produced white flowers.
        1   What percentage of the seeds produced purple flowers ?
        2   What percentage of the seeds produced white flowers ?
        3   What percentage of the seeds did not grow ?

15.   This graph shows the cost of buying small plant pots from the local garden
        centre.

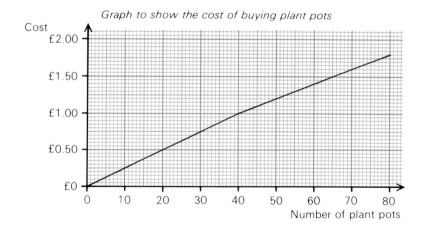

Graph to show the cost of buying plant pots

        Notice that the graph is not straight. This is because Mr Jones charges less for
        pots if a customer buys more than 40.
        1   What does one small square on the vertical axis represent ?
        2   What is the cost of 30 plant pots ?
        3   What is the cost of 55 plant pots ?
        4   How many plant pots can you buy for 25p ?
        5   How many plant pots can you buy for £1.50 ?

Exercise C4   Activities

1. **Computer work**

    Different computers may work slightly differently. This is because there are slight differences in the BASIC language used in various machines. If you have any trouble ask your teacher for help.

    Try entering this BASIC program into your computer.

    ```
    10  FOR I = 1 TO 5
    20  E = I * 2
    30  PRINT I,E
    40  NEXT I
    ```

    I = INPUT and E = OUTPUT (It would be confusing to use 0).

    To make the program work type RUN.
    You should get an INPUT—OUTPUT table which looks like this.

1	2
2	4
3	6
4	8
5	10

    Try changing the program and see what happens.

    Examples

    1 Change line 10 from FOR I = 1 TO 5 to FOR I = 1 TO 10
    2 Change line 20 from E = I * 2 to E = I * a number of your choice.

    How can you make an OUTPUT which is in descending order ?
    Try to explain what each line of the program is doing.

    Here is another program for you to try.

    ```
    10  FOR I = 1 TO 5
    20  E = I * 3 + 2
    30  PRINT I,E
    40  NEXT I
    ```

    Experiment with the program to make different INPUT—OUTPUT tables.
    Do not worry if you go wrong. It does not take long to type a new program in.

2. **Write a fractions and percentages booklet**

Write a small booklet that will help young children to understand fractions and percentages.
Use colourful diagrams in your booklet to make it look interesting.
Give practical examples of where fractions and percentages are used.

Perhaps you could design a game that young children could play to help their understanding of fractions and percentages.

3. **A biased die**

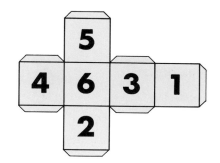

A biased die is an unfair die.
Each number will not have the same chance of landing on the top.

Draw a net for a cube on thin cardboard.
Add tabs to the net and score all the edges.
Mark the numbers on each face.
What do the numbers on opposite faces of a die add up to ?

To make the die biased, fix a weight, such as a small piece of plasticine, to the inside of the face with the number 1 on.
Make the die.

Can you predict the effect of the weight when you roll the die several times ?

Make a data collection sheet to record the results of each roll of the die.
Roll the die 60 times.

Roll an ordinary die 60 times.

PUZZLE

38. Write the next line in this number pattern.

```
                        1
                    1       1
                1       2       1
            1       3       3       1
        1       4       6       4       1
    1       5      10      10       5       1
```

Index

Answers

Some answers have been corrected to a reasonable degree of accuracy, depending on the questions.
There may be variations in answers where questions involve drawings, graphs or measurements.

Page 3   Exercise 1.1

1. **1** 24   **5** 50   **8** 45
   2 17   **6** 98   **9** 22
   3 86   **7** 31   **10** 63
   4 74

2. **1** thirteen   **6** eighty-one
   2 twenty-seven   **7** forty
   3 thirty-eight   **8** thirty-three
   4 fifty-two   **9** ninety-five
   5 seventy-nine   **10** sixty-seven

3. **1** 53   **2** 64   **3** 18   **4** 59

4. **1** seventy-three   **3** sixteen
   2 eighty-eight   **4** forty

Page 5   Exercise 1.2

1. **1** 5   **6** 3   **11** 60 000
   2 60   **7** 600   **12** 300
   3 300   **8** 7   **13** 1 000 000
   4 2   **9** 4000   **14** 2000
   5 800   **10** 20   **15** 90

2. **1** 126   **5** 1639   **8** 49 500
   2 317   **6** 4800   **9** 167 212
   3 509   **7** 15 000   **10** 1 000 042
   4 740

3. **1** two hundred and forty-five
   2 one hundred and fifty
   3 two hundred and seventy-eight
   4 nine hundred and two
   5 one thousand, four hundred and twenty
   6 two thousand, five hundred
   7 three thousand, seven hundred and sixty-eight

    8 twelve thousand five hundred
    9 twelve thousand, three hundred and forty-nine
    10 one hundred and fifty-six thousand, four hundred and thirty-seven

4. **2** 504

5. **1** 3 hundreds + 7 tens + 4 units
   2 5 hundreds + 2 tens + 6 units
   3 3 hundreds + 4 units
   4 7 hundreds + 2 tens
   5 1 thousand + 4 hundreds + 3 tens + 7 units
   6 5 thousands + 7 tens

Page 7   Exercise 1.3

1. **1** 15, 26, 34
   2 24, 38, 59, 78
   3 127, 130, 131, 141
   4 2745, 2746, 2753, 2764
   5 14 726, 14 762, 15 014, 15 135

2. **1** 7, 15, 29, 37
   2 70, 86, 94, 99
   3 5, 108, 110, 120
   4 3399, 3400, 3406
   5 999 064, 1 000 001, 1 001 078

3. **1** 75, 63, 57, 39, 19
   2 87, 67, 53, 48, 45
   3 178, 145, 137, 129, 102
   4 2739, 2638, 1726, 1426, 1324, 989
   5 143, 134, 123, 34, 4, 3, 1

4. **1** 124   **5** 147   **8** 2349
   2 135   **6** 3568   **9** 1447
   3 247   **7** 1234   **10** 34 589
   4 368

5. **1** 742   **5** 984   **8** 5210
    2 932   **6** 8751   **9** 64 431
    3 753   **7** 6431   **10** 98 743
    4 983

Page 8   Exercise 1.4

2. **1** 1, 3, 5, 7, 9
    2 15
    3 60, 62, 64, 66, 68, 70
    4 40, 42, 44, 46
    5 91, 89, 87, 85, 83
    6 46

3. **1** 162   **4** 998
    2 171   **5** 5
    3 299   **6** 11

Page 9   Exercise 1.5

1. **3** 19   **4** 20

2. **1** 9   **4** Larry
    2 Roy   **5** Hanif
    3 Georgina, Rachel,   **6** Robert
        Robert, George   **7** Helen

3. Laughing Gas
    Laughing Gas, Air Balloon, Kaleidoscope,
    Dynamo, Braille System,
    Bunsen Burner, Aeroplane.

4. Superior, Michigan, Erie, Huron, Ontario.

Page 14   Exercise 2.1

2. **1** number 96

3. **1** Alf   **4** Laura
    2 Laura   **5** Laura
    3 Sally   **6** Sally

Page 18   Exercise 2.2

1. 180°

2. 90°

3. East

4. SW

5. **1** NW   **2** SE

6. **1** 90°   **2** 270°

7. **1** 90°, 270°   **4** 45°, 315°
    2 135°, 225°   **5** 270°, 90°
    3 225°, 135°   **6** 180°, 180°

8. **1** Headly   **6** South-East
    2 Baylea   **7** North-East
    3 Lighthouse   **8** Headly
    4 Windmill   **9** East
    5 North-West

Page 21   Exercise 2.3

1. acute angles **1**, **3**, **4**
    obtuse angles **2**, **5**, **6**

2. acute angles **1**, **6**   right-angle **4**
    obtuse angle **3**   reflex angle **2**, **5**

3. **1** 54°, 7°, 45°, 1°
    2 138°, 178°, 100°
    3 290°, 300°, 272°, 315°, 182°
    4 180°, 90°, 360°

Page 24   Exercise 2.4

1. **1** *CD, IJ*   **2** *EF, GH, KL*

2. **2** and **3** are perpendicular

3. **2** and **4** are parallel

4. **1** *AB*   **3** *M*   **5** *J*
    2 *L*   **4** *N*   **6** *K*

5. **1** right   **4** intersection
    2 ninety   **5** horizontal
    3 parallel lines   **6** set-square

Page 26   Exercise 2.5

1. **1** obtuse   **4** obtuse   **7** acute
    2 right   **5** straight **8** obtuse
    3 acute   **6** acute

2. **5** 1 mile north, 3 miles
            east, 4 miles south, 1 mile west
    6 9 miles
    7 *B*
    8 *D* and *E* or *E* and *D*
    9 28 miles
    10 30 miles

Page 33   Exercise 3.1

1. 77

2. 33

3. 73

4. **1** 46   **3** 61   **5** 73
   2 41   **4** 53   **6** 92

5. **1** 10   **2** 325

6. 632

Page 35   Exercise 3.2

1. **1** 3   **2** 2   **3** 23

2. 23

3. 243

4. **1** 13   **2** 24   **3** 12   **4** 22

5. 17

6. 18

7. 26

8. **1** 15   **3** 16   **5** 56
   2 28   **4** 46   **6** 16

9. 148

Page 39   Exercise 3.3

1. 77   6. 31   11. 206
2. 81   7. 45   12. 176
3. 450   8. 508   13. 282
4. 425   9. 387   14. 347
5. 644   10. 175   15. 368

Page 41   Exercise 3.4

1. **1** 35   **2** 38

2. **1** 44   **2** 52

3. **1** 39   **3** 53   **5** 73
   2 34   **4** 66   **6** 62

4. **1** 32   **2** 25

5. **1** 28   **2** 22

6. **1** 12   **3** 15   **5** 18
   2 24   **4** 32   **6** 28

Page 42   Mental calculations

1. 9   5. 29   8. 80
2. 8   6. 38   9. 70
3. 12   7. 50   10. 100
4. 13

Page 43   Exercise 3.5

1. **1** 27   **3** 56   **5** 61
   2 38   **4** 32   **6** 75

2. **1** 43   **2** 64   **3** 82   **4** 81

3. **1** 18   **3** 44   **5** 53
   2 16   **4** 19   **6** 38

Page 45   Exercise 3.6

1. 31

2. 31

3. 30

4. February

5. 21

6. 7

7. Feb 6th

8. March 7th

9. March 8th

10. April 18th

11. April 29th

12. April 3rd

13. 31 days

14. Dec 3rd

15. 34

Page 46   Exercise 3.7

1. 72p

2. **1** 43   **2** 258   **3** 29   **4** 272

3. 13p

4. **1** 3   **5** 6   **8** 4
   2 2   **6** 5   **9** 2
   3 4   **7** 5   **10** 1
   4 7

5. **1** 25   **2** 39

7. There are other possible answers to parts
   1 to **6**.
   1 close the door
   2 save £5
   3 empty the kettle
   4 get undressed
   5 undo your shoelace
   6 add 5
   7 7 + 4 = 11 or 4 + 7 = 11
   8 15 + 8 = 23 or 8 + 15 = 23
   9 11 + 6 = 17 or 6 + 11 = 17
   10 15 − 7 = 8 or 15 − 8 = 7
   11 29 − 8 = 21 or 29 − 21 = 8
   12 26 − 12 = 14 or 26 − 14 = 12

Page 53   Exercise 4.1

1. **1** 47
   2 51
   3 249, 233, 254, 211, 207
   4 229, 229, 230, 245, 221
   5 1154

2. **1** £10.25   **7** extra large
   2 £11.20   green
   3 £12.75   **8** 80p
   4 £10.90   **9** £1.85
   5 £10.60   **10** £20.85
   6 medium red

3. **1** £142   **6** £62
   2 £168   **7** £52
   3 £85   **8** 10 nights
   4 £280   **9** June, 7 nights
   5 £216

Page 55   Exercise 4.2

1. **1** 6   **5** 15   **8** 28
   2 12   **6** 17   **9** 23
   3 4   **7** 11   **10** 20
   4 9

Page 57   Exercise 4.3

1. **1** Totals: Cats 5, Dogs 7, Neither 8
   2 20
   3 Dog

Page 58   Exercise 4.4

1. **1** Mercury   **9** Pluto
   2 687 days   **10** Jupiter
   3 1 427 000 000 km   **11** 42 000 000 km
   4 48 000 km   **12** Earth, Pluto
   5 18 hours   **13** 700 km
   6 Uranus   **14** 83 years
   7 2   **15** Mercury, Venus
   8 Venus

Page 63   Exercise 5.1

1. **1** 60   **5** 300   **8** 6500
   2 600   **6** 12 400   **9** 730
   3 1740   **7** 30 600   **10** 748 600
   4 2700

2. £80

3. £400

4. 1200

5. 80 miles

6. **1** 130   **3** 10   **5** 10
   2 10   **4** 100   **6** 100

7. **1** £1500   **2** £230   **3** £1730

Page 66   Exercise 5.2

1. **1** 69   **5** 72   **8** 344
   2 48   **6** 140   **9** 486
   3 96   **7** 234   **10** 455
   4 75

2. 72p

3. 70

4. 168

5. 318

6. 128

7. 73

8. 94

9. **1** 108   **2** 12 and 9

10. **1** 15
    2 3 and 5
    3 60
    4 3, 5 and 4 or 15 and 4
    5 150
    6 30 and 5
    7 450
    8 30, 5 and 3 or 150 and 3

Page 68   Exercise 5.3

1. **1** 4, 2, 232   **3** 2, 12, 2, 6, 3, 408
    2 2, 74, 222   **4** 4, 10, 1240

2. **1** 172   **4** 312   **7** 304
    2 216   **5** 690   **8** 1640
    3 126   **6** 492

Page 70   Exercise 5.4

1. **1** 13   **5** 13   **8** 15
    2 12   **6** 18   **9** 12
    3 12   **7** 18   **10** 21
    4 13

2. 14 weeks

3. £12

4. 16 conkers

5. £16

6. £16

7. 43 miles

8. 12

9. 25 weeks

10. 28

Page 72   Exercise 5.5

1. **1** 3   **3** 4   **5** 10
    2 5   **4** 6   **6** 12

2. **1** 22 ÷ 4   **2** 5   **3** round down

3. 8

4. 6

5. 13

6. 12

7. 14

8. 3

Page 73   Exercise 5.6

1. 30 years

2. £96

3. **1** 59   **2** 442

4. 9

5. 315

6. £23

7. 7

8. **1** same
    2 18 ÷ 6 = 3 or 18 ÷ 3 = 6
    3 20 ÷ 4 = 5 or 20 ÷ 5 = 4
    4 72 ÷ 8 = 9 or 72 ÷ 9 = 8
    5 48 ÷ 8 = 6 or 48 ÷ 6 = 8
    6 6 × 2 = 12 or 2 × 6 = 12
    7 5 × 6 = 30 or 6 × 5 = 30
    8 6 × 7 = 42 or 7 × 6 = 42
    9 12 × 4 = 48 or 4 × 12 = 48

Page 79   Exercise 6.1

1. **1** (1, 2)   **4** (2, 0)
    2 (4, 1)   **5** (0, 4)
    3 (5, 4)

2. **1** (0, 0)   **5** (4, 4)
    2 (1, 1)   **6** (5, 5)
    3 (2, 2)   **7** They are the same
    4 (3, 3)

3. **1** *E*   **3** *C*   **5** *B*
    2 *D*   **4** *A*   **6** *D*

4. **1** LEEDS
    2 OBAN
    3 YORK
    4 GLOUCESTER
    5 MARGATE

6 HIGH WYCOMBE
7 (9, 4) (6, 3) (1, 9) (5, 6) (2, 0) (7, 7) (10, 6)
8 (6, 5) (5, 0) (6, 3) (0, 6) (1, 9) (8, 9) (8, 9)

Page 82   Exercise 6.2

2. **4** an arrow

3. **7** a face

4. a dog

Page 84   Exercise 6.3

1. **1** Sand Bay   **4** 0401
   2 Greenfield   **5** 0702
   3 Clifford   **6** 0605

2. **1** Bywell 4743, Ford 4637, Waine 4340
   2 Ford Farm 4838, Hill Farm 4639, Peck's Farm 4840, Waine Farm 4139
   3 Waine Station 4341, Ford Station 4736
   4 4142, 4340, 4637
   5 Church
   6 Castle
   7 Bridge over the railway

Page 85   Exercise 6.4

1. **1** 25   **6** (5, 4)   **10** (3, 4)
   3 (2, 5)   **7** (4, 4)   **17** (5, 5)
   4 (5, 2)   **8** (5, 3)   **18** 17
   5 (2, 3)   **9** (3, 1)

2. **1** THIS QUESTION IS ABOUT COORDINATES
   2 WHERE WILL YOU FIND ZEBRAS AND PELICANS?
   3 CROSSING THE ROAD

3. **1** Gatehouse   **2** Gate   **3** Junction
   4 Alternative answers possible
   ① 362516, ② 367523,
   ③ 370529, ④ 374516,
   ⑤ 375527

Page 95   Exercise 7.1

1. **1** 5 cm   **3** 1 cm
   2 8 cm   **4** 5 cm

2. **1** 7 cm   **2** 74 mm   **3** 74 mm

3. **1** 10   **2** 1 mm   **3** 8 cm 2 mm

4. 10 cm 5 mm

5. **1** 67 mm   **3** 38 mm   **5** 148 mm
   2 24 mm   **4** 19 mm

6. **2** 62 mm

Page 98   Exercise 7.2

1. **1** 500 g   **3** 10 g   **5** 300 g
   2 5   **4** 130 g   **6** 390 g

2. **1** 1 kg 500 g
   2 4 kg 200 g
   3 5 kg 740 g

3. **1** 3 kg 500 g
   2 4 kg 750 g
   3 6 kg 50 g

4. **1** 1500 g   **3** 5375 g   **5** 7050 g
   2 3700 g   **4** 1080 g   **6** 10 005 g

5. 200 g

6. 750 g

7. 229 g

8. **1** 3 kg   **5** 1 kg 800 g
   2 10   **6** 1 kg 200 g
   3 100 g   **7** 300 g
   4 2 kg 500 g

9. **1** 10 kg   **5** 5 kg 800 g
   2 10   **6** 2 kg 100 g
   3 100 g   **7** 700 g
   4 7 kg 500 g

10. **1** 4600 g
    2 4 kg 600 g
    3 1800 g

11. **1** 5570 g   **2** 5 kg 570 g

12. **1** 4500 g   **2** 4 kg 500 g

13. **1** 400 kg   **2** 100 kg

14. **1** 12 000 g   **2** 200

15. 5 kg

Page 101   Exercise 7.3

1. **1** 1 litre   **3** 50 ml
    2 2   **4** 750 ml

2. **1** 200 ml   **3** 20 ml
    2 5   **4** 140 ml

3. **1** 100 ml   **4** 90 ml   **6** 24 ml
    2 10   **5** 67 ml   **7** 7 ml
    3 1 ml

4. **1** 4 litres   **3** 10 litres
    2 7 litres   **4** ½ litre

5. **1** 5000 ml   **3** 3500 ml
    2 8000 ml   **4** 5500 ml

6. **1** 1 litre   **4** 3 litres   **7** 11 litres
    2 4 litres   **5** 2 litres   **8** 12 litres
    3 2 litres   **6** 5 litres

7. 230 ml

8. **1** 2000 ml   **4** 260 ml
    2 2 litres   **5** 4
    3 80 ml

9. 7 litres

10. 800 ml

11. 80

12. **1** 11 360 ml   **2** 11 litres

13. 36

14. **1** 60   **2** Yes   **3** 200 ml

Page 107   Exercise 7.4

1. **1** 8.50 am   **3** 3.30 pm
    2 7.25 pm   **4** 4.55 pm

2. **1** 03.00   **4** 17.15   **7** 10.45
    2 16.00   **5** 11.23   **8** 00.30
    3 06.20   **6** 15.30

3. **1** 4.00 pm   **5** 12.15 am
    2 2.00 am   **6** 9.24 am
    3 7.30 pm   **7** 5.15 pm
    4 1.20 pm   **8** 5.55 am

4. **1** 2 minutes 10 seconds
    2 15 minutes 43 seconds
    3 27 minutes 17 seconds

5. **1** 120   **3** 15
    2 90   **4** 1440

6. **1** 180   **3** 1800
    2 150   **4** 3600

7. 65 minutes

8. 3 hours 15 minutes

9. 55 minutes

10. 2 hours 35 minutes

11. 1 hour 50 minutes

Page 109   Exercise 7.5

1. **1** 6000 kg   **4** 12 175 kg
    2 5260 kg   **5** 500 kg
    3 7830 kg   **6** 1010 kg

2. **1** 20 tonnes 200 kg
    2 19 tonnes 350 kg
    3 16 tonnes 800 kg
    4 36 tonnes 700 kg
    5 7 tonnes 350 kg
    6 20 tonnes 500 kg
    7 21 tonnes 890 kg
    8 12 tonnes 770 kg

4. **1** 2000 ml   **5** *B* and *E*
    2 2 litres   **6** *C* and *E*
    3 320 ml   **7** *A*, *B* and *D*
    4 *E*

6. **1** 35 minutes   **4** 6.40 pm
    2 35 minutes   **5** 12.05 am
    3 Comedy   **6** 2 hours 35 minutes

Page 112   Exercise A1

1. 36   9.   60
2. West   10. 5 kg
3. 24   11. 1500
4. 200   12. 2.30 pm
5. acute angle   13. 1500 ml
6. 5   14. 147
7. 360°   15. 380 g
8. 60p

Page 113   Exercise A2

1. 59
2. 140
3. 25
4. 90°
5. 27th August
6. South-West
7. 6.20 pm
8. 6
9. acute angle
10. 3000 m
11. 18.30
12. 15 minutes
13. 13, 15, 17, 19, 21
14. 200 ml
15. 32

Page 113   Exercise A3

1. **1** 414   **2** 138

2. **1** 4   **2** 0   **3** 7   **4** 7

3. **1** 5°, 72°, 87°
   2 124°, 91°, 130°
   3 194°, 276°, 358°, 184°

4. **1** 3000 g   **2** 3 kg

5. **1** 470   **3** 222   **5** 18
   2 2300   **4** 36   **6** 16

6. **1** W **2** CD and RS **3** 4

7. 135

8. 40

9. 29th March

10. **1** 8 cm   **2** 8 cm 4 mm

11. 7

12. $A(0, 3)$, $B(4, 0)$, $C(5, 5)$, $D(1, 2)$

13. **2** 13, 5, 10, 6, 11, 6
    3 8, 4, 11, 5, 6, 17
    4 Total amount of milk delivered each day during the week.
    5 51 pints

14. **1** 25 minutes
    2 15 minutes
    3 51 minutes

15. **1** Totals: U5, A6, H14, P9
    2 Hardwood
    3 34

Page 121   Exercise 8.1

1. <u>2</u>5, 20
2. <u>3</u>8, 30
3. <u>7</u>5, 70
4. <u>9</u>1, 90
5. <u>1</u>7, 10
6. <u>1</u>35, 100
7. <u>2</u>54, 200
8. <u>1</u>09, 100
9. <u>7</u>99, 700
10. <u>1</u>435, 1000
11. <u>3</u>764, 3000
12. <u>1</u>76, 100
13. <u>3</u>1, 30
14. <u>7</u>890, 7000
15. <u>8</u>3, 80

16. **1** 6   **2** 600

17. **1** 9   **2** 900

Page 122   Exercise 8.2

1. 20
2. 30
3. 40
4. 60
5. 90
6. 120
7. 440
8. 280
9. 70
10. 110
11. 170
12. 110
13. 4380
14. 1310
15. 1470
16. 60°C
17. 90 m

Page 123   Exercise 8.3

1. 300
2. 400
3. 300
4. 600
5. 700
6. 900
7. 1800
8. 3300
9. 800
10. 4400
11. 1000
12. 14 400
13. 27 800
14. 39 500
15. 124 500
16. 1400 m
17. 7200 km

Page 125   Exercise 8.4

1. **1** 70   **4** 30
   2 110   **5** 60
   3 110

2. **1** 700   **4** 300
   2 900   **5** 600
   3 300

3. **1** 4000   **4** 5000
   2 8000   **5** 11 000
   3 5000

4. **B**   6. **C**

5. **A**   7. **B**

Page 127   Exercise 8.5

1. 2   5. 5   9. 104
2. 1   6. 1   10. 411
3. 3   7. 16   11. 183
4. 1   8. 14   12. 42

Page 127   Exercise 8.6

1. 440 m, 410 m, 380 m, 350 m, 340 m, 320 m, 320 m

2. 32 600, 14 800, 37 600, 8600, 21 100, 23 900, 9500

Page 133   Exercise 9.1

1. **1** Jam   **3** Peanut butter
   2 Ham   **4** 14

2. **1** Totals: 3, 6, 4, 1

3. **1** 4   **2** 4
   3 Sea-side (if by majority)

Page 136   Exercise 9.2

1. **1** 1 book   **3** 4   **5** 3
   2 Bill   **4** 9   **6** 33

2. **1** 10   **4** 30
   2 1989   **5** 190
   3 60

3. **1** 4 hours   **5** 9
   2 8.30 am–9.00 am   **6** 11
   4 24   **7** 175

4. **3** 115

Page 140   Exercise 9.3

1. **1** 2   **4** 1
   2 Saturday   **5** 13 pints
   3 Sunday

2. **3** 28

3. **2** 22 hours

4. **1** Saturday
   2 Thursday
   3 Monday, Tuesday, Friday, Sunday
   4 37 hours

Page 141   Exercise 9.4

1. **1** 21   **4** 35   **7** 36
   2 23   **5** 34   **8** 69
   3 13   **6** 33

Page 147   Exercise 10.1

1. **1** 2, 5   **4** 6, 11   **7** −2, 4
   2 4, 4   **5** 3, 6   **8** 1, 2
   3 −1, 1   **6** 0, 10

2. **1** Alvington   **2** 4°C

3. **1** Box was 9 cm too wide to fit.
   2 Box would just fit leaving a 2 cm gap.

4. **1** −5
   2 The bird went 5 m under the water.

5. Andrea was 7 cm taller than her brother.

6. **1** −3
   2 Opposing sides scored a total of 3 more goals than Hackington.

7. 40

8. **1** more   **2** 38

9. **1** Rovers −8, City 4, United −9, Town −6
   2 United

Page 149   Exercise 10.2

1. **1** 50°F   **2** 10°C

2. *A* 55°C, *B* 47°C, *C* 35°C, *D* 25°C, *E* 17°C, *F* 6°C, *G* −2°C, *H* −7°C, *I* −13°C, *J* −17°C

4. **1** *E*   **6** *B*
   2 *F*   **7** Living room/dining room
   3 *A*   **8** Bedrooms
   4 *B*   **9** 15°F
   5 *B*

5. **1** $B - 35°C$, $C - 4°C$, $D - 22°C$,
        $E - 11°C$, $F - 28°C$
    2 C
    3 B

Page 152   Exercise 10.3

1. **1** 7   **6** ⊞ and ④
    2 FLOOR 3   **7** ⊟ and ④
    3 FLOOR -2 **8** ⊟ and ③
    4 ⊞ and ④   **9** ⊞ and ②
    5 ⊟ and ②   **10** ⊟ and ⑥

2. **1** 3°C   **3** 8°C   **5** 7°C
    2 5°C   **4** 7°C   **6** Wednesday

4. **1** -3 **5** -7 **9** 18
    2 18   **6** 22   **10** 18
    3 0   **7** 5   **11** 4
    4 15   **8** 10   **12** 14

Page 159   Exercise 11.1

1. **1** 500p   **5** 1275p   **8** 107p
    2 800p   **6** 72p   **9** 1006p
    3 247p   **7** 5p   **10** 5110p
    4 350p

2. **1** £4 (£4.00)   **6** £0.11
    2 £2.50   **7** £0.06
    3 £5.75   **8** £2.08
    4 £16 (£16.00)   **9** £10.01
    5 £37.50   **10** £21.10

3. 46p

4. £1.25

Page 160   Exercise 11.2

1. **1** ②.⑤⑧
    2 ①.②⑦
    3 ⑤.⑥③
    4 ④⑤.③⑨
    5 ③.⓪④
    6 ⓪.②⑥ (.26)
    7 ⓪.⓪① (.01)
    8 ①⓪.⓪④
    9 ②⓪⑤.③⓪ (205.3)
    10 ①⓪①.⓪①

2. **1** 2.87   **5** 5.06   **8** 100
    2 0.7   **6** 0.06   **9** 105.9
    3 2.55   **7** 76   **10** 160.1
    4 4.6

3. **1** £0.90   **6** £12.80
    2 £0.89   **7** £0.02
    3 £1.50   **8** £7 (£7.00)
    4 £2.36   **9** £4.20
    5 £0.15   **10** £0.10
    (Answers could be given in pence.)

Page 162   Exercise 11.3

1. **1** 70p   **3** 55p   **5** 13p
    2 25p   **4** 64p   **6** 37p

2. **1** £3   **3** £3.75   **5** £0.74
    2 £1.50   **4** £2.63   **6** £4.15

3. **1** 69p   **2** 31p

4. **1** £2.51   **2** £2.49

5. **1** £12.20   **2** £7.80

6. **1** £10.25   **2** £9.75

7. £1.40

8. £19.72

9. **1** £83.40   **2** £4.17

10. £6.45

11. 29, 7p

12. 7, 20p

13. £10.75

14. **1** £98.83   **2** £1.17

15. **1** £23.93   **2** £6.07

Page 164   Exercise 11.4

1. **1** 70p, 50p + 20p
    2 75p, 50p + 20p + 5p
    3 54p, 50p + 2p + 2p
    4 24p, 20p + 2p + 2p
    5 93p, 50p + 20p + 20p + 2p + 1p
    6 £1 + £5
    7 50p + £1 + £1

8 5p + 20p + 50p + £1 + £1 + £5
9 2p + 2p + 20p + 10p + 50p + £1
10 2p + 20p + 50p + £1 + £1 +
       £1 + £5

2. **2** £7.50, £9.00, £3.00, £2.80, £3.60,
        £1.64, £3.40
    3 Stuart   3, 0, 0, 0, 0, 0
         Lesley   2, 1, 3, 0, 0, 0
         Bill   1, 1, 0, 0, 0, 0
         Dawn   1, 1, 3, 0, 0, 0
         Lucy   3, 1, 1, 0, 0, 0
         Gary   1, 1, 1, 0, 2, 0
         George   3, 0, 4, 0, 0, 0
    4 19
    5 5 × 50p, 20 × 10p, 1 × 5p, 2 × 2p,
        1 × 1p
    6 £23.60

3. **1** 25p, 24p, £1.20 for 5
    2 69p, 67p, 67p per carton
    3 28p, 28p, £2.76 for 10 tins
    4 26p, 26p, £1.55 for 6 cans
    5 18p, 17p, £1.20 for 7 packets

4. **1** £1.50   **3** 16, 20p   **5** £90
    2 3, 10p   **4** £555   **6** £465

Page 173   Exercise 12.1

1. **1**, **2**, **4**, **5** have line symmetry

2. **1**, **2**, **3**, **4** have plane symmetry

3. **1** 6   **4** 4
    2 3   **5** 2
    3 8

4. **1** *B*, *M*   **2** *H*   **3** *J*, *Z*   **4** *H*, *Z*

Page 176   Exercise 12.2

1. **1** *B*, *J*   **9** *B*, *E*, *G*, *J*
    2 *B*, *E*, *G*, *H*, *J*   **10** *A*, *C*, *F*
    3 *A*, *C*   **11** *A*
    4 *D*, *F*   **12** rectangle
    5 *C*, *D*, *F*   **13** square
    6 *A*, *B*, *C*, *G*   **14** pentagon
    7 *D*, *F*, *H*   **15** hexagon
    8 *E*, *G*, *H*, *J*

2. *A* and *H*, *B* and *F*, *C* and *E*, *D* and *J*,
    G and *I*

Page 179   Exercise 12.3

1. **1** cube   **4** pyramid
    2 cuboid   **5** cylinder
    3 triangular prism **6** sphere

2. **1** cylinder   **5** disc
    2 cone   **6** cuboid
    3 sphere   **7** triangular prism
    4 cube

3. **1** die, brick, chocolate
    2 baked bean tin, ice cream cone,
        football, coin
    3 die
    4 baked bean tin, coin,
        (ice cream cone has no surface)
    5 brick, chocolate
    6 chocolate

4. **2** cube, 12, 8, 6
    3 pyramid, 8, 5, 5
    4 cuboid, 12, 8, 6
    5 triangular prism, 9, 6, 5

5. **1** 6   **2** 4   **3** 4   **4** 60 cm

Page 181   Exercise 12.4

1. **5** 8 cm 1 mm (8.1 cm)

2. **5** 7 cm 1 mm (7.1 cm)

5. **2** 10 cm 3 mm (10.3 cm)

Page 187   Exercise 12.5

1. **1**, **3**, **5**, **6** are nets of a cube

2. cuboid

3. **1** 2   **2** 3   **3** 5 cm by 2 cm

4. **1** 8   **2** 18   **3** 12

Page 189   Exercise 12.6

2. **1** A, B, C, D, E, K, M, T, U, V, W, Y
   2 H, I, X (possibly O as well)
   3 F, G, J, L, N, P, Q, R, S, Z
   5 H, I, N, S, X, Z
   6 O (depending on type)

Page 194   Exercise 13.1

1. **1** 6.4 cm **3** 8.8 cm
   2 12.1 cm **4** 3.3 cm

2. 2.8 cm

3. **1** 7.5 cm **5** 0.8 cm **8** 1.4 cm
   2 6.1 cm **6** 0.9 cm **9** 1.6 cm
   3 4.2 cm **7** 1.5 cm **10** 9.1 cm
   4 2.6 cm

4. **1** 5.6 cm **3** 4.4 cm
   2 6.3 cm **4** 16.3 cm

5. There are other possible answers.
   2 m, fibre tape
   3 m, fibre tape
   4 cm, ruler
   5 m, trundle wheel
   6 m, fibre tape
   7 cm, metre rule
   8 cm, steel tape
   9 cm, steel tape
   10 mm, ruler

Page 197   Exercise 13.2

1. **1** 2 m 45 cm
   2 15 m 21 cm
   3 5 m 7 cm

2. **1** 4 m 18 cm **4** 9 m 73 cm
   2 12 m 7 cm **5** 7 m 9 cm
   3 2 m 30 cm **6** 29 m 83 cm

3. **1** 158 cm **6** 40 cm
   2 326 cm **7** 330 cm
   3 1281 cm **8** 603 cm
   4 509 cm **9** 12 640 cm
   5 200 cm **10** 3 cm

4. 1 m 47 cm

5. 70 cm

6. 1 m 98 cm

7. **1** 5 m 40 cm **2** 2 m 37 cm

Page 198   Exercise 13.3

1. **1** 3 m 48 cm
   2 0 m 37 cm
   3 9 m 6 cm

2. **1** 5 m 25 cm **4** 0 m 7 cm
   2 1 m 20 cm **5** 27 m 35 cm
   3 0 m 52 cm **6** 15 m 6 cm

3. **1** 3.56 m **6** 14.7 m
   2 5.04 m **7** 1 m
   3 2.6 m **8** 0.15 m
   4 0.9 m **9** 10.5 m
   5 13.62 m **10** 0.04 m

4. 2.7 m

5. **1** 1.45 m **2** 0.75 m

6. 2.4 m

7. **1** 15.5 m **2** 4.5 m

Page 201   Exercise 13.4

1. **1** 2.22 m **3** 2.41 m **5** 2.32 m
   2 2.37 m **4** 2.29 m **6** 2.19 m

2. **1** 9.04 m **3** 9.17 m **5** 9.11 m
   2 8.98 m **4** 9.24 m **6** 8.97 m

3. **1** 1.13 m **3** 0.93 m **5** 1.09 m
   2 1.01 m **4** 0.87 m **6** 0.99 m

4. **1** 113 cm **3** 93 cm **5** 109 cm
   2 101 cm **4** 87 cm **6** 99 cm

Page 203   Exercise 13.5

1. **1** 155 cm **2** 1.55 m
2. **1** 90 cm **2** 0.9 m
3. **1** 125 cm **2** 75 cm
4. **1** 44 cm **2** 0.44 m
5. 1.9 m
6. 6.1 m

7. 1.25 m

8. 8.69 m

9. **1** 244 cm   **2** 2.44 m

10. **1** 3.05 m   **2** 1.29 m   **3** No

11. **1** 0.04 m   **5** 0.09 m   **8** 0.13 m
    2 0.08 m   **6** 0.05 m   **9** 0.15 m
    3 0.08 m   **7** 0.14 m   **10** 0.24 m
    4 0.02 m

12. 13.3 m

13. **1** 220 cm   **2** 2.2 m

Page 206   Exercise 13.6

1. **1** 125 cm   **2** 1.25 m

2. **1** 450 cm   **2** 25 cm

3. **1** 225 cm   **2** 2.25 m

4. 49.2 m

5. **1** 375 cm   **3** 755 cm
   2 380 cm   **4** 7.55 m

6. 202.8 m

7. **1** 6.4 m   **2** 640 cm

8. **1** 6.25 m   **2** 625 cm

9. **1** 150 cm   **2** 144 cm   **3** 36 cm

10. **1** 450 cm   **2** 4.5 m

11. **1** 720 cm   **2** 7.2 m

12. **1** 14   **2** 20 cm

13. **1** 2500 cm   **2** 25 m

14. 80 cm

Page 208   Exercise 13.7

1. **1** 6.01 m   **2** 4.55 m

2. **1** Yes   **3** 10 cm
   2 0.69 m (69 cm)   **4** 5 cm

3. **1** 18   **2** 4   **3** 5   **4** £10

4. **1** 8   **4** 17.1 m
   2 90 cm   **5** 51.3 m
   3 16.9 m

5. **1** 135 cm   **2** 1.35 m   **3** 22

Page 213   Exercise 14.1

1. **1** □ = 5   **6** □ = 8
   2 □ = 4   **7** □ = 15
   3 □ = 9   **8** □ = 6
   4 □ = 10   **9** □ = 25
   5 □ = 3   **10** □ = 28

2. **1** △ = 5   **6** △ = 8
   2 △ = 9   **7** △ = 15
   3 △ = 10   **8** △ = 23
   4 △ = 18   **9** △ = 57
   5 △ = 8   **10** △ = 81

3. **1** * = 2   **6** * = 4
   2 * = 4   **7** * = 7
   3 * = 7   **8** * = 8
   4 * = 8   **9** * = 8
   5 * = 9   **10** * = 9

4. **1** △ = 4   **6** △ = 4
   2 △ = 8   **7** △ = 9
   3 △ = 3   **8** △ = 45
   4 △ = 16   **9** △ = 80
   5 △ = 30   **10** △ = 12

5. **1** □ = 25   **6** * = 27
   2 △ = 12   **7** △ = 0
   3 * = 1   **8** * = 50
   4 □ = 100   **9** □ = 1
   5 △ = 41   **10** △ = 80

Page 215   Exercise 14.2

1. **1** $a = 10$ **2** $b = 14$

2. **1** $c = 4$ **2** $d = 1$

3. **1** $e = 15$ **2** $f = 27$ **3** $g = 30$

4. **1** $h = 7$ **3** $j = 3$
   2 $i = 4$ **4** $k = 1$

5. **1** $m = 7$ **2** $n = 13$ **3** $p = 23$

6. **1** $q = 10$ **3** $s = 4$
   2 $r = 8$ **4** $t = 2$

Page 218   Exercise 14.3

1. **1** subtract seven
    2 add nine
    3 divide by six
    4 multiply by three
    5 subtract 2 then divide by 3
    6 add 3 then divide by 4
    7 subtract 5 then multiply by 2
    8 divide by 2 then multiply by 3

2. **1** divide by 4   **3** $b = 8$
    2 $a = 5$ **4** $c = 10$

3. **1** add 7   **3** $e = 17$
    2 $d = 10$ **4** $f = 31$

4. **1** subtract 5 then divide by 4
    2 $g = 4$
    3 $h = 7$
    4 $i = 10$

5. **1** multiply by 4 then subtract 3
    2 $j = 9$
    3 $k = 37$
    4 $m = 45$

6. **3** 5

7. **3** 9

8. **1** 6   **2** 9

Page 221   Exercise 14.4

1. add 4

2. subtract 10

3. divide by 3

4. multiply by 4

5. **1** multiply by 3 then add 1
    2 multiply by 2 then add 3
    3 divide by 2 then subtract 1
    4 multiply by 3 then subtract 3 (subtract 1 then multiply by 3)

Page 223   Exercise 14.5

1. **1** 14 cm   **2** 20 cm   **3** 22 cm

2. **1** 12 cm   **3** 28 cm
    2 16 cm   **4** 40 cm

3. **1** £28   **4** 5 days
    2 £43   **5** 8 days
    3 2 days

4. $\triangle = 4$

5. **1** $\square = 5$ **6** $\triangle = 2$
    2 $\triangle = 6$ **7** $* = 4$
    3 $* = 5$ **8** $\triangle = 3$
    4 $\triangle = 7$ **9** $\square = 9$
    5 $\square = 8$ **10** $\triangle = 12$

6. **1** 8 g
    2 25 minutes
    3 Bill 6, Cyril 24, Total 32
    4 12 years
    5 12 years
    6 64 years

7. **1** 10
    2 15
    3 10, 15, 20, 40
    4 7
    5 12
    6 the number of tables by 5.
    7 To find the number of tables divide the number of chairs by 5.

Page 226   Exercise B1

1. square   9. 800
2. 680 m   10. £20
3. 12   11. 10
4. 70 minutes   12. 6 minutes
5. 12   13. 5°C
6. 260   14. sphere
7. £4.50   15. 24.5 cm
8. 6

Page 227   Exercise B2

1. 415p   9. 12
2. 8   10. 20p
3. 7   11. 80
4. 75p   12. 8°C
5. 40 cm   13. 4
6. 9   14. 195 cm
7. 5   15. 50 m
8. 3.5 cm

Page 227   Exercise B3

1. **1** 106   **2** 113

2. 5

3. 18

4. **1** 7°C, 7°C, 9°C, 6°C, 7°C, 3°C, 8°C
   2 Saturday

5. **1** 240   **2** 23   **3** 15 700

6. **1** 45 minutess   **2** 15 minutes

7. **1** subtract 5 then divide by 3
   2 $a = 17$
   3 $b = 9$
   4 $c = 44$
   5 $d = 15$
   6 $e = 77$

8. **1** 32p   **2** 33p   **3** £1.62 for 5

9. **1** C **3** South-West
   2 North-East   **4** West

10. **1** 250   **3** 2000
    2 1000   **4** 3275

11. **1** F **4** G **7** A
    2 I **5** H **8** C
    3 D **6** E

12. **1** £15.45   **2** £4.55

13. **1** 9   **2** 21   **3** 14

14. **1** 3 million
    2 Italy
    3 Austria, Canada, UK
    4 17 million

15. **4** E

Page 238   Exercise 15.1

1. **1** 3 cm   **3** 10 cm
   2 2 cm   **4** 6 cm^2

2. **1** 18 cm   **2** 8 cm^2

3. **1** 20 cm   **2** 15 cm^2

4. **1** 18 cm, 22 cm, 16 cm, 24 cm
   2 T
   3 S
   4 T J E S
   5 8 cm^2, 10 cm^2, 7 cm^2, 11 cm^2
   6 T
   7 S
   8 T J E S

5. **1** 18 cm   **2** 20 cm^2

6. **1** 16 cm   **2** 16 cm^2

7. **1** 14 cm, 10 cm^2 **5** 22 cm, 30 cm^2
   2 14 cm, 12 cm^2 **6** 26 cm, 40 cm^2
   3 12 cm, 9 cm^2 **7** 24 cm, 27 cm^2
   4 20 cm, 25 cm^2 **8** 30 cm, 56 cm^2

8. length 4 cm, breadth 2 cm

Page 241   Exercise 15.2

Answers may vary for this exercise.
1. **1** 4   **3** 4   **5** 15
   2 4   **4** 3   **6** 15 cm^2

2. 20 cm^2

3. **1** 1 km^2 **2** 21 km^2

4. **1** 1 m^2 **2** 26 m^2

5. **1** 1 mm^2 **2** 4 mm^2 **3** 26 mm^2

Page 244   Exercise 15.3

1. **1** 6 cm^3 **4** 21 cm^3
   2 7 cm^3 **5** 20 cm^3
   3 14 cm^3

2. **1** 6   **2** 6   **3** 12 cm^3

3. **1** 6 cm   **2** 2 cm   **3** 12 cm^3

4. **1** 4 cm   **4** 12
   2 3 cm   **5** 24 cm^3
   3 2 cm

5. **1** 8 cm   **4** 40
   2 5 cm   **6** 160 cm^3
   3 4 cm

6. **1** cube   **2** 8 cm^3

7. **1** 18   **2** 18 cm^3

8. **1** 27 cm³   **2** 3 cm
9. **1** 6   **3** 30   **5** 90
    2 5   **4** 3   **6** 90 cm³
10. 1000

Page 246   Exercise 15.4

1. **1** 28 mm   **2** 48 mm²
2. **1** 16 cm   **3** 16 cm
    2 15 cm²   **4** 14 cm²

Page 251   Exercise 16.1

1. **1** $\frac{1}{2}$ **4** $\frac{1}{6}$
    2 $\frac{1}{4}$ **5** $\frac{1}{9}$
    3 $\frac{1}{5}$
2. **1** $\frac{2}{5}$ **5** $\frac{5}{9}$ **8** $\frac{3}{5}$
    2 $\frac{3}{4}$ **6** $\frac{5}{9}$ **9** $\frac{3}{8}$
    3 $\frac{3}{7}$ **7** $\frac{7}{12}$ **10** $\frac{11}{20}$
    4 $\frac{5}{8}$
3. **1** 12   **3** $\frac{5}{12}$
4. **1** 8   **3** $\frac{3}{8}$

Page 254   Exercise 16.2

1. **1** $\frac{6}{8} = \frac{6 \div 2}{8 \div 2} = \frac{③}{4}$

    2 $\frac{10}{15} = \frac{10 \div ⑤}{15 \div 5} = \frac{2}{③}$

    3 $\frac{16}{20} = \frac{16 \div 4}{20 \div ④} = \frac{④}{⑤}$

2. **1** $\frac{1}{2}$ **6** $\frac{2}{3}$ **11** $\frac{2}{3}$
    2 $\frac{1}{3}$ **7** $\frac{3}{4}$ **12** $\frac{3}{4}$
    3 $\frac{1}{4}$ **8** $\frac{5}{6}$ **13** $\frac{8}{9}$
    4 $\frac{1}{4}$ **9** $\frac{4}{5}$ **14** $\frac{2}{3}$
    5 $\frac{1}{2}$ **10** $\frac{2}{3}$ **15** $\frac{7}{8}$

3. **1** $\frac{6}{7}$ **5** $\frac{7}{8}$ **8** $\frac{2}{3}$
    2 $\frac{9}{11}$ **6** $\frac{1}{6}$ **9** $\frac{3}{8}$
    3 $\frac{5}{11}$ **7** $\frac{3}{4}$ **10** $\frac{3}{4}$
    4 $\frac{3}{7}$

4. **1** $\frac{1}{2} = \frac{②}{4}$ **4** $\frac{⑤}{6} = \frac{10}{12}$

    2 $\frac{2}{5} = \frac{6}{⑮}$ **5** $\frac{4}{⑦} = \frac{12}{21}$

    3 $\frac{5}{8} = \frac{20}{㉜}$

5. **1** $\frac{1}{3} = \frac{②}{6} = \frac{3}{⑨} = \frac{④}{12}$

    2 $\frac{④}{7} = \frac{8}{14} = \frac{⑯}{28} = \frac{20}{㉟}$

    3 $\frac{40}{60} = \frac{⑳}{30} = \frac{10}{⑮} = \frac{②}{3}$

Page 256   Exercise 16.3

1. **1** 7   **5** 3   **8** 6
    2 3   **6** 5   **9** 4
    3 4   **7** 6   **10** 3
    4 3
2. **1** 10   **2** 20
3. **1** 7   **2** 21
4. **1** 6   **3** 18
    2 12   **4** 24
5. **1** £10   **6** 15 kg
    2 15 m   **7** 12 cm
    3 15 mm   **8** 35 miles
    4 32 tonnes   **9** £18
    5 6 km   **10** 56 km

Page 258   Exercise 16.4

1. **1** 40%   **5** 47%   **8** 75%
    2 50%   **6** 6%   **9** 1%
    3 80%   **7** 39%   **10** 100%
    4 35%

2. 15%

3. 63%

4. 72%

5. **1** $\frac{11}{50}$ **2** 2   **3** 22%

6. **1** $\frac{7}{10}$ **2** 10   **3** 70%

7. **1** 60%   **5** 50%   **8** 65%
   2 90%   **6** 48%   **9** 80%
   3 80%   **7** 40%   **10** 75%
   4 20%

Page 260   Exercise 16.5

1. **1** $\frac{50}{100} = \frac{1}{2}$ **6** $\frac{45}{100} = \frac{9}{20}$
   2 $\frac{25}{100} = \frac{1}{4}$ **7** $\frac{5}{100} = \frac{1}{20}$
   3 $\frac{20}{100} = \frac{1}{5}$ **8** $\frac{12}{100} = \frac{3}{25}$
   4 $\frac{60}{100} = \frac{3}{5}$ **9** $\frac{2}{100} = \frac{1}{50}$
   5 $\frac{75}{100} = \frac{3}{4}$ **10** $\frac{28}{100} = \frac{7}{25}$

2. 40%

3. 72%

4. 25%

5. 30%

6. 40%

Page 261   Exercise 16.6

1. **1** 16   **4** 50%
   2 8   **5** 50%
   3 $\frac{1}{2}$

2. **1** $\frac{1}{3}$ **2** 16 hours   **3** $\frac{2}{3}$

3. **1** 4 hours   **4** 7 hours
   2 10 hours   **5** $\frac{7}{24}$
   3 3 hours

4. **1** 5   **3** 70%
   2 80%   **4** Freda

5. **1** 20%   **2** $\frac{39}{50}$ **3** 98%

6. **1** 25%   **4** $\frac{50}{100} = \frac{1}{2}$
   2 $\frac{20}{100} = \frac{1}{5}$ **5** $\frac{70}{100} = \frac{7}{10}$
   3 $\frac{30}{100} = \frac{3}{10}$ **6** $\frac{95}{100} = \frac{19}{20}$

Page 267   Exercise 17.1

1. **1** 4 litres   **4** lunch-time
   2 7 litres   **5** machine was filled
   3 3 litres   **6** all gone home

2. **1** 18   **2** 7   **3** 22

3. **1** 3 hours
   2 Saturday
   3 $2\frac{1}{2}$ hours
   4 Wednesday and Friday
   5 2, $2\frac{1}{2}$, 1, 3, 1, 0, 4 hours
   6 $13\frac{1}{2}$ hours

4. **1** £10   **2** £150   **3** £290
   4 (£100), £150, £250, £290, £230, £250, £70, £0, £100, £180, £130, £0
   5 £1750   **6** August   **7** Christmas

Page 272   Exercise 17.2

1. **1**

mark	1	2	3	4	5	6	7	8	9	10
f	0	1	2	5	4	5	4	4	3	2

2. **1** 8
   2

No. of appliances	1	2	3	4	5	6	7	8
frequency	6	12	11	14	9	4	3	1

Page 275   Exercise 17.3

1. **1** 19   **2** 66

2. **1** Frequencies 4, 8, 9, 9, 4, 4, 2

Page 279   Exercise 17.4

1. **1** 6   **2** 5

2. **1** 10   **2** 52   **3** 13

3. **1** £13   **4** 6 miles   **7** 2 cm
   2 7 m   **5** 5 kg   **8** 13 litres
   3 4 years   **6** 11 p

4. **1** 14 cm   **3** £6.50   **5** 5 litres
   2 39.5 kg   **4** 5.5 miles   **6** 6.5 years

5. **1** £1.78   **2** 65p

6. **1** 16 seconds   **2** 83 seconds

7. 36

8. **1** 8   **4** 11   **7** 13.3
    2 9   **5** 13   **8** 13.5
    3 8   **6** 13.4   **9** April

Page 281   Exercise 17.5

1. **1** 50
    2 1200 seconds
    3 24 seconds
    4 Frequencies: 2, 19, 9, 4, 7, 3, 2, 3, 1
    6 3p   **7** 45p   **8** 42p
    9 Columns: 96p, 77p, 64p, 71p, 84p,
         79p, 114p, 88p, 88p, 94p Total £8.55
    10 17p

Page 284   Exercise C1

1. 23   9. 7
2. 22 cm   10. 8
3. 21.30   11. 14
4. £1.20   12. 45 years
5. 70%   13. $\frac{1}{2}$
6. $\frac{1}{4}$ 14. 998
7. North-West   15. 2.7 cm
8. 3

Page 285   Exercise C2

1. 45   9. 41
2. 14   10. 45
3. 10 cm   11. 14
4. 15   12. 42
5. 200   13. East
6. 4   14. -4
7. £24   15. 3
8. $\frac{1}{6}$

Page 285   Exercise C3

1. 3076

2. **1** 28   **3** 84 cm^3
    2 7 and 4   **4** 7, 4 and 3 (28 and 3)

3. **1** 18   **3** 28   **5** 40
    6 4, 10, 18, 28, 40, 54, 70, 88, 108,
         130

4. **1** 28°F   **2** -2°C

5. **1** 2.17 m   **2** 0.18 m

6. **1** $\frac{3}{7}$ **3** $\frac{8}{15}$
    2 $\frac{1}{2}$ **4** $\frac{3}{5}$

7. **1** 0   **2** 2nd   **3** 15

8. 4

9. **1** 13   **2** 5p

10. **1** 28   **4** 42.8

11. **1** 18 cm   **2** 8 cm^2

12. **1** 3   **3** 5
     2 6   **4** Rule 2

13.   9999 × 9999   = 99980001
         99999 × 99999   = 9999800001
        999999 × 999999   = 999998000001
       9999999 × 9999999 = 99999980000001

14. **1** 50%   **2** 40%   **3** 10%

15. **1** 5p   **4** 10
     2 75p   **5** 65
     3 £1.30